MAJOR CRIMINAL JUSTICE SYSTEMS

SAGE FOCUS EDITIONS

MAJOR CRIMINAL JUSTICE SYSTEMS

Edited by
George F. Cole
Stanislaw J. Frankowski
Marc G. Gertz

Foreword by **GERHARD O. W. MUELLER**

 SAGE PUBLICATIONS   Beverly Hills   London

For information address:

SAGE Publications, Inc.
275 South Beverly Drive
Beverly Hills, California 90212

SAGE Publications Ltd
28 Banner Street
London EC1Y 8QE, England

Printed in the United States of America

Library of Congress Cataloging in Publication Data
Main entry under title:

Major criminal justice systems.

    (Sage focus editions; 32)
    Bibliography: p.
    1. Criminal justice, Administration of—Addresses, essays, lectures. I. Cole, George F., 1935-   . II. Frankowski, Stanislaw. III. Gertz, Marc G. IV. Series.
K5001.Z9M34   364'.9   81-9211
ISBN 0-8039-1671-X   AACR2
ISBN 0-8039-1672-8 (pbk.)

THIRD PRINT'NG, 1984

CONTENTS

FOREWORD

A book on major criminal justice systems would have been an impossibility a generation ago. The term "criminal justice," by itself, would not have been properly understood. When used at all, it was used in reference to the juridical apparatus with jurisdiction in criminal matters. The use of the term "systems" in reference to criminal justice would have prompted a blank stare, because the various agencies concerned with crime prevention and control were not viewed as parts of an interdependent system. Comparison was in its infancy—at least as far as crime prevention was concerned—and was restricted to law comparison. Yet even there the systematic, dogmatic, and political differences were regarded as so overwhelming as to cause many scholars to regard comparative studies in criminal law as esoteric and virtually fruitless.

All this has changed in a single generation, largely due to the efforts of a handful of scholars, at a few research centers, in a few countries mostly in the northern tier of the world. Today, thanks to the phenomenal growth of scientific criminology, criminal justice has become a political reality that encompasses all of society's attempts to come to grips with the crime problem. The agencies of criminal justice are now being viewed as parts of a system, an entire sector of public—and, to some extent, private—endeavor to deal with unacceptable deviance in a humane yet effective and efficient manner. Above all, the value of comparison has been discovered and is being appreciated. Social, economic, ideological, or political differences are no longer being viewed as an obstacle to comparison. On the contrary, they are seen for what they are: variables worthy of analysis in an effort to determine why countries have such widely varying crime problems—ranging from insignificant to catastrophic.

A whole new methodology for the comparative study of criminal justice systems, all their component parts and all their strategies, had to be created. The interaction of the criminal justice sector with all other sectors of public life began to be investigated in an effort to turn criminology, as the science of criminal justice, from a theoretical discipline into a practical tool of social engineering. It is at this point that the United Nations has entered the picture. The world organization, having achieved virtual universality of representation with its 151 member states, is deeply committed to the proposition that all nations should be able to enjoy the benefit of the experience of all other nations. In the field of crime prevention and criminal justice, for which the Crime Prevention and Criminal Justice Branch is the Secretariat's administrative organ, this means that the aggregate of world experience must be presented in a meaningful and comparable manner so that each nation can profit from the success—and failures—of all other nations, so that no nation need repeat the costly mistakes made elsewhere. Experience does show that, on the natural path of socioeconomic development, crime becomes a problem whenever crime prevention and the criminal justice system are not built into the overall national development effort.

The United Nations' first world crime survey, with the participation of 66 states, has been approvingly received by the General Assembly (A/Res/32/60). For the first time nations can gauge their own position on the region-by-region charts showing both the extent of criminality and the investment in personnel devoted to crime prevention. The General Assembly has also adopted the first international plan of action, for the remainder of the twentieth century, which is calculated to guide international and national efforts for efficient crime prevention and criminal justice administration (A/32/58, adopting E/CN.5/536, annex IV).

The experiences in crime prevention and control, criminal justice, offender treatment, and criminal policy are now being widely distributed through the quinquennial world congresses of the United Nations; through the work of the interregional and regional institutes in Europe, Asia, and Latin America; through the publications of the Secretariat—including the international *Review of Criminal Policy*—and through regional and interregional meetings of experts. Technical assistance, providing for a transfer of technology, strategy, and experience in the field of crime prevention and control, is now available to all governments requesting it. In sum, the academic discipline of comparative criminology has become the practical intergovernmental and governmental instrument of crime prevention and control.

It is most timely, therefore, that a group of distinguished scholars from countries which played a leading role in the field—in theory and in practice—have pooled their efforts in the production of this important volume on comparative criminal justice systems. It is my fervent hope that through this volume the expertise necessary for improving national criminal justice systems by comparison may be more widely spread. I wish the authors every success in their contribution to the important world effort to reduce the human and material waste and suffering which criminality brings with it.

Gerhard O. W. Mueller
Chief, Crime Prevention and
Criminal Justice Branch
United Nations

PREFACE

As events of recent decades have demonstrated, the world is a small space in which travel and communication make it possible for important events to transcend national and even regional concerns. The simple fact that more than 150 countries belong to the United Nations indicates that Earth is comprised of an interdependent network of nations where no one country stands completely alone. This is a dramatic change from just 50 years ago, when many nations followed isolationist policies, believing that they could remove themselves from the problems of other states. Only in recent decades has it been recognized that most of the pressing social matters on the contemporary scene—pollution, resource allocation, poverty, and crime—are universal problems.

During the past decade scholarly activity with regard to crime and the administration of justice has greatly increased. Responding to the growth of crime, a concern that affects all developed countries, scholars have conducted research examining the causes of crime, the treatment of offenders, and, as indicated in the foreword by Professor Mueller, such a volume would have been an impossibility a generation ago.

As Mueller also notes, the United Nations "is deeply committed to the proposition that all nations should be able to enjoy the benefit of the experience of all other nations." This international perspective is the basis upon which this book is organized. We all need to know the experiences of other countries with regard to their criminal justice system so that we can better understand our own approach to the problem of crime. This concern for an international perspective on criminality has been demonstrated by the increase in the number of courses on comparative criminal justice that are now being offered in universities throughout the world. Unfortunately, there does not seem to be a comprehensive book that adequately deals with a representative cross-section of the criminal justice systems of the international community. We hope that *Major Criminal Systems* will help to fill this void.

The book was designed primarily to introduce American students of crime to the criminal justice systems of some of the major countries of the world. It is intended to be introductory and descriptive, in keeping with what we believe is the level of theory and evidence currently available on criminal justice in most countries. Each chapter was written by a distinguished scholar who describes the administration of criminal justice in his native land. The book is organized into three parts that correspond to the major legal systems, and the chapters are grouped so that comparisons can be made among the countries of a particular family of law and then among these families.

Anthologies using multiple authors often run the risk that each chapter will be written along different lines and thus the opportunities for comparisons are reduced. We hope we have solved this problem by presenting eight chapters which follow a common outline. On the assumption that the book will be read principally by Americans who know about their own criminal justice system, the chapter on the United States was written in a different style so that it can serve as a benchmark for comparative purposes.

Some may question our choice of countries for inclusion. Certainly it would increase the value of the book if selections were included from countries subscribing to Islamic law, those in Africa and South America, and the world's most populous nation, The People's Republic of China. Unfortunately, we were unable to solicit chapters from scholars in these areas. As will be discussed in the Introduction, many of the countries in the Third World have legal systems that are based on procedures brought by colonial powers which have been adopted to contemporary local and political conditions. We hope that this fact will help to alleviate this lacunae.

Readers may find that some of the authors have written chapters that do not comply with the dominant scientific paradigms of the West. It is important that these chapters not be dismissed but studied so that it will be possible for the student to understand the author's perspective and the assumptions concerning law and justice in that country. It is our thesis that despite ideological, socioeconomic, and cultural differences, which in the final instance determine the methods and functions of each criminal justice system, there exists at least one common denominator which makes our attempt as editors meaningful; the administration of justice in every country is supposed to protect the set of social relationships and values, the maintenance of which seems desirable for those holding power. As such, the criminal law is used to protect these values and to prohibit, under the threat of penalty, the commission of certain forms of behavior perceived as dangerous.

As noted above, we hope that readers will become more acquainted with the criminal justice systems of a variety of countries and that the book will help to foster an international and comparative perspective among students of criminology. It is also our hope that this volume will serve as a first step toward the development of such an international approach to the problems of crime and justice.

G.F.C.
S.J.F.
M.G.G.

COMPARATIVE CRIMINAL JUSTICE: AN INTRODUCTION

George F. Cole,
Stanislaw J. Frankowski,
and Marc G. Gertz

Given the prevalence of crime in all societies, it is perhaps somewhat strange that there has been little or no attempt to compare, at a sophisticated and systematic level, the administration of criminal justice in various countries and especially to make these analyses across the spectrum of socioeconomic systems. Certainly there has been extensive research on the causes of crime and the policies of enforcement, adjudication, and correction of offenders in specific countries, but there is lacking a body of literature that contributes to a cross-cultural theory of criminal justice. It would appear that such a comparative approach is in its infancy largely because of a number of methodological problems that have impeded development of such a perspective. It is only when these difficulties are understood that we may proceed to examine the wide implications for a comparative study of criminal justice.

SOME METHODOLOGICAL PROBLEMS

One of the central concepts necessary for comparative analysis of criminal justice is that of system. Based on concepts drawn from the biological sciences, the systems perspective has been extensively developed by such social scientists as Parsons (1951), Blau (1964), and Merton (1957). It gained greatest acceptance in the United States during the past two decades, while its application in Europe has been most recent. In fact, it is interesting to note that it is difficult to find a suitable equivalent of the English term "criminal justice system" in most other languages of the developed world. Traditionally, scholars have examined each component of criminal justice— police, courts, corrections—without taking into account its functional relationship to the other parts and the sociopolitical environment within which it operates. It is now recognized that there is a linkage, an interdependence, of these components, and such an analysis requires that a systems framework be used. Given the recent nature of this development, it is not surprising that there are few studies using the comparative approach and the system concept when no serious analysis exists at the national level.

All of the difficulties involved in the study of one system of criminal justice exist when ventures are made into the comparative framework. In addition, new conceptual problems appear. These difficulties are related to a variety of factors, including the assumption that seemingly identical organizational structures are in fact the same, that language differences may play tricks on us, and that the cultural settings within which the systems operate produce very different outputs. As a result, one may be easily misled into assuming that two institutions perform the same function in different countries because they bear the same name and the "official" statement of their operations would seem to indicate that they are identical. The exact work of a given institution can be grasped only when the researcher has a full knowledge of the legal system of which criminal justice is a part, the political and cultural environment in which it functions, and the actual operations of the system as compared to formal statements describing the operation. Given these problems, it is necessary to analyze the institutions of a given country at both the normative, or formal, level and then at the substantive level, where it is possible to take into account the operations in practice.

Herrmann (1977), for example, notes that each criminal justice system has to face the fact that there cannot be a full trial for every case. In common law countries this problem is solved through extensive use of the guilty plea, while the Federal Republic of Germany has developed a so-called "penal order procedure," in which the prosecutor asks the judge for issuance of such an order. From a formal perspective the guilty plea and the penal order have nothing in common. In fact, German scholars have emphasized that the guilty plea could never be reconcilable with the criminal procedures of that country, yet when one studies the actual functioning of the two practices one finds striking similarities.

A second reason for the slowness with which scholars of criminal justice have used the comparative approach may be related to philosophical assumptions concerning the nature of law. It is suggested that those using the common law approach have been influenced to take a more pragmatic or realistic view of criminal justice. Certainly the works of American scholars such as Pound, Llewellyn, and Cardozo influenced a legion of researchers who wanted to understand the law in action rather than the law on the books. Scholars have argued that, by comparison, European thought—for some time influenced by the German idealism of Kant and Hegel—emphasized a highly speculative mode of thinking that concentrated on building abstract concepts without reference to the social context. This approach reached its peak at the beginning of this century; it was argued that the law as passed by the legislature was elevated and thus considered an absolute value with the concomitant demand that there be obedience. The continental approach seems to have greatly influenced the development of a socialist way of viewing law, especially in the Soviet Union during the Stalinist period. Here one has the sense that the law was viewed as omnipotent and that absolute obedience was the utmost duty of each citizen. It was stated that socialist law was always just, always proper, since it was passed in accordance with the will of the people. One result of these philosophical differences has been that empirical research on the administration of justice has been a fairly recent phenomenon in many countries.

In addition to these reasons for the slowness with which a cross-national approach to the administration of justice has developed, it is necessary to consider several concepts that have heuristic value for comparative studies. As will be developed in a later portion of this essay, it seems useful to divide the criminal justice systems of the developed world according to three families of law—common, civil, and socialist. By clustering systems in this manner it is then possible to make comparisons that we will call "internal" and "external." A comparison of at least two systems of criminal justice belonging to the same legal family—for example, the American and the English—may be called an internal cross-national comparison. Alternately, comparisons between or among systems of different legal families may be defined as external cross-national comparisons.

At a different level of analysis it may also be important to compare only portions of two systems—courts of the USSR and Japan—while on other occasions cross-national statements about two or more criminal justice systems in their entirety may be appropriate. The first we will designate as "micro"; the latter would be a "macro" comparison. Even though it may be desirable to study a particular institution in different countries, it must still be recognized that they are linked to other parts of their criminal justice systems and to the sociopolitical environment.

THE VALUE OF
COMPARATIVE CRIMINAL JUSTICE RESEARCH

Why should we undertake the enterprise of comparative research? Some might argue that crime in one's own country is such a serious problem that only the dilettant would try to understand the administration of criminal justice in similar nations, let alone those with completely different legal and political structures. On the contrary, it can be argued that comparative research in the field of criminal justice is not only a desirable undertaking but one that is necessary. At the pragmatic level it is possible to show that certain operations in other states will have direct application if adopted in one's own country. At a theoretical level it can be hoped that progress in the development of a science of criminology will be advanced through comparative undertakings. To understand the ramifications of these proposals, let us look at a few of the expected values of comparative research in more detail.

INTERNATIONAL COOPERATION

As already mentioned, through comparative research a knowledge of foreign systems of criminal justice is attained. This knowledge is, in fact, a prerequisite for obtaining the other values to be discussed, but it is also profitable in itself. Comparative research expands our knowledge of the contemporary world with its complexity, speed of communication, and the internationalization of many social problems. It is hoped that such knowledge contributes to a better understanding of other countries and their cultures. It contributes to a more international, less parochial perspective. But although these are valued goals, it must also be recognized that crime has become an international concern. Since the end of World War II we have become much more aware of the extent to which criminal operations are carried out on a transnational basis. International terrorism, air hijacking, and drug smuggling have all become recognized as problems that require international cooperation if they are to be prevented. With the ease of modern transportation come increased problems with regard to foreign nationals who have committed offenses abroad. Often cultural differences are the basis for commission of the crime, but questions of extradition and the execution of foreign judicial orders require an understanding by criminal justice officials of the procedures of the other nation.

UNDERSTANDING ONE'S OWN SYSTEM

Just as it is important to learn about the criminal justice system of others, it can also be stated that through the comparative approach we can achieve a better understanding of our own system. There is a common tendency to be uncritical of the system in one's own country if one is ignorant of the ways of others. There is an inclination to think that the solutions to problems in one's own legal order are the only possible answers. This can lead to idealization of one's native legal institutions and the tendency to treat them as inherent in the general nature of law. In the words of Lepaulle (1922: 858), "Where one is immersed in his own law, in his own country he is unable to see things from without, he has a psychologically unavoidable tendency to consider as natural, as necessary, as given by God, things which are simply due to historical accident or temporary social situations." Here is a leading scholar who admitted that he never completely understood French law until he came to the United States to study another system. As discussed by David and Brierley (1968:8), legal parochialism is "irreconcilable with a truly scientific spirit since it impoverishes, and indeed is dangerous to the development and application of national law." The discovery of other legal possibilities thus not only stimulates students' curiosity and imagination but also puts into question the solutions defined by their own national law. They are compelled to question the soundness of the solutions, norms, and many other aspects of their own law, to inquire into the whys and wherefores of the institutions.

It is especially important that we gather knowledge of a foreign system when our own is derived, through transplantation, from that other system. Americans recognize that their legal institutions have their roots in those of England, yet through time certain aspects have changed. Visiting Englishmen, for example, often see in the American state judicial system a model of the prereform courts of their native country. Likewise, Americans can get a much better insight into their institutions—for example, public prosecution—when they become aware of the historical background of the colonial period. Similarly, after World War II Japan inherited criminal procedures that borrowed heavily from the United States. It is highly probable that the inability of these procedures to function under Japanese conditions was caused by a lack of knowledge of the American criminal justice system and culture as a whole. Such an example of legal transplantation is of particular importance for many Third World countries that have attempted to adopt elements of either the common law or continental systems, institutions from the colonial periods, and new procedures based on customary law, to create a system that meets their needs and conforms to their values.

Finally, the comparative approach to criminal justice forces us to identify and explain the differences and similarities of our own and other systems. As a result, there may be a greater appreciation of the fact that the reason for particular legal institutions and practices must be understood as evolving from the socioeconomic and cultural environment. As Kamba (1974:493) noted, "comparative law serves to emphasize the interdependence between law and other social phenomena." Given this reality, it becomes clear that the machinery of criminal justice is actually an instrument of social control and is thus influenced by and influences social life in numerous ways.

REFORM OF ONE'S OWN SYSTEM

Every nation has portions of its criminal justice system that can be improved. One of the values of comparative research is the opportunity to benefit by learning of the experiences of others who may have faced similar problems. As Maine (1871:4), one of the early exponents of comparative law, said, "The chief function of comparative jurisprudence is to facilitate legislation and the practical improvement of the law."

Currently those countries with a high degree of industrialization and urbanization face a number of similar crime problems, such as increases in white-collar criminality, crimes of violence, and those related to the use of drugs. The criminal justice systems of these countries face similar difficulties, such as court congestion, law enforcement inefficiency, and correctional ineffectiveness. Socialist countries also have many shared problems—alcohol-related, economic criminality, and motor vehicle offenses are growing concerns. Although the criminal justice systems of these countries function quite smoothly in terms of the efficiency of courtroom procedures, in some of them the number of incarcerated offenders compared with the general population is very high. Finally, in the Third World there are problems of corruption and abuse of power as these countries move toward full economic and political independence.

It is obvious that knowledge of the experiences of other nations is invaluable when attempts are made to reform existing systems. Although procedures and institutions used in one culture may not flower in the same manner in another environment, often elements can be shifted, resulting in improvements in attempts to prevent crime and administer justice in the new setting. Likewise, knowledge of the experience of others can point to actions that should be avoided. However, it must be emphasized that when the procedures of one country have been adopted by another without adjustments for local circumstances, the effects are often disastrous. As observed by Tallon:

> Assuredly, to resort to a foreign legislation is not an innovation. . . . Its aim is not to find a foreign institution which could be easily copied, but to acquire ideas from a careful survey of similar foreign institutions and to make a reasonable transportation of those which may be retained according to local conditions [1969: 265-266].

UNIFICATION AND HARMONIZATION OF LAWS

One of the early reasons espoused for the comparative study of criminal justice was that it would lead to unification and harmonization of laws on a cross-national basis. As early as the 1900 Paris International Congress of

Comparative Law, it was urged by Lambert that the purpose of comparative law was to provide

> material which would form the basis of a general unification of those national systems of law which have attained the same degree of development or "civilization" and their replacement by an international common law [Kamba, 1974: 501].

This hope, which reflects much of the international sentiment following World War I, has not been realized, but there are indications that in some specialized areas unification of laws is possible. The harmonization of the laws of several countries with others has a greater potential for fulfillment.

A distinction must be made between unification, the adoption of identical laws by different countries, and harmonization, the elimination of major differences by minimizing existing legal obstacles. Efforts to bring about these goals can be seen at the international, regional, and national levels. For example, the United Nations has been active in promoting the adoption of minimum standards for the treatment of prisoners. Likewise, regionally or culturally linked nations—for example, the Scandinavian countries and members of the European Economic Community—have attempted to coordinate many activities in the criminal justice field. At the national level, especially in federations such as the United States, model codes have been developed to guide state legislatures so that their actions will be consistent with those of their sister states. Even in a unitary country such as the United Kingdom, where there are separate criminal justice systems for England and Wales, Scotland, and Northern Ireland, attempts are made to ensure the coordination among these entities.

Although the dreams of many who have advocated the unity of law at an international level have not been realized, there are many examples of nations seeking to unify or harmonize their criminal justice systems with those of others. What must be emphasized is that knowledge of comparative law is a prerequisite for such activities.

SCIENTIFIC PROGRESS

Thus far we have outlined a number of purposes that might justify the study of criminal justice systems on a comparative basis. Each function may be viewed as oriented toward the achievement of some instrumental purpose that would improve the rule of law. However, knowledge of the major criminal justice systems of the world and the use of the comparative perspective are important for the development of theories that will contribute to the broader purposes of science. For, as Rheinstein (1952:98) argued, comparative law belongs to the realm of the exact sciences "when its cultivator tries to observe, describe, classify and investigate in their relations among themselves and to other phenomena, the phenomena law." Thus the comparative approach to law uses the scientific method.

The mere knowledge of the functions and processes of criminal justice systems in a number of countries will not contribute to science unless the comparative approach is undertaken in a systematic manner. This means that research on criminal justice must conform to the accepted standards of the scientific enterprise in which findings accumulated following specific experimental procedures are used to develop concepts that can link hypotheses in order to develop theories. This movement from the plane of observation to that of the theoretical is essential if we are to understand our world. Use of the comparative approach as a means of studying criminal justice is one of the most important tools that can be used to achieve that goal.

In seeking to contribute to a scientifically based theory of criminal justice it is important that regularities observed in one system be examined to determine if they are found in other countries. For a theory or model to be viewed as reliable it will be necessary for its validation to be accomplished on a cross-national basis. As explained by Clinard and Abbott (1973:2), the aim of comparative research "is to develop concepts and generalizations at a level that distinguishes between universals applicable to all societies and unique characteristics representative of one or a small set of societies."

CLASSIFICATION OF CRIMINAL JUSTICE SYSTEMS

The division of this book into three sections denoting the common law, civil law, and socialist criminal justice systems follows the typology normally accepted by Western specialists in the field of comparative law. According to this scheme, elaborated by French scholar Rene David (1968), there exist in the contemporary world three main systems, which may be called groups or "families" of law. David uses two criteria in formulating this scheme. First, he asks if someone educated in one law would be able to handle another. If this is not possible, the two laws must belong to different families. Second, laws cannot be considered as belonging to the same family if they are based on opposing philosophical, political, or economic principles and if they seek to achieve two entirely different types of societies. When used cumulatively these criteria, David argues, result in the threefold division of the criminal justice systems of the developed world. In addition, he notes that there are supplementary systems based strictly on religious tenets found, for example, in the Muslim countries, as well as those emerging systems in the developing countries of Africa and Asia that are evolving out of their colonial past.

Many scholars contend that a distinctive category of socialist law does not exist, since the foundation of the legal systems of the Soviet Union and the countries of Eastern Europe can be traced to the continental (Roman-Germanic) family. Similarly, the threefold classification is usually criticized by socialist scholars (Szabo and Peteri, 1977) who, drawing inferences from their Marxist view of the world, point out that the typology is based only on formal elements such as the sources and structures of law, organization of the judiciary, and ways of legal reasoning. They claim that we must understand the essence of law, and thus the continental and Anglo-Saxon legal systems are merely various appearances of the same type of law based on a particular social order. Thus from a socialist perspective the basis for the demarcation should result in two legal families, one based on the private ownership of the means of production and the corresponding social system (common law and continental), and the other founded on the social ownership of property (socialist). As Szabo said, "Any approach differing from this will blur the differences arising from the social categories and is likely to lead, owing to its false start, to false conclusions" (Szabo and Peteri, 1977:13).

Some "bourgeois" scholars seem to be of the same opinion. For example, E. L. Johnson, an English specialist on the Soviet legal system, says that

> although we correctly place Soviet law within the continental group of legal systems, there is another factor of the greatest importance to be considered, for Soviet law claims to be an entirely new type of legal system based on the Marxist political philosophy and the socialist type of economy [1969:5].

He believes that, from this perspective, Soviet law bears no resemblance to continental systems, since it has aims and purposes different from those of capitalist states.

With regard to this controversy the name of Karl Renner, the Austrian jurist, is often mentioned. Renner elaborated the doctrine of the "neutrality of legal concepts." In his view legal concepts, like bricks, can be used for the construction of a building that can serve different purposes. In the same way legal concepts may be used to construct various legal systems. Johnson (1969:5), for example, claims that "the fact that the traditional civil law concepts have not been used for the purpose of constructing a system based on Marxist philosophy and socialist economics seem to many a striking justification of Renner's thesis." Hungarian scholar Szabo (Szabo and Peteri, 1977) also emphasizes the correctness of Renner's observation that the legal institutions will, in time, undergo functional changes, while their normative definition remains the same.

Another viewpoint, such as the one advanced by French comparative law specialist Marc Ancel, suggests that there are two main types of legal systems in the developed world: one found in Western countries, including the common law and continental systems, based on the ideas of liberalism and individualism and on Christian traditions; and the socialist system, being the reflection of current socioeconomic conditions, viewed in an instrumental way as a tool in building a new society and not as an expression of any abstract concept of justice. Ancel (1971) points out that the unity of the Western system has deep historical roots. For example, immediately following the American Revolution some leaders, such as Jefferson, urged that the common law be rejected and that the French pattern be adopted. At the time, it must be remembered, the French legal structure had been greatly influenced by the French Revolution. The arguments advanced by the two American jurists Story and Kent won, however, and there was popular support for retaining the common law. It was pointed out that the common law system, as well as the French legal reforms, aimed at the protection of civil liberties and rights. It is clear, says Ancel, that the ideological unity of the Western world stems from an older period. In conclusion, he claims that in the contemporary world there are two basic types of legal systems—the liberal and the socialist. As Ancel notes, in the future a third type probably will emerge to serve the needs of the peoples of Africa and Asia. This form, while retaining some elements of customary law, probably will be a model with characteristics placing it between Western liberalism and the socialist structures of the East.

In summary, we are brought back to this question: Is the socialist system a distinctive system or is it just a civil law system adapted to another circumstance? It is our belief that the thesis supported by the majority of scholars reflects reality: The socialist law, because of its distinctive philosophical background and ideology and the radically different functions it is supposed to perform, should be considered as a separate type of law as opposed to the common law and the continental law that exist in other developed countries. It is with the knowledge of this controversy that we have adopted the traditional three-system division in this book. In our view this formulation is a reflection of the reality of the existing world order—at least as far as the countries under discussion are concerned.

REFERENCES

ANCEL, M. (1971) Utilite et methodes du droit compare. Neuchatel: Editions Ides et Ca-
    lendes, Universite de Neuchantel.
BLAU, P. (1964) Exchange and Power in Social Life. New York: John Wiley.
CLINARD, M. B. and D. J. ABBOTT (1973) Crime in Developing Countries. New York: John
    Wiley.
DAVID, R. and J. E. BRIERLEY (1968) Major Legal Systems in the World Today. London:
    Free Press.

HAZARD, J. (1951) "Comparative law in legal education." University of Chicago Law Review 18:264.

HERRMANN, J. (1977) "Teaching and research in comparative and international criminal law." Revue International de Droit Penal 48:304.

JOHNSON, E. L. (1969) An Introduction to the Soviet Legal System. London: Methuen.

KAMBA, W. J. (1974) "Comparative law: a theoretical framework." International and Comparative Law Quarterly 23:485.

LEPAULLE, P. (1922) "The function of comparative law." Harvard Law Review 35:838.

MAINE, H. J. (1871) Village Communities in the East and West. New York: Holt, Rinehart, & Winston.

MERTON, R. (1957) Social Theory and Social Structure. New York: Free Press.

PARSONS, T. (1951) The social system. Glencoe: Free Press.

RHEINSTEIN, M. (1952) "Teaching tools in comparative law." American Journal of Comparative Law 1:95.

SZABO, I. and Z. PETERI (1977) A Socialist Approach to Law. Budapest: Akademiai Kiadó.

TALLON, D. (1969) "Comparative law: expanding horizons." Journal of the Society of Public Teachers of Law 10:265.

PART I

COMMON LAW SYSTEMS

The common law system originated in England following the Norman Conquest and today is found in all English-speaking countries with the exception of Scotland and South Africa. Through colonial expansion it was transferred to those Third World countries formerly linked to England. However, in many of these countries, particularly those with a Muslim population and in India, the transplantation was not complete, with the result that portions of the common law system existed along with the existing traditional forms of law.

Common law is referred to as "judge-made law," in that it developed out of decisions made in individual cases which then became precedent for the resolution of future disputes. It is thus characterized by an emphasis on solving the present case rather than on articulating a rule of conduct for the future. Thus it is less abstract than the legal rule found in the civil law systems. For common law jurists matters concerning the administration of justice, evidence, procedure, and the execution of penal decisions are more important than the articulation of substantive rules.

Part I begins with a description of criminal justice in the United States. Because it is assumed that most readers will be American students, this chapter should serve as the basis for comparisons with the other countries discussed in the book. The English and Canadian chapters describe systems that are most nearly similar to that of the United States, yet there are important differences that should be noted. In particular, it must be noted that England is a unitary political system, while the United States and Canada are federations; yet all three are industrial and urbanized countries with many similar crime problems.

1

UNITED STATES OF AMERICA

George F. Cole

At some point in the 1960s, Americans awoke to a startling acceleration in the amount of crime. As shown by such statistics as those in the FBI's *Uniform Crime Reports,* crimes of violence rose 156 percent from 1960 to 1970. In a 1968 Gallup survey, "crime and lawlessness" were mentioned as a cause of apprehension more often than any other local problem. This may be constrasted with a similar poll taken in 1949, when only four percent of big-city residents felt that crime was their communities' worst problem. The rise in crime coincided with a series of libertarian decisions by the Supreme Court, racial violence, urban change, and protests against the war in Vietnam. Demographers were also able to point to a startling bulge in the portion of the population in the high-risk crime group (15-24-year-olds). As a result political leaders found that the issues of "law and order" and "crime in the streets" hit a responsive chord.

Always quick to sense certain types of public unease, Congress and the president responded by creating the President's Commission on Law Enforcement and the Administration of Justice, and by establishing the Law Enforcement Assistance Administration (LEAA) with yearly appropriations reaching over $700 million by 1978 to help fight crime. In the states, similar efforts were undertaken to implement this major response to lawlessness. During the past 10 years the war on crime has become one of the major domestic policy efforts supported by the Johnson, Nixon, Ford, and Carter administrations.

I. GENERAL INFORMATION

Comprised of 230 million people who live in 50 states and 5 territories, the United States of America contains almost every topographical feature and extends from the frozen wastes of the Arctic to the semi-tropical zones of Puerto Rico. During the past 50 years there has been a continuing shift of the population from rural to urban areas. In addition, black citizens, who prior to World War II lived mainly in the South, have moved in dramatic numbers to the northern cities. There have been other population shifts from the older sections of the Northeast to the "sunbelt" of the Southwest. More Spanish-speaking citizens are now living in many parts of the country, particularly as a result of migrations from Puerto Rico, Cuba, and Mexico. Given this heterogeneity in a multiracial "nation of immigrants," it is of interest that public opinion surveys have shown there is near-unanimity as to the major sociopolitical values. These studies note a high level of agreement among the citizenry on the types of behavior that should be labeled as criminal.

CRIMINAL JUSTICE IN A FEDERAL SYSTEM

A federal governmental structure was created in 1789 with the ratification of the U.S. Constitution. This instrument created a delicate political bargain in which it was agreed that the national government would have certain powers—to raise an army, to coin money, to make treaties with foreign countries, and so on—but that all other powers would be retained by the states. Nowhere in the Constitution does one find specific reference to criminal justice agencies of the national government, yet the Federal Bureau of Investigation is widely known, criminal cases are often tried in U.S. District Courts, and the Federal Bureau of Prisons operates institutions from coast to coast that hold offenders who have violated national laws.

For conceptual purposes it is useful to think of two distinct criminal justice systems: national and state. Each performs enforcement, adjudication, and correctional functions, but they do so on different authority and their activities are vastly dissimilar in scope. Criminal laws are primarily written and enforced by agencies of the states, yet the rights of defendants are protected by the constitutions of both state and national governments. Although approximately 85 percent of criminal cases are heard in state courts, there are certain offenses—narcotics violations and transportation of a kidnap victim across state lines, for example—that are infringements of both state and federal laws.

As a consequence of the bargain worked out at the Constitutional Convention, the general police power was not delegated to the federal government. No centralized national police force with broad enforcement powers

may be established in the United States. It is true that the national government has police agencies such as the FBI and the Secret Service, but they are
authorized to enforce only those laws prescribed under the powers granted to
Congress. Because Congress has the power to coin money, it also has the
authority to detect and apprehend counterfeiters, a function performed by
the Secret Service of the Treasury Department. The FBI, part of the Department of Justice, is responsible for the investigation of all violations of
federal laws, with the exception of those assigned by Congress to other
departments. The FBI has jurisdiction over fewer than 200 criminal matters,
including offenses such as kidnapping, extortion, interstate transportation of
stolen motor vehicles, and treason.

The role of criminal justice agencies following the assassination of President John F. Kennedy in November 1963 illustrates the federal-state jurisdictional division. Because Congress had not made it a federal offense to kill
the president of the United States, Lee Harvey Oswald would have been
brought to trial under the laws of the state of Texas. The Secret Service had
the job of protecting the president, but apprehension of the killer was the
formal responsibility of the Dallas police and other Texas law enforcement
agencies.

As American society has become interdependent, with constant movement of people and goods across state lines, federal involvement in the
criminal justice system has increased. No longer is it useful to assume that
acts committed in one state will not have an impact on the citizens of another
state. This is seen especially in the area of organized crime, where gambling
or drug syndicates are established on a national basis. Congress recently
passed laws designed to allow the FBI to investigate situations where local
police forces are likely to be less effective. For example, under the National
Stolen Property Act, the FBI is authorized to investigate thefts of over
$5,000 when the stolen property is likely to have been taken across state
lines. In such circumstances jurisdictional disputes are possible because the
offense is a violation of both state and national laws. The court to which a
case is brought may be determined by the law enforcement agency making
the arrest. It is possible for a defendant to be tried under state law and then
retried in the federal courts for a violation of the laws of the national government. In most instances, however, the two systems respect each other's
jurisdictional lines.

It is important to emphasize that the American system of criminal justice
is decentralized. Two-thirds of all criminal justice employees work for
county and municipal units of government. This is not a result of the fact that
any one subunit of the system, such as the police, is primarily employed at
the local level; but, with the exception of corrections, at least a majority of

the workers in each of the subunits—police, judicial, prosecution, public defense—have ties to local government. It is in the states and communities that laws are enforced, violators brought to justice; consequently, the formal structure and actual processes are greatly affected by local norms and pressures—that is, the needs and demands of local people who are influential and the community's interpretation of the extent to which the laws should be enforced.

EXTENT OF CRIMINALITY

As discussed above, the United States has experienced a dramatic increase in the amount of crime during the last 10 years. Although this rise seems to have been halted, and for some crimes decreased, crime remains a serious national problem.

One of the frustrations of studying criminal justice is that there is no accurate means of knowing the amount of crime. Surveys that have asked members of the public if they have ever committed a breach of the law indicate that there is much more crime than is reported. Until recently, measurement of crime was limited to those incidents that were known to the police. Beginning in 1972, however, the LEAA sponsored ongoing surveys of the public to determine the amount of criminal victimization experienced. Comparing these studies with what appears in the FBI-produced *Uniform Crime Reports* (UCR) shows that there is a significant discrepancy between the occurrence of crime and offenses known to the police.

One of the main sources of crime statistics is maintained by the FBI and published annually, the *Uniform Crime Reports*. Authorized by Congress in 1930, this national and uniform system of compiling crime data is the product of a voluntary national network through which local, state, and federal law enforcement agencies transmit information to Washington concerning seven major crimes, "Index Offenses," and 22 other offense categories. Scholars have pointed out that the UCR data concern only those crimes reported to the police, that submission of the data is voluntary, that the reports are not truly uniform because events are defined according to differing criteria in various jurisdictions, and that upper-class and "white-collar" crimes are not included.

Although questions have been raised about the accuracy of the data concerning crime, it is broadly accepted that there has been a rise in actual crime in the United States during the past decade. The crime rate (amount of crime adjusted for population) for 1976 was up 42 percent over 1968; crimes of violence were up 39 percent, and those against property were up 44 percent.

The public most fears crimes of violence, such as murder, rape, and assault; yet these made up only nine percent of the incidents cited by the UCR in 1976. These are also the crimes that have been committed at a fairly constant rate over the years; although some, such as murder, are lower now than in times past. It is among crimes involving theft that the most dramatic increases have occurred. But here the reports may fool us. Burglary rates may have risen statistically not because there are more criminals but because more things are insured, because there are more opportunities for criminal activity in an affluent society, and because the FBI's definition of "serious" crime (theft of more than $50) is inconsistent with the realities of inflation.

AGENCIES OF CRIMINAL JUSTICE

Society has commissioned the police to patrol the streets, prevent crime, arrest suspected criminals, and enforce the law. It has established courts to determine the guilt or innocence of accused offenders, to sentence those who are guilty, and to "do justice." It has created a correctional system of prisons and programs to punish convicted persons and to try to rehabilitate them so that they may eventually become useful citizens. These three components— law enforcement, law adjudication, and corrections—combine to form the American system of criminal justice. It would be incorrect, however, to assume that system to be monolithic or even consistent. It was not fashioned in one piece at one time. Rather, various institutions and procedures that are the parts of the system were built around the core assumption that a person may be punished by government only if it can be proved by an impartial process that he or she violated a specific law. Some of the parts, such as trial by jury and bail, are ancient in origin; others, such as juvenile courts and community-based corrections, are relatively new. The system represents an adaptation of the institutions of the English common law to the American social and political environment.

Public organizations numbering 40,000 with 670,000 employees and total annual budgets of over $3 billion in four levels of government are charged with enforcing the law and maintaining order in the United States. The local nature of police efforts can be seen in the fact that the federal government contains only 50 law enforcement agencies and the states have 200. The other 39,750 are dispersed throughout the counties, cities, and towns.

The responsibilities of law enforcement organizations fall into four categories. First, they are called upon to "keep the peace." This is a broad and most important mandate and involves the protection of rights and persons in a wide variety of situations ranging from street-corner brawls to domestic quarrels. Second, the police must apprehend law violators and combat crime. This is the responsibility the public most often associates with police work, yet it accounts for only a minuscule portion of police time and resources. Third, the agencies of law enforcement are expected to engage in crime prevention. Through public education about the threat of crime and by reducing the number of situations in which crimes are most likely to be committed, the police can lower the incidence of crime. Finally, the police are charged with providing a variety of social services. In fulfilling these obligations a policeman recovers stolen property, directs traffic, provides emergency medical aid, gets cats out of trees, and helps people who have locked themselves out of their apartments.

Entrusted with the enforcement of a list of specific federal penal statutes, police organizations of the national government are part of the executive branch. Other than the FBI, which has the broadest purview—investigation of all federal crimes not the responsibility of another agency—there are also (1) units of the Treasury Department concerned with violations of laws relating to the collection of income taxes (Internal Revenue Service), alcohol and tobacco taxes, and gun control (Bureau of Alcohol, Tobacco, and Firearms), and customs (Customs Service); (2) the Drug Enforcement Administration of the Justice Department; (3) the Secret Service Division of the Treasury, concerned with counterfeiting, forgery, and protection of the president; (4) the Bureau of Postal Inspection of the Postal Service, concerned with mail offenses; and (5) the Border Patrol of the Department of Justice.

Each state has its own police force, yet here also the local nature of law enforcement may be seen by the fact that state police forces were not established until the turn of the century, and then primarily as a wing of the executive branch that would enforce the law when local officials did not. In all states this force is charged with the regulation of traffic on the main highways, and in two-thirds of the states it has been given general police powers; yet in only about a dozen populous states is it adequate to the task of general law enforcement outside the cities. Where the state police are well developed—such as in Pennsylvania, New York, New Jersey, Massachusetts, and Michigan—they tend to fill a void in rural law enforcement. American reluctance to centralize police power means that the state forces generally have not been allowed to supplant local officials. For the most part they operate only in those areas where there is no other form of police protection or where the local officers request their expertise or the use of their facilities.

Sheriffs are found in almost every one of the more than 3,000 counties in the United States. They have the responsibility for law enforcement in rural areas, yet over time many of their functions have been assumed by the state or local police. This is particularly true in portions of the Northeast. In parts of the South and West, however, the sheriff's office remains a well-organized force. In 33 of the states sheriffs have broad authority, are elected, and occupy the position of chief law enforcement officer in the county. Even when the sheriff's office is well organized it may lack jurisdiction over municipalities and incorporated areas. In addition to having law enforcement responsibilities, the sheriff is often an officer of the court and is charged with holding prisoners, serving court orders, and providing bailiffs.

Police departments exist in over 1,000 cities and 20,000 towns, yet only in the cities where they have the resources can it be said that they perform all four of the law enforcement functions. Although established by local government, the police of the cities and towns are vested by state law with general authority. Usually, the larger the community, the more police workers. Nearly one-third of the police personnel in the United States are employed by the 55 cities with populations over 250,000, resulting in a ratio of officers to residents of 2.9 per thousand, which is almost twice the average for cities of less than 100,000. In the metropolitan areas, where law enforcement may be fragmented among agencies of all governmental levels, jurisdictional conflict may inhibit the efficient use of police resources. The United States is essentially a nation with small police forces, each operating independently within the limits of its jurisdiction.

The United States has a "dual court system": a separate judicial structure for each of the states in addition to a national structure. In each of the systems is a series of trial and appellate courts, with the United States Supreme Court being the only body in which the systems are "brought together." It is important to emphasize that the U.S. Supreme Court, although commonly referred to as "the highest court in the land," does not have the right to review all decisions of state courts in criminal cases. It will hear only those cases where a federal statute is involved or where a right of the defendant under the U.S. Constitution has been allegedly infringed. This usually means the accused claims that one or more of his due process rights were denied during the state criminal proceeding.

With a dual court system, interpretation of legal doctrine can differ from state to state. Although states may have statutes with similar wording, none of them interprets the laws in exactly the same way. To some extent these variations reflect varying social and political conditions. They may also represent attempts by certain state courts to solve similar problems through different means. But primarily the diversity of legal doctrine results simply from fragmentation of the court system; within the framework of each jurisdiction the judges have discretion to apply the law as they feel it should be applied, until overruled by a higher court.

The national court system is arranged in a hierarchical manner, with the *district courts* at the base, the *courts of appeals* at the intermediate level, and the *Supreme Court* at the top. The 95 district courts are the tribunals of original jurisdiction, or the first instance. Distributed throughout the country, with at least one in each state, they constitute the judicial body that hears the great majority of civil and criminal cases arising under federal law.

Above the federal district courts are the 11 United States Courts of Appeals, each with jurisdiction for a geographic portion of the country, and one for the District of Columbia. Created in 1891 as a means of reducing the case burden of the Supreme Court, this intermediate level of the judiciary hears appeals from the district courts and from administrative bodies like the United States Tax Court and the National Labor Relations Board. From three to nine judges are assigned to each court of appeals, and normally three jurists sit as a panel.

The Constitution gives original jurisdiction to the U.S. Supreme Court for only a few types of cases; hence, the primary task of the high court is to hear appeals from the state courts of last resort and the lower federal courts. But as the highest appellate court, it still retains discretion over the cases it will hear. Each year it rejects as unworthy of review three-fourths of the 2,000 cases reaching it. With nine justices appointed for life, the Supreme Court is probably the most influential judicial tribunal in the world, exercising review and attempting to maintain consistency in the law within the federal structure.

One of the difficulties in describing the structure of state courts is that while they all are somewhat alike, they are all somewhat different. The laws of each state determine the organization of these courts; thus their names, their relationships to one another, and the rules governing their operation vary considerably. Still, one usually finds three levels of courts and a close resemblance between the pattern in the states and the organizational framework of the national judiciary. It should be emphasized that the state courts operate under the authority of state constitutions and should not be considered "inferior" to comparable courts in the national structure.

The *courts of first instance,* often referred to as the "inferior" trial courts, have powers limited to arraignment of all cases, preliminary hearings involving crimes that must be adjudicated at a higher level, disposition of summary offenses (where a jury is not allowed), and, in some states, trial of persons accused of some misdemeanors. Generally, the law defines the jurisdiction according to the maximum jail sentence that may be imposed. Six months in jail is commonly the greatest penalty that these courts may confer.

Especially in urban areas, the observer at these courts will find very little that resembles the dignity and formal procedures of higher bodies. These are not jurisdictions of record (no detailed account of the proceedings is kept), and the activities are carried out in an informal atmosphere. In most urban areas endless numbers of people are serviced by these courts, and each defendant gets only a small portion of what should be his "day in court."

The *courts of general jurisdiction* are above the courts of first instance and have the authority to try all cases, both civil and criminial. They are courts of record and follow the formal procedures of the law. In large metropolitan areas it is common to have divisions specializing in different kinds of cases. In addition to the original jurisdiction that such courts exercise, and which is their principal function, they also act on appeals, hearing those defendants who contest decisions made at the inferior level.

The *appellate courts* have no trial jurisdiction but hear only appeals from the lower courts. In some states only the state's supreme court is found at this level; in others there may be an intermediate appellate court in addition to its highest judicial body.

On any given day approximately 1.3 million offenders are under the care of America's system of corrections. Through a variety of institutions and treatment programs at all levels of government attempts are made to restore people to society. Of interest is the great number of approaches employed by correctional personnel to bring about the rehabilitation of offenders. The average citizen probably equates corrections with prisons, but only about one-third of convicted offenders are actually incarcerated; the remainder are under supervision in the community. The use of probation and parole has increased dramatically, as has the creation of community-based centers, where those who have been incarcerated may maintain ties with families and friends so reintegration into society can be more successful.

The federal government, all of the states, most counties, and all but the smallest cities are engaged in the correctional function. In small communities facilities are usually limited to jails that are used to hold persons awaiting disposition. As in the police and court functions, each level of government acts independently. Although the states operate prisons and parole activities, probation is frequently tied to the judicial departments of counties or municipalities.

II. SUBSTANTIVE CRIMINAL LAW

In the American system violators of the laws are prosecuted and tried according to rules. The ancient Latin maxim, *nullen crimen, nulla poena, sine legel* (there can be no crime, and no punishment, except as the law prescribes), is basic to the system. The criminal code therefore not only embodies a view of the forbidden behavior and the punishment to be administered but describes the ways officials may deal with defendants.

The mere description of criminal offenses does not give a full understanding of the law's content. The criteria used to decide whether a specific act is a crime must be more precise than the statements of the general characteristics of a body of rules. More important, it is necessary to understand the principles buttressing these definitions because the principles assist in differentiating those who should be labeled offenders. For every crime there are theoretically seven interrelated and overlapping principles. Ideally, behavior cannot be called a crime unless all seven principles are present:

(1) Legality—a law defining the crime.
(2) *Actus reus*—behavior of either commission or omission by the accused that constituted the violation.
(3) *Mens rea*—a guilty state of mind.
(4) Fusion of *actus reus* and *mens rea*—the intention and the act must both occur.
(5) Harm—a crime has a harmful impact on certain legally protected values.
(6) Causation—a causal relationship between the act and the harm.
(7) Punishment—the sanctions to be applied for the proscribed behavior must be stipulated in the law.

Over time the seven principles of a crime have been interpreted to meet changing conditions. In particular, the concept of a guilty state of mind *(mens rea)* has been adapted to the lessening of religious influences (sin) on the law and the emergence of psychology as a prominent field of knowledge. The idea of *mens rea* as an actual consciousness of guilt has been abandoned in favor of intentional, or even reckless or negligent, conduct. The new doctrine, called "objective" *mens rea,* asks "not whether an individual defendant has consciousness of guilt, but whether a reasonable man in his circumstances and with his physical characteristics would have had consciousness of guilt." The traditional notion of *mens rea* has thus been replaced by the requirement that the act be voluntary and that the so-called "general defenses" do not apply. The general defenses include such conditions as insanity, immaturity, intoxication, coercion, and mistake of fact. In contemporary terms, *mens rea* has evolved to a concept of objectivity without the ethical or moral connotations attached to the original idea.

SOURCES OF CRIMINAL LAW

In recent years there has been increased academic debate concerning the sources of criminal law. This question has come to the forefront as minority groups have become more vocal and as the sanctions imposed on white-collar offenders has been contrasted with those imposed on street criminals. Why are some types of human behavior and not others declared criminal by law? What are the social forces that are brought to bear on legislators as they write the criminal code? Why are activities that are labeled criminal during one era found to be acceptable in another? Such issues require the development of a theory explaining the sources of the criminal law because they have an impact on the assumptions concerning the nature of crime and the sources of criminal behavior.

For much of American history there was a tendency to think of crime as pertaining only to criminals rather than to some other units of society. Most Americans seem not to separate the concept of crime from that of "criminal" and believe that criminals are a group set off from the mainstream of society. In Puritan Massachusetts crime was viewed in theological terms, and the criminal was a creature of the devil. Most provisions of the Puritans' legal code were annotated to show the biblical source of the injunctions. In a later era the medically oriented saw crime as arising from some biologically inherited abnormality. Psychologists in the nineteenth and twentieth centuries described crime as resulting from mental or personality defects. More recently, social scientists have looked to social situations—neighborhood, school, gang, and family—as predisposing persons to be either law-abiding or criminal. Throughout all of these approaches runs the idea that criminality is a characteristic of individuals and not a consequence of a label imposed by the community.

It is most important to recognize that the definition of behavior as criminal stems from a social process in which rules are developed and applied to particular people. This means that as well as the person who commits a crime there must first be a community and process that has called the commission of that act criminal. In addition, someone must have observed the act or its consequences and applied the community's definition to it. Third, a crime implies a victim. Finally, punishment implies that someone is responsible for carrying out the community's will. All of this signifies that crime is a social phenomenon arising from the complex interactions of a number of individuals and social situations.

Theories have been developed to explain the focus and functions of criminal laws and the social processes by which they evolve. These ideas may be divided into a consensus model and a conflict model. The consensus model argues that the criminal law is a reflection of the will or values of society. This assumes that the society has achieved a well-integrated and relatively stable agreement on basic values. Studies have shown very high public agreement on the seriousness of crimes, and the norms concerning crime seriousness are widely diffused throughout the subgroups of society. The conflict model emphasizes the role of political interests in the formulation of the law and points to the dominance of powerful groups in structuring the law to meet their own needs. As an example, it has been shown that a variety of elements influenced the development and enforcement of prohibitions against narcotics, including the relations among nations, controversies between druggist and physician interest groups, the bureaucratic politics of enforcement agencies, and the fear of racial and ethnic minorities.

At this point in the development of a sociology of law it is impossible to reach a conclusion as to the theoretical value of the consensus and conflict models. Certainly with some laws, especially those prohibiting crimes that are *mala in se,* there is consensus in most Western societies as to the values espoused. It is also very easy to demonstrate how the laws prohibiting cattle rustling, the consumption of alcohol, vagrancy, and the sale of pornography—crimes *mala prohibita*—have their source in the political power of special interests. Because the great bulk of criminal violations are now those of the latter type, attention logically focuses on the conflict model.

III. CRIMINAL PROCEDURE

Although a formal diagram of the criminal justice process may appear streamlined, with cases of the accused entering at the left and swiftly moving toward their disposition at the right, the fact remains that the system is detailed and fraught with detours. At every point along the way decision makers have the option of moving a case on to the next point or dropping it from the system. The formal blueprint of the administration of justice does not include the influences of the social relations or political environment within which the system operates.

The popular and even the lawbook conception of the criminal justice machinery supported by a due process ideology and reinforced by the "Perry Mason" image of an adversary system oversimplifies in some respects and overcomplicates in others. Theory holds to an ideal of law enforcement in which the police arrest those suspected of committing infractions of the law and promptly bring them to a magistrate. If the offense is minor, the magistrate disposes of it immediately; if it is serious, the accused is held for further action and is admitted to bail. The prosecutor is next given the case and charges the offender with the specific crime after a preliminary hearing of the evidence. If the defendant pleads "not guilty" to the charge, he is bound over for trial. In the courtroom a "fight," supervised by the judge, is staged between adversaries—defense counsel and prosecutor—so that the truth becomes known. If the jury finds the defendant guilty, he is sentenced by the judge or the jury and correctional officials impose the prescribed sanctions.

Although many cases do proceed as described above, for most cases this conception of the criminal justice flow makes fundamental assumptions that do not correspond to reality. It fails to take note of the many informal arrangements that occur through negotiations among the principal actors.

Only a small number of cases ever reach the trial stage. Rather, decisions are made early in the process on the basis of discretion so that cases that may not result in conviction are filtered out by the police and prosecutor. In addition, in some jurisdictions up to 90 percent of the defendants plead guilty, thus obviating the need for a trial. Through bargaining between the prosecutor and defendant, a guilty plea is exchanged for reduction of the charges or a sentencing recommendation. The size of the prison population can be used as a justification to influence sentencing or parole decisions.

Social scientists have recognized that discussion of an organization solely in terms of its structure is inadequate for a full appreciation of its dynamic process. Although the term "organization" suggests a certain bareness—a lean, no-nonsense construct of consciously coordinated activities—all organizations are molded by forces tangential to their rationally ordered structures and stated ends. The formal rules do not completely account for the behavior of the actors because an informal structure also exists that results from the social environment and the interaction of these actors. Organizations have formal decision-making processes, but these may serve mostly to legitimize organizational goals and act to enhance the symbolic needs of authority. Emphasis on the prescribed structure may neglect the fact that the achievement of goals is dependent upon the behavior of actors who have their own requirements, which may run counter to the manifest aims of the organization. Further, it must be recognized that the organization itself has survival needs that must be fulfilled. Thus the realization of system aims is but one of the several important purposes of the organization. The system makes adaptive responses to meet its needs because informal arrangements arise to meet the goals of both the organization and its actors.

The administration of criminal justice may be characterized by certain essential features. First, it should be noted that it is an open system; new cases, changes in personnel, and different conditions in the political system mean that it is forced to deal with constant variations in its milieu. Second, there is a condition of scarcity within the system; shortages of resources such as time, information, and personnel are characteristic. Every case cannot be processed according to the formally prescribed criteria. This affects the subunits of law enforcement—police, prosecutor, courts—so that each competes with the others for the available resources. Central to this analysis is the politics of administration; the varied range of interactions between an agency and its environment that augment, retain, or diminish the basic resources needed to attain organizational goals.

The President's Crime Commission has referred to the legal process as a continuum—an orderly progression of events. Like all legally constituted structures, there are formally designed points in the process where decisions are made concerning the disposition of cases. To speak of the system as a continuum, however, may underplay the complexity and the flux of relationships within it; although the administration of criminal justice is composed of a set of subsystems, there are no formal provisions for the subordination of one unit to another. Each has its own clientele, goals, and norms, yet the outputs of one unit constitute the inputs to another.

We should not be surprised by the fact that conflicts exist among the various actors in the criminal justice process. Each sees the problem of crime and the administration of justice from a different perspective. The daily experiences, social background, and professional norms of the policeman, prosecutor, defense attorney, and judge exert an influence on the way each makes decisions. The policeman who has seen the agony of crime victims and risked his life to protect society may be unable to understand why defendants are released on bail or why prosecutors willingly reduce charges to gain guilty pleas. At the same time, the prosecutor may be concerned by the policeman's lack of attention to detail in collecting evidence, while the judge may be upset by a failure to maintain the civil liberties of defendants. A characteristic of the criminal justice process is that each participant is dependent upon others to assist him in doing his work. At every stage from arrest to sentencing, a variety of actors with different viewpoints and goals are involved in making decisions about the disposition of each case.

Given the fragmentation of the system, we may ask how decisions are made. As interdependent subunits of a system, each organization and its clientele is engaged in a set of exchange relationships across boundaries. The necessary interactions among participants means that bargains are made that stipulate the conditions under which a defendant's case will be handled. The police, charged with making decisions concerning the apprehension of suspects, interact with the prosecutor's office when presenting evidence and recommending charges. The defendant, through his counsel, may exchange a guilty plea for a reduction of the charges by the prosecutor. Likewise, the courts and prosecutor are linked by the decision to bring charges, the activities of the courtroom, and disposition of the case.

Although the formal structures of the judicial process stress antagonistic and competitive subunits, the interaction of exchange may strengthen cooperation within the system, thus deflecting it from its manifest goals. For example, although the prosecutor and defense counsel occupy roles that are prescribed as antagonistic, continued interaction on the job, in professional associations, and in political or social groups may produce a friendship that greatly influences role-playing. Combat in the courtroom, as ordained by the formal structure, not only may endanger the personal relationship but may also expose weaknesses in the actors to their own clientele. An outcome, rather than the unpredictability and professional distance stressed by the system, is that decisions on cases may be made to benefit mutually the actors in the exchange.

The most distinctive feature of the administration of criminal justice is that it is marked by a high degree of discretion. As in few other social organizations, discretion in law enforcement and judicial agencies increases as one moves down the administrative hierarchy. In most organizations, the observer usually finds the lowest-ranking members performing the most routinized tasks under supervision, with various mechanisms of quality control employed to check their work. With the police, prosecutor, and lower-court judges, discretion is exercised more frequently by those who are newest to the organization, who maintain the primary organizational contact with the public, and whose work is usually shielded from the view of supervisors and outside observers. Thus, the patrolman has wide discretion in determining whom he should arrest and on what charges, the deputy prosecutor makes vital decisions concerning indictments, and lower-court judges operate without the dominating influence of higher courts.

A final characteristic of the administration of justice is that the process resembles a filter through which cases are screened: Some are advanced to the next level of decision-making, while others are either rejected or the conditions under which they are processed are changed. As the President's Crime Commission noted, "Approximately one-half of those arrested are dismissed by the police, prosecutor, or magistrate at an early stage of the case." Other evidence is equally impressive, showing that a preponderance of adult felony arrests do not go to the grand jury for indictment. Typically, jury trials account for a minuscule percentage of the guilty convictions in criminal courts. Sentences are mostly imposed following a plea of guilty.

Criminal justice is greatly affected by the values of each decision maker, whose career, influence, and position may be more important than are considerations for the formal requirements of the law. Accommodations are sought with those in the exchange system so that decisions can be made that are consistent with the values of the participants and the organization. A wide variety of departures from the formal rules of the ideology of due process are accepted by judicial actors but are never publicly acknowledged. Because of the strain of an overwhelming caseload and the adversary nature of the formal structure, members of the bureaucracy can reduce stress while maximizing rewards by filtering out those cases viewed as disruptive or as potential threats to the established norms. Because defendants pass through the system and the judicial actors remain, the accused may become second-ary figures in the bureaucratic setting. The administrative norms are so well established that judges may agree that defendants surviving the scrutiny of the police and prosecutor must be guilty.

IV. EXECUTION OF PENAL MEASURES
(CORRECTIONS)

Since 1870, when the American Prison Association proclaimed that "reformation, not vindictive suffering, should be the purpose of the penal treatment," the rehabilitative ethos and the organizational structures created to achieve its aims have been the dominant purpose of the criminal sanction. As recently as 1973 a national commission demonstrated the almost complete acceptance of this medical model by the correctional community by recommending additional measures to implement the rehabilitative goal more fully. During the past decade, however, there has been a growing literature pointing to the ineffectiveness of treatment programs on recidivism, to concern about the pervasiveness of the discretion required by this goal and its impact on civil rights, and to evidence that rehabilitation has had little impact on the control of crime.

Legislatures in over 20 states are now considering as a substitute for the dominance of the rehabilitative schema proposals that emphasize "deserved punishment" as the goal of the criminal sanction. To implement this new focus, reformers have called for definite sentences, revitalized systems of probation, and the abolition of parole. The speed with which this reversal of correctional policy is occurring and the nature of the forces working for this change may have a far-reaching impact on all facets of the criminal justice system.

RETHINKING THE REHABILITATIVE MODEL

The treatment model of the criminal sanction is most beguiling. Crime is diagnosed as a disease; punishment, the treatment. Release from punishment is then related with cure. On the basis of this simple schema the goal of rehabilitation achieved a position of priority in the United States during the late 1950s. Under the banner of the social and behavioral sciences a new breed of penologist helped to shift the emphasis of the postconviction sanction to treatment of the criminal, an offender whose social, intellectual, or biological deficiencies had caused him to engage in illegal activity. A historical review of social values might suggest that during different eras justifications for the criminal sanction have been advanced that fit the dominant ethical ideals of the day. Given the special position of science in the twentieth century, it is not surprising that the medical model of corrections should have had such an appeal.

So pervasive has been the rehabilitative goal that structures to enhance its achievement—indefinite sentences, treatment programs, and parole—have been incorporated into the criminal justice system of every state as well as that of the federal government. By sentencing the guilty to indefinite periods of incarceration, judges are able to give correctional officials the freedom to determine when the offender has been "cured." Elaborate classifications have been developed so that institutional personnel may prescribe the treatment that it is hoped will correct the social or psychological difficulties that lie at the base of the offender's problem. Vocational training and education, individual counseling and psychotherapy, honor farms, group therapy, work-release, halfway houses, behavior modification—all have been incorporated into the modern penal system. Parole boards are authorized to decide when the inmate is sufficiently reformed so that he may reenter society. Each of these structural features of the rehabilitative model requires that decision makers have an ability to predict future behavior. It is doubtful that there is a scientific basis for such predictions, and increasingly there is realization that organizational needs have a crucial influence on decision-making.

PROPOSALS FOR CHANGE

Although the general public may be alarmed by high crime rates and newspaper accounts of parole violations, serious questions are being raised by practitioners and scholars about the optimistic assumptions of the rehabilitative model and its impact on measures to prevent and control crime. Persons concerned by the inability of corrections to reduce the crime rate are not the only ones critical of the rehabilitation model. A wide-ranging group of humanists, scholars, and former offenders believe that the discretion accorded judges and correctional administrators has led to an unjust postconviction process.

By recommending that correctional policy shift away from the goals and organizational structures of rehabilitation, contemporary reformers are advocating a return to a more classical approach to wrongdoing. Predominance is given to a model of human behavior as volitional and the concept of punishment as proportionate to the seriousness of the crime. Past conduct is stressed, not the potential for future conduct. Punishment expresses moral disapproval for criminal activity. In addition, it is argued that deserved punishment should be applied only for the wrong inflicted and not to achieve utilitarian benefits (deterrence, incapacitation, rehabilitation).

Already the states of California, Indiana, Illinois, and Maine have enacted legislation that incorporates this new focus. Although differing in some respects, the focus of these reforms is on narrowing discretion through definite sentences, voluntary access to treatment programs, and the abolition of release by the parole board. In each of the states legislative debate has surrounded the question of the time to be served. It has been recognized that this is the ingredient that exerts a tremendous influence on the functioning of all parts of the criminal justice system. In most states where reform is under consideration the actual time now being served has been the basis for the proposals.

One can discern a major difference in the rhetoric of contemporary correctional reform and that of prior eras. In the post-Attica climate of the 1970s, the assumptions of the past have lost their credibility. The research of the recent few years has awakened many from the dream that the cause of criminal behavior could be diagnosed and cured. No quick and easy solutions are offered, and claims about crime reduction are noticeably absent. What is claimed is that simple justice should be the goal and that this may be achieved largely by harnessing discretion through definite sentencing. Thus the goal is a postconviction process that is humane, visible, and just.

2

ENGLAND

John C. Freeman

I. GENERAL INFORMATION

England, for the purposes of this chapter, is taken to include the Principality of Wales. Northern Ireland and Scotland, while part of the United Kingdom, have a largely separate system of law and criminal administration and are therefore excluded.

The area of England and Wales is 50,053 square miles (including 7,969 square miles in Wales) and its population is 48,593,658 (including 2,723,596 Welsh). Thus the country has a relatively high density of population, 971 per square mile. Immigration, coming largely from the countries of the British Commonwealth in the last two or three decades, has resulted in a nonwhite population widely estimated at about two million. London is England's capital and it has a population of about seven million.

Although the country was invaded by the Romans from 55 B.C., there has been no significant reception into England of Roman Law. The influence of Roman Law doctrines in Scotland is much more pronounced.

England may now be described as a country with a Christian tradition and as a constitutional monarchy with an unwritten and hence flexible constitution. To become effective, legislation must be passed by the House of Commons (composed of 635 elected members) and the House of Lords and receive the Royal assent. In practice, the latter cannot be withheld, and the blocking powers of the House of Lords are extremely limited. The members of the House of Commons are democratically elected, all citizens over the age of 18 years being eligible to vote. Elections are held at least once every five years; most of those elected belong to either the Conservative or the Labour Party. An independent and permanent Civil Service is a strong factor in maintaining a fairly consistent and progressive policy toward criminal justice, whichever party is in power.

There is no Ministry of Justice in England. The functions normally exercised by such a ministry in other countries are carried out chiefly by the Home Office (whose minister, the Secretary of State for the Home Department, is one of the principal members of the Cabinet) and by the Lord Chancellor's Office (the Lord Chancellor also being a senior cabinet minister as well as filling other major constitutional positions).

A number of bodies such as the Criminal Law Revision Committee and various ad hoc committees review the criminal law and make recommendations for change. Since the passing of the Law Commissions Act of 1965 there has been a Law Commission for England and Wales with the express task of keeping the law up-to-date. Some major reforms in the criminal law have been instigated by this body in recent years.

It is perhaps unnecessary here to detail the complicated structure of local government and administration that exists in England. Suffice to say that there are elected county councils, district councils, and similar bodies with wide-ranging control over such matters as local planning, housing, fire services, and highways. In many of these activities, such as the police, authority is shared with the central government.

SCOPE OF CRIMINAL SANCTIONS

In common with all developed countries, England has seen a great growth of criminal law in recent years. The handful of major crimes against the king, persons, and property that emerged many centuries ago when criminal law parted from civil law has grown into the usual confusion of restraints and punishments thought to be required by a sophisticated modern state. No really adequate definition of a crime exists, and sociologists differ from lawyers as to how a crime may properly be recognized and defined. Many offenses were created in the nineteenth century in response to social pressures, and many more have been created recently to impose some limits on the potential harm of motor vehicles and kindred contemporary vexations. Truly, nobody now knows how many offenses there are.

In company with other nations with a similar inheritance, England is now scrutinizing her straggling criminal law quite closely. The work of the Law Commission has already meant much consolidation and abolition of many obsolete crimes. England has no law of desuetude, so prosecutions are occasionally based on statutes centuries old. A Criminal Policy Department exists with the Home Office. Persistent consideration is being given to decriminalization and to the future shape of the criminal law. In the future more attention may be paid to offenses against the environment and to certain far-reaching white-collar crime. At the same time, there may be a corresponding withdrawal from enforcement of criminal sanctions for petty crimes against individuals. It is, of course, unrealistic to imagine that all social problems are solved by a withdrawal of criminal law. They merely become the responsibility of an alternative agency. The frequent offense of drunkenness is a case in point. Yet the decriminalization thesis may win some acceptance in England for other good reasons.

GENERAL DESCRIPTION OF THE LEGAL SYSTEM

England is a common law country, and courts are bound by earlier decisions of superior courts on similar facts. Many crimes, including some of the most serious (such as murder), are still not defined by statute, but modern Acts of Parliament are gradually replacing the common law, as well as creating many new offenses. Two contemporary trends may be noted. First, Parliament, with increasing frequency, lays down the outline of legislation to be filled in by delegated or subordinate legislation, often in the form of multitudinous rules and regulations promulgated by ministerial departments. Road traffic legislation and the Bail Act of 1976 are two examples among many. Second, legislation is sometimes passed by Parliament to become effective when later announced by ministerial decision. As in the case of the Children and Young Persons Act of 1969, it is not unusual for many sections of acts to remain inoperative for years because of changes in policy, lack of resources for implementation, or other reasons.

AMOUNT, STRUCTURE, AND DYNAMICS OF CRIMINALITY

Social attitudes change. Few today would agree with the order of crimes discussed by Sir William Blackstone in his widely published *Commentaries* at the turn of the eighteenth century, which put first those crimes immediately injurious to God and His holy religion and second those violating and transgressing the law of nations.

A recently successful prosecution for blasphemous libel was the first in many years and there was widespread public dismay that such a crime should still exist at all. English criminal law has often been criticized for apparently placing more emphasis on offenses against property than upon offenses against the person, and there is wide concern that persons convicted of a serious robbery, for example, may serve longer terms of imprisonment than some who have murdered.

Perhaps the biggest change in crime and criminal law has resulted from the Industrial Revolution, urbanization, and the need to control and administer an increasingly complex society. With motoring offenses running at about half of the court convictions in England and Wales, underdeveloped countries wishing to curtail conviction statistics might well eschew the introduction of the motor vehicle.

STRUCTURE AND FUNCTIONING OF LAW ENFORCEMENT AGENCIES

There are over 111,000 police (including some 5,000 women) organized in 43 regular forces throughout England and Wales. The largest force is the Metropolitan Police Force of London, which has almost 21,000 men covering an area with a radius of about 15 miles. Responsibility for, and control of, the police is shared between local and central government.

Prosecution is a matter for discretion, which usually rests with the police, although in a few special cases decisions are made by the attorney-general or the director of public prosecutions. Most prosecutions are conducted before the courts by the police themselves, but counsel drawn from private practice are briefed in serious cases.

The legal profession in England and Wales is divided in two. Barristers (counsel) are chiefly advocates before the higher courts and provide opinions on difficult questions of law. Solicitors, usually practicing in partnerships, sometimes appear in certain courts but more often advise lay clients on everyday legal affairs. Lay clients obtain the services of barristers through the intermediary offices of a solicitor. The most senior barristers are designated Queen's Counsel (silks), and most judicial appointments are made from the ranks of the barristers. At the close of 1976 there were 3,881 barristers in practice, including 313 women; and at the end of 1977 32,812 solicitors were practicing, of whom 2,130 were women. Free, or substantially subsidized, legal aid is widely available to defendants.

About 98 percent of those convicted of crimes are dealt with by magistrates' courts, of which there are about 900 throughout the country. They are staffed by over 23,000 lay magistrates (justices of the peace), who voluntarily take time off from their normal occupations to do this work. In addition, about 50 stipendiary magistrates (full-time salaried lawyers) man some of the courts in large urban areas. Appeal from the magistrates' courts lies to the crown courts, which also have original jurisdiction in serious criminal cases. Appeal lies further to the Court of Appeal (Criminal Division) and thence to the House of Lords in certain cases. In the Crown Courts the judge sits with a 12-man jury which is the arbiter of facts at the trial. Judges of the higher courts are appointed by the Crown, and the removal of a judge from office would be constitutionally extremely difficult and exceptionally rare. Persons under the age of 17 are brought before juvenile courts, where three specially appointed lay justices sit. Both sexes must be represented on such a bench.

II. SUBSTANTIVE CRIMINAL LAW

GENERAL PRINCIPLES OF LIABILITY

It goes almost without saying that in England there can be no conviction for crime save for proven infractions of preexisting substantive offenses. An apparent attempt in the House of Lords to recognize the power of the courts to create new heads of liability retrospectively was widely criticized and eventually denied in the more recent case of *Knuller* v. *D.P.P.* (1972, 3 W.L.R. 143). So far as statutory offenses are concerned, a number of presumptions have been acknowledged by the courts—for example, (1) against the restriction of individual liberty, (2) that penal statutes are to be strictly construed, (3) against retrospective effect, (4) that *mens rea* is required for liability, and so on. Thus we were reminded by Lord Reid in *Sweet* v. *Parsley* (1969, 2 W.L.R. 470) that "it is a universal principle that if a penal provision is reasonably capable of two interpretations, that interpretation which is most favourable to the accused must be adopted." It remains a seemingly insuperable task for all the law of a complex society to be so expressed and so accessible that the common man knows all his rights and duties in advance.

CLASSIFICATION OF OFFENSES

Offenses in England may be classified in different ways for different purposes. Many distinctions are largely procedural. Crimes may be regarded philosophically as dealing with things either *mala en se* or *mala prohibita;* they may be thought of as either statutory or common law. The ancient divisions of treasons, felonies, and misdemeanors were abolished by the Criminal Law Act of 1967 and replaced by the new categories of arrestable offenses and nonarrestable offenses.

Perhaps the most useful (though confusing) distinction exists between indictable and nonindictable offenses, the former being eligible for trial by jury. Although this provides an apparent guide to the seriousness of an offense, indictable offenses could include relatively minor thefts, robberies, and assaults; in certain circumstances many such crimes may be tried summarily before the magistrates. The Criminal Law Act of 1977, by provisions not yet operative, is intended to obviate these anomalies by spelling out offenses triable only summarily, offenses triable only on indictment, and offenses triable either way.

AGE OF CRIMINAL RESPONSIBILITY

Although persons under the age of 17 are dealt with in juvenile courts, they are considered in law to be fully responsible for their crimes if they are over the age of 14. Children under 14 are not held to be liable unless, in addition to having ordinary *mens rea,* they also have a "mischievous discretion." This latter is generally taken to be present if a child admits to knowing that what he was doing was wrong. Under the age of 10 children are entirely exempt from criminal liability.

LIABILITY OF CORPORATIONS

A corporation is recognized as having a legal existence with rights and duties separate from that of its members. Early jurisprudential difficulties concerning, *inter alia, mens rea* and the *ultra vires* doctrine having been overcome or overlooked, corporations may now be regarded as generally liable to the same extent as an individual. This result has been achieved by extending the doctrine of vicarious liability and by visiting responsibility on the high officers of a company who direct its activities. Although it has been remarked that a corporation has no body to be kicked nor soul to be damned, this has not prevented the imposition of apposite sanctions.

THE MENTAL ELEMENT

> It is of the utmost importance for the protection of the liberty of the subject that a court should always bear in mind that, unless a statute, either clearly or by necessary implication, rules out *mens rea* as a constituent part of a crime, the court should not find a man guilty of an offense against the criminal law unless he has a guilty mind [Brewd v. Wood, 1946, 175 L.T. 306].

Nevertheless, there have been many offenses in the last 50 years that have been held to be offenses of strict (sometimes wrongly called "absolute") liability. This doctrine has been held to be necessary in the public interest: It is said to promote higher standards of safety, hygiene, and welfare by dispensing with the need to prove intent and thus facilitating prosecution. But this is seen as working injustice on, for example, an honest trader who is already doing his best, or indeed upon anybody who has taken all reasonable care to do nothing wrong. In more recent statutes, defenses equivalent to due diligence are beginning to appear, as the injustice of the full rigor of the strict liability doctrine becomes apparent even to the common layman.

There has been, in general, no liability for negligence in English criminal law.

ATTEMPT AND CONSPIRACY

The law of attempt and conspiracy has become very complicated and confused. Since mere intention to commit a crime is in itself insufficient for liability, there must be evidence of the commission of some act directly connected with the offense for attempt to be charged. But some acts of the accused that may show the necessary connection might be considered too remote to constitute a true attempt. For a long time the courts have dwelt on the proximity of the acts in question. More recently the courts have toyed with the notion of the "unequivocal act" and also with the "substantial step theory." In truth, no one theory seems yet to have been consistently accepted and the matter is surrounded by a considerable incrustation of academic literature.

The law of conspiracy has also been widely criticized. According to the common law, one was guilty of conspiracy who agreed with another to commit an unlawful act or a lawful act by unlawful means. The Criminal Law Act of 1977 now provides, in effect, that a charge of conspiracy can be lodged only in respect to an agreement to commit a criminal offense.

DEFENSES

Where a defendant is suffering from mental illness or severe subnormality, the Home Secretary may, acting on the advice of two medical practitioners, order his detention in a hospital. If the accused, being brought to trial, is found incapable of pleading, understanding the charge, and following the proceedings, he may be found unfit to plead on arraignment under the Criminal Procedure (Insanity) Act of 1964.

If he is able to stand trial, the accused may still wish to raise insanity as his defense. This happens very rarely. The rules are ancient and amount to this:

> That every defendant is presumed sane until the contrary be proved to the satisfaction of the jury.

> It should be ascertained whether the accused was labouring under such a defect of reason from disease of the mind as not to know the nature and quality of his act. If he is found to have understood the nature and quality of his act, the court has further to be satisfied that he knew that it was wrong.

> If the accused is found to be suffering under an insane delusion, he is under the same degree of responsibility as he would have been on the facts as he imagined them to be [R. v. M'Naghten, 1843, 10 Cl. & F. 200].

In 1957 the Homicide Act was passed which *inter alia* borrowed from Scots law the doctrine of diminished responsibility. This is a limited defense, which provided that murder may be reduced to manslaughter where the accused "was suffering from such abnormality of mind (whether arising from a condition of arrested or retarded development of mind or any inherent causes or induced by disease or injury) as substantially impaired his mental responsibility."

In practice, this defense seems virtually to have replaced the use of the M'Naghten Rules, and there is also some suspicion that pleas of guilty to manslaughter based on diminished responsibility are being accepted in lieu of pleas of not guilty to murder. The flexible sentencing powers of the courts, which may impose up to life imprisonment for manslaughter (which sentence is mandatory for murder), ensure that elements of justice and security are satisfied and a court is enabled to deal mercifully with, for example, a "mercy killing."

Automatism, in the sense of involuntary movement of the body or limbs, or acts done while unconscious or in a convulsion or spasm, may be a defense.

As such, irresistible impulse is no defense, but it might amount to diminished responsibility.

An honestly held mistake of fact, even though unreasonable, might serve as a defense. A mistake of law never will (even though the state of the law at any given time must surely be regarded as a fact!).

Self-induced (as opposed to involuntary) intoxication due to drink or drugs which falls short of bringing about actual insanity seems to be defense only where it negates specific intent in crimes held to require this. The law as stated in *D.P.P.* v. *Beard* has been interestingly discussed in *R.* v. *Lipman* (a drugs case) and by the House of Lords recently in *R.* v. *Majewski*.

Fear of dire threats and some other forms of duress may be a defense to some crimes but not to murder. Coercion is a somewhat obsolete defense available only to wives who commit offenses under the moral persuasion of their husbands.

What scant authority there is on the defense Superior Orders suggests that if it exists at all, it does so in a manner most restricted.

The defense of necessity is illustrated in one of the most poignant cases in English legal history. Some survivors of the shipwrecked *Mignonette* (1884), after 20 days at sea with virtually no food and water, killed and ate the youngest of their number, a cabin-boy. They were later rescued, to be tried and convicted of murder. From that day until the present no place has been found for any defense of necessity.

PUNISHMENTS AND PENAL MEASURES

For the purposes of the present discussion, penal measures are taken to embrace all the sentencing options open to the courts from absolute discharge to capital punishment.

A recent Home Office Working Paper describes policy objectives as follows: (1) to protect society from the dangerous offender; (2) to reduce the incidence of offending (particularly among juveniles); (3) to reduce the prison population and the use of imprisonment; and (4) to improve the efficiency and enhance the humanity of the system. This policy rests on a number of assumptions about the efficacy of general and particular deterrence; it reveals a certain official ambivalence toward the positive and negative consequences of imprisonment; it illustrates also the now-evident conflict between the two philosophies of treatment and punishment or "just deserts."

It is important to note that there are no general minimum penalties laid down by law, although there may be statutory limits on maximum sentences.

PRINCIPAL PENAL MEASURES

Capital punishment for murder has not existed since the Murder (Abolition of Death Penalty) Act of 1965. It still survives for the outdated offenses of high treason and piracy with violence. Whipping was abolished in 1948. The gravest punishment at the present time is life imprisonment, which is mandatory on conviction for murder and may also be passed on conviction for certain other very serious crimes, such as manslaughter, rape, violent robbery. It serves as an indefinite preventive measure. Life imprisonment does not necessarily imply incarceration for the term of one's natural life.

Imprisonment is available as a punishment in a wide variety of cases involving offenders over the age of 17; the sentence may be either immediate or suspended. Although it has been accepted policy for years that no one under the age of 21 should be sent to prison unless no alternative appears open to the courts, there is still a large and growing number of this age group going into this form of custody; about 5,000 were committed to immediate imprisonment in 1976.

The Powers of Criminal Courts Act of 1973 provides a consolidation of much previous penal legislation and, by section 22, confirms the power of courts to suspend sentences of imprisonment in certain categories of cases. The Criminal Law Act of 1977 contains further restrictions on the courts' power to order imprisonment; it also contains two new provisions enabling the court itself (not the Parole Board) to suspend the remainder of a prison sentence after part of it has been served. These measures reflect not only the continued growth of humanitarian and reformist considerations but also the continued growth of the present prison population, which has reached limits almost incapable of further extrapolation.

Similar influences have led to the increase of noncustodial sentences. The fine is the traditional mainstay of the system. It is overwhelmingly the most commonly employed penalty. It has not proved easy to devise entirely efficient modes of collecting outstanding fines, and fines totaling several million pounds may be unpaid and awaiting enforcement at any one time. The Swedish day-fine system has been discussed but not adopted.

Probation is also very widely used and provides skilled supervision for a period of up to three years, generally in lieu of any other sentence. The Probation Service is also responsible for the care of prisoners released from prison, as well as for many other functions in the penal system. Most of the modern alternatives to imprisonment call upon the resources of the Probation Service in one way or another.

It is possible for courts "to do nothing." This may happen by their awarding either an absolute or a conditional discharge. The former would be appropriate where an offense was seen as extremely trivial or purely technical. The latter is a discharge subject to a condition that the offender not commit any further offenses for a period of up to three years. This is somewhat similar to a bind over, which is an ancient power of the court to obtain an undertaking (on a recognizance, or money pledge) from an offender that he will be of good behavior and keep the peace. It is thus wider than a conditional discharge in its terms and is preventive in its policy.

Motoring offenders are normally dealt with by fines and by disqualification from driving and/or imprisonment in more serious cases.

The Criminal Justice Act of 1972 introduced a number of new modes of dealing with offenders. Most of these methods are now reproduced in the Powers of Criminal Courts Act of 1973. They give the criminal courts themselves power to order the defendants to pay restitution and compensation to the victims of their crimes. Criminal bankruptcy might be ordered in cases where loss or damage of more than 15,000 pounds has been caused. These are important incursions of the criminal process into what has for a long time been the province of the civil law, and they are directed toward a long overdue recognition of the plight of victims. Experimental day training centers have been set up to try to break patterns of recidivism. It is also possible to make community service orders compelling offenders to do between 40 and 240 hours of unpaid work for the community in their spare time. There are, in addition, powers for deprivation of offenders' property used for crime, and powers for imposing disqualification from driving where a vehicle has been used for crime. It will be seen that the government has not been altogether timid in its experimentations in recent years. Courts now have many more alternatives to the traditional sanctions. Moreover, if they wish to test a convicted person before final disposition, they may now defer sentence for a period of not more than six months.

SENTENCING TRENDS

Unfortunately, the creation of new sentences and the increasing unwillingness of courts to resort to imprisonment is offset by the steady increase in many forms of criminality with a consequent increase in the total number of persons passing through the system.

SPECIAL CATEGORIES OF OFFENDERS

Juveniles, those under 17 who are brought before the juvenile courts, may, like adults, be subject to absolute or conditional discharges, bound over, or ordered to pay compensation. Fines may be adjudged and, in some cases, ordered to be paid by their parents.

Additionally, boys may be ordered to spend some of their Saturday afternoons at attendance centers, and children of both sexes may be placed on supervision, which is generally undertaken by a social worker employed by the local authority instead of the Probation Service. The juvenile courts also have power to sentence boys over the age of 14 to detention centers, where they are held in custody for a few weeks; in the case of boys and girls aged 15 to 21, the juvenile courts may ultimately send serious offenders to the Crown Court with a recommendation for Borstal training. The Crown Court then reviews the sentencing decision to decide whether this form of semi-intermediate sentence (from six months to two years) is really appropriate or whether some other form of disposition could be employed.

The effective limit of a juvenile court's powers is reached when it makes a care order which places the ordinary powers of the parents in the hands of the local authority whose social workers decide in case conferences the best disposition of their charges under the age of 18. They will consider placement of the children in community homes and schools, foster placements, return to their natural parents, and other options.

The maximum duration of sentences of imprisonment laid down for certain offenses may be exceeded by the courts in the case of some recidivists by means of extended sentences.

The Mental Health Act of 1959 enables courts to make hospital orders or guardianship orders with respect to mentally disordered offenders. Where a person is convicted of an offense punishable by imprisonment and is considered mentally ill by court standards, the court may hospitalize him or assign guardianship to a social services agency. In certain cases where the protection of the public is required, a restriction order may be added to a hospital order so that a patient is not discharged without the consent of the Home Secretary.

The Misuse of Drugs Act of 1971 draws a distinction between those who possess controlled drugs and those who supply them. Drugs are thus listed in classes. For example, class A includes the opiates, class B contains cannabis, and class C such substances as benzphetamine. If someone comes before the courts for possession of a small amount of cannabis for his own use, he would normally be fined. At the other end of the range, someone convicted of trafficking in heroin could expect a custodial sentence of several years. When appropriate, offenders are given probation and/or referred to special treatment centers. Special treatment has been provided in some penal institutions but, particularly for those addicted to hard drugs, the success rate cannot be claimed as high.

No law—certainly not the penal law—has yet proved capable of significantly affecting alcoholics. At present they pass through the magistrates' courts getting small fines or drying out in prisons for short terms. Successive legislative endeavors have attempted to better the situation. A few experimental treatment centers have been set up to provide an alternate to prosecution, but they are expensive to operate effectively and the prognosis remains poor.

Special hospitals exist for those who are mentally ill and dangerous. The head of one of these was said recently to have observed that he could release half of his inmates with complete safety to the public forthwith; his difficulty was that he could not tell which half. Many regarded as psychopathic are detained in prison and, indeed, the response to treatment elsewhere is so minimal that this has been deemed the best place for them. Other persons clearly regarded as dangerous at the present time include terrorists, bombers, and similarly violent political fanatics, who have been given very long terms of imprisonment following conviction for the gravest kinds of violence. But in other respects the whole concept of dangerousness is undergoing continued and urgently needed reappraisal.

DISCHARGED OFFENDERS

Those discharged from institutions may have after-care provided by the Probation Service. Attention is also drawn to the Rehabilitation of Offenders Act of 1974, which provides that many people convicted of certain classes of crimes may regard their convictions as "spent" after given periods of crime-free life. They may not have to reveal or admit their convictions and can be protected from any unjustified revelation of their spent convictions being made by other people.

PAROLE

Parole was introduced by the Criminal Justice Act of 1967. The legislation provides that prisoners may become eligible for consideration for release on license (and supervision undertaken by the Probation Service) after they have served one-third of their sentence, or 12 months, whichever is the longer.

DIVERSION FROM CRIMINAL JUSTICE

Diversion has been described as a way to reduce the volume of persons circulating through the criminal justice process while reducing recidivism and reducing the risk of getting a criminal record. Viewed thus widely, diversion properly embraces more than schemes and projects created in parallel to the criminal justice system. In time such schemes will almost inevitably come to be regarded as part of the system. True diversion must mean expelling culprits from the criminal justice system altogether. In this wide sense much has been achieved in England.

III. CRIMINAL PROCEDURE

GENERAL PRINCIPLES

The adversary system of justice obtains in criminal trials as in civil. The presumption of innocence is paramount. The rule against double jeopardy is fully recognized, so that no man can be charged twice for substantially the same offense. The charge would be met by the ancient plea of autrefois acquit (or convict).

PHASES OF CRIMINAL PROCEEDINGS

It has been explained that magistrates' courts hear and dispose of about 98 percent of all criminal cases. The magistrates do, however, also sit as examining justices in serious indictable cases: They determine whether there is a *prima facie* case against the accused such as to justify his subsequent trial in a crown court. The sentencing power of magistrates is very limited. At the present time they may not impose more than six months' imprisonment nor a fine of more than 400 pounds.

The process of the trial proceeds according to certain stages. The prosecutor outlines his case with a short speech and calls witnesses and other evidence to support it. The defense may then submit that the case is insufficient for conviction as it stands. If this application is rejected, the defense witnesses and evidence are called and the defense then makes a final speech. At that stage the magistrates give their decision or, if the case has been a trial before the crown court, the judge sums up the evidence for the jury and explains to them the law, leaving the jury to decide upon the facts. Each witness is examined by the side producing him, cross-examined by the other side and then reexamined by the first side again. The court has little power to call evidence of its own volition.

RIGHTS OF THE ACCUSED

Appeals lie from the Crown Court to the Court of Appeal (Criminal Division) and from there to the House of Lords, if a point of general public importance is involved. While it is possible for an accused person to appear in the courts without any representation, it is most common, especially in the more serious cases, for barristers or solicitors to be engaged. If the accused is unable to afford the fees himself, they are met by legal aid. It is a fundamental right that every defendant should be entitled to a lawyer of his choice.

The laws regarding arrest, search, and seizure are too complicated to be expressed in a short compass. Basically, the citizen's right to move about freely is protected by law. Restraint can only be justified on certain grounds.

So far as search and seizure are concerned, subject to exceptions, the police have no power to search anyone not under arrest, nor in general have they any power to enter and search premises, save by authority of a search warrant. The power to seize property is similarly curtailed. It is right to observe, however, that statutory exceptions to these important freedoms are becoming increasingly common—some would say too common. Unlike the position in some other jurisdictions, in cases where police in England have obtained evidence unlawfully, the courts have a discretion to receive that evidence notwithstanding the improper mode by which it was obtained. Some of the protections intended to be afforded to individuals are contained in what are known as the *Judges' Rules*.

PRETRIAL DETENTION

A person arrested without a warrant must either be released on bail by the police or brought before a magistrates' court within 24 hours. A person arrested on a warrant must then either be granted bail (if the warrant so provides) or be brought to the magistrates' court at once.

Detention of persons in custody should be the exception and not the rule. As it is, about 80 percent of persons remanded by the magistrates are remanded on bail. But this still means that 44,501 persons were remanded in custody in 1972, and anxiety is increased by the fact that, of the number, 2,186 were found not guilty or had their cases dropped. A further 15,648 were convicted but received noncustodial sentences. At the present time, defendants in custody spend an average of 9.6 weeks awaiting trial (or 16 weeks in London), and those on bail wait for 14.6 weeks (or 27 weeks in London). This position is seen as unjust and unsatisfactory. One reason it is unsatisfactory is that those remanded in custody aggravate the numbers of those already in overcrowded prisons and add to the prisons' administrative problems.

SPECIAL PROCEEDINGS

Courts-martial have jurisdiction over members of the armed forces and are governed principally by the Army and Air Force Acts of 1955 and the Naval Discipline Act of 1957. The accused may be arrested by a superior officer for any offense against military law, and the form of trial is similar in many respects to that in the civil courts. Courts-martial have jurisdiction over civilians only when Her Majesty's forces are in armed occupation of hostile territory. Appeals lie to the Courts-Martial Appeal Court, which is composed of ordinary members of the Court of Appeal nominated by the Lord Chief Justice. There may be a right of further appeal to the House of Lords.

LAY PARTICIPATION IN CRIMINAL PROCEEDINGS

The contribution of the laity in criminal proceedings is extensive, through jury service and through the lay magistracy. As already mentioned, more than 23,000 lay justices (justices of the peace) sit in over 900 courts in different parts of the country and they may also sit with the judge in the crown court. This office of justice of the peace is an ancient one, with a more or less direct lineage going back to 1362 and still further in a less direct way. They are appointed by the Lord Chancellor and serve until the age of 70. They have, as a rule, no formal legal training, though they do nowadays undergo short courses prior to appointment, and they are kept up-to-date through publications and by ad hoc lectures and conferences. They are guided on law by lawyers appearing before them and by trained clerks of the court.

There are many criticisms of the lay magistracy. It is not as representative of all social classes as it might be, but the demands are onerous for certain categories of workers. In many ways it is perhaps remarkable that the quality of these benches of unpaid, part-time justices is as good as it is. Certainly, by years of experience, many become very capable and give good service. There is, after all, a right of appeal to the crown court by way of complete rehearing of a case, and the infrequency of such appeals may reflet some satisfaction with the outcome of the trials. At the present time, it is difficult to see how the necessary judicial manpower could be provided if the vast amount of work now undertaken by law magistrates were to be placed in professional hands.

This principle of trial by one's peers, or lay participation in criminal justice, is also preserved in the ancient jury system. Juries of 12 people are used in the crown courts and most citizens aged between 18 and 65 are eligible to serve. People in certain occupations are barred from taking part, as are people with some kinds of criminal records. Juries are now able to reach majority verdicts.

JUVENILE COURTS

As was stated, those under 17 may be brought before a juvenile court. The courts are less formal than adult magistrates' courts, although, understandably, some children and their parents may still be bemused by what is going on around them. The Children and Young Persons Act of 1969 represents a difficult compromise between those who see the juvenile courts as another arm of social services with a protective role toward children in trouble and others (largely lawyers) who see it as an affront to justice that children may be dealt with in ways which they (the children) perceive as punitive without having the procedural protections afforded by a proper criminal trial. The position at the present time remains that the procedure of the juvenile courts is very little different from that in the adult courts, except that the atmosphere is more relaxed, some strict rules are a little less rigidly enforced, and the courts—uniquely in the English criminal justice system—are not open to the general public.

IV. EXECUTION OF PENAL MEASURES (CORRECTIONS)

The aims of penal measures no doubt embrace the usual hodge-podge objectives: deterrence (general and individual), prevention, reformation, retribution, denunciation, compensation, expiation, and so on. The sentencer may not always be overt in taking these goals into account, but they are behind every sentence in greater or lesser proportion according to circumstance.

EXECUTION OF DEPRIVATION OF LIBERTY

It is for the judiciary to pass sentence in England and it is not the practice for prosecutors to call for any particular sentence or form of punishment. However, once the court has pronounced sentence, the role of the judge is virtually at an end in that case.

The executive plays an increasingly large part. Thus, for example, after a judge says a prisoner is to be imprisoned for five years, an executive decision determines where the sentence will be served, whether under open conditions or closed; what "treatment" might be accorded the convicted person in prison, whether he will receive the usual one-third remission for good conduct or be deemed to forfeit any part of it; whether he will be paroled; and so on. Similarly, once a juvenile court has used its gravest power (the making of a care order passing parental rights to the local authority), it is a matter for the authority as to how those rights are exercised, whether the child is allowed home, placed in an institution, and, if so, for how long. An increasing number of other situations make it true to say that the control of sentences is passing from the judiciary to the executive and that the judge is being left merely to create a sentence framework to be filled in by others. This trend may have implications for justice that must be carefully borne in mind.

ADMINISTRATION AND SUPERVISION OF PENAL INSTITUTIONS

The Home Secretary is the minister ultimately responsible for penal institutions and the treatment of offenders in England and Wales. He receives advice from the Advisory Council of the Penal System, a body comprised of distinguished judges, criminologists and penologists, psychiatrists, lawyers, and others. Prison policy and the administration of custodial institutions are carred out by the Home Office Prison Department, and probation is administered by the Home Office Probation and After-Care Department.

CLASSIFICATION OF OFFENDERS

The classification of offenders by age has already been referred to above. Entirely different processes and institutions are relevant to those of less than adult age. All offenders are segregated according to sex. In general, there are separate institutions for each sex. In the case of adult offenders this is certainly so. Some dispositions, such as detention centers, are not available for females.

So far as adult prisoners are concerned, they are segregated into those convicted and those unconvicted, and those convicted are separated into security categories that considerably influence the type of prison to which they may be sent and the regime to be employed there:

Category A: Prisoners whose escape would be highly dangerous to the public or the police or to the security of the state (approx. 1%).

Category B: Prisoners for whom the very highest conditions of security are not necessary but for whom escape must be made very difficult (approx. 30%).

Category C: Prisoners who cannot be trusted in open conditions but who do not have the ability or resources to make a determined escape attempt (approx. 50%).

Category D: Those who can reasonably be trusted to serve their sentences in open conditions (approx. 20%).

TYPES OF PENAL INSTITUTIONS

The main distinction is made between open and closed prisons. Most are of the latter category. Some are very modern (and the building program continues), but many were built during the last century. Most are seriously overcrowded; more than one-third of those in custody sleep two or three to a cell that was originally designed for one. There are prisons especially designed for those on remand, for those with psychiatric problems, for those deemed suitable for certain industrial conditions, and others. There are also prisons with special units to contain certain prisoners in Category A. All prisoners receive one-third remission of their sentences, so long as they do not forfeit all or part of this by infringing rules while in custody.

RIGHTS AND DUTIES OF INCARCERATED OFFENDERS

These are governed largely by the ordinary law of the land and by the Prison Rules. Infringement of the rules amounting to offenses against the criminal law may be prosecuted before the ordinary courts. Lesser offenses may be adjudicated by the governor of an institution, and if his own powers of action are insufficient, severer penalties may be imposed by visiting magistrates. Inmates also have the right to bring complaints to the visiting magistrates.

Rule 43, which provides for the segregation of certain prisoners in certain circumstances, may be invoked by prisoners themselves to obtain enhanced protection from victimization by fellow inmates.

Some prisoners operate a "hostel scheme." Here a segregated part of the prison is set aside for a small number of offenders in the concluding months of their sentences, and those selected are able to sleep in the "hostel" at night, while working freely in the community outside the prison by day. There are other schemes for the employment of inmates outside institutions.

EXECUTION OF NONCUSTODIAL MEASURES

These depend in almost all cases on the support of the Probation Service and have been outlined already. Community service orders have met with some success. Some offenders have become so involved in their projects that they have asked to remain active after the expiry of their court orders.

3

CANADA

Brian A. Grosman

I. GENERAL INFORMATION

Canada occupies most of the northern half of the North American continent, stretching over 4,000 miles from the Atlantic Ocean in the east to the Pacific Ocean in the west, and from its southern border with the United States, past the Arctic Circle in the north. The geographical land area of Canada is 9.22 million square kilometers.

The population of Canada is small in relation to the country's geographical size. The most recent national census, taken in 1976, indicates a total population for Canada of 23,243,000 persons, reflecting a low population density. The population, however, is concentrated along Canada's southern border, where the climate is the mildest and where most of Canada's arable land and industry are located.

The northern two-thirds of Canada is sparsely settled but is rich in mineral resources which will play a large part in Canada's future development. Unlike central Canada's industrial and manufacturing concentrations, the extreme east, north, and west of Canada have economic bases more centered on primary production and resource extraction.

The Canadian economy, like those of many Western nations, has experienced difficulty over the past five years in maintaining full employment while controlling inflation. Despite these problems, however, the country's population maintains a relatively high standard of living even compared to other developed nations.

Two important demographic characteristics of the Canadian population are relevant to Canada's legal system. The first has to do with the Province of Quebec's origin as a French colony. This province of Canada is predominantly French-speaking and has retained French legal institutions. The civil laws of the Province of Quebec are found in the Quebec Civil Code. Quebec's Civil Code is generally similar to the types of civil codes found in civil law countries. This basic difference in the civil law of Quebec as compared to the rest of Canada does not affect the central issues discussed below, however, because the power to make criminal laws in Canada is within the jurisdiction of the federal government according to Canada's constitution. Criminal law and criminal procedure are the same throughout all of the provinces of Canada, notwithstanding Quebec's social, political, and institutional uniqueness within Canada.

The second demographic characteristic which is of relevance to Canada's legal system has to do with the Native population of Canada. At the time when the North American continent was settled by Europeans, from the seventeenth until the early twentieth century, the land area was already inhabited by North American Indians. These first inhabitants of Canada live outside of the social mainstream, often under inferior economic conditions. In part, because Canada's Native population is economically disadvantaged, Natives make up a disproportionate share of Canada's criminal offenders.

The Government of Canada is a federal system based upon the British model of parliamentary democracy. The Dominion of Canada consists of ten provinces and two territories. The two territories are under federal control, although local territorial councils are empowered to govern these areas. The territories are located in the northernmost part of Canada, have the smallest populations, and are the least developed.

Powers of government in Canada are shared by the federal government, located in Ottawa, and ten provincial governments, located in provincial capitals. The powers of government are divided between the two levels of government in accordance with Canada's constitution, the British North American Act. The constitution is an Act of the Parliament of Great Britain. The act dates from 1867, when Canada was granted independence by Britain. Prior to this date, Canada had been first a French and then a British colony. Canada's early history as a British colony has resulted in the nation having characteristically British political and legal institutions, such as parliamentary governments and the adversary and common law system of litigation and adjudication.

GENERAL DESCRIPTION OF THE LEGAL SYSTEM

Canada's legal system is based, to a large extent, on British legal institutions. For example, Canada's civil law, with the exception of the Province of

Quebec, is derived from and continues to develop along lines similar to those of the common law of England. Decisions of Britain's higher courts are still given weight when argued before a Canadian court, if no other Canadian decision is binding on that court. Canada has followed the British system of *stare decisis*. Under this system of law, all judicial decisions are binding on their facts, on all other courts lower in the judicial hierarchy than the one rendering the decision. It is this system of *stare decisis* which is chiefly responsible for the development of Canadian common law.

It is within the power of the federal government of Canada and provincial governments to vary or abolish the common law as they choose. Each level of government is limited to its constitutionally prescribed sphere of legislative activity. Where disputes arise as to whether or not a given law is within the jurisdiction of the level of government which has proposed or enacted it, it is the task of the country's highest court, the Supreme Court of Canada, to rule on the proper interpretation to be placed on those sections of Canada's constitution, as well as on the validity of the challenged legislation.

A tendency to vary the common law by way of legislative enactment has increased in recent years. Examples of this tendency are the creation of new causes of action for parties especially disadvantaged, such as the surviving family of an individual who has died as a result of an actionable civil or criminal wrong (fatal accidents legislation and criminal injuries compensation legislation), and the creation of special courts and special procedures dealing with specific areas of the law (family law courts and labor relations boards).

The creation of criminal law offenses in Canada has been completely removed from the common law. All Canadian criminal offenses and most criminal procedure are contained in the Criminal Code of Canada, an act of the federal Parliament of Canada. Section 8 of the Criminal Code states that there are no criminal offenses in Canada except as provided in the code. However, common law defenses are retained (section 7(2) as they existed under the criminal law of England that was in force in a province on the first day of April 1955.

CRIMINALITY OVER THE PAST 50-100 YEARS

Changes in the pattern or amount of criminal activity in Canada over the past century do not lend themselves to precise analysis, due to a lack of reliable statistical data. Only recently have criminal statistics been collected in Canada in a comprehensive manner. In the past 15 years, for example, the framework of definitions used as a base for statistical collection have been varied twice, with the uniform crime reporting categories being adopted only in 1972.

In general terms, there has been an increase in crimes of violence in Canada as the urban areas of the country have grown in size and population density. In addition, there has been an increase in legislation creating quasi-criminal or regulatory offenses. However, such regulatory offenses are not generally viewed by society as "criminal."

SCOPE OF CRIMINAL LAW

In terms of a basic philosophy, the classification of acts as criminal in Canada is sought to be limited to those acts which Canadian society views as morally wrong and therefore meriting punishment and which have a potential to do substantial damage to society. The designation of conduct as criminal is seen as an instrument of last resort for reaffirming the values of Canadian society and registering social disapproval of those acts which are morally revolting to society. The goal of those enforcing the criminal law is to administer criminal justice in such a manner that humanity, freedom, and justice are maximized for the greatest number of citizens.

In Canada recently there has been a tendency toward narrowing the scope of the criminal law, in accordance with these philosophical principles. These changes, however, are not being effected through altering offenses so much as through provision in the Criminal Code for more various and less stigmatizing sentences.

STRUCTURE AND FUNCTIONING OF
LAW ENFORCEMENT AGENCIES

There are three levels of law enforcement agencies in Canada. At the federal level, the Royal Canadian Mounted Police (RCMP) is charged with protecting national security and enforcing certain federal legislation such as the Narcotic Control Act. At the provincial level, the provinces of Quebec and Ontario administer their own provincial police forces. In the other eight provinces, the role of a provincial police force is filled by the RCMP on a contract basis, between the federal and provincial governments. Provincial police forces are charged with enforcement of the Criminal Code within the province, as well as provincial legislation such as traffic and highways legislation and liquor legislation. At the local level, large urban centers operate their own municipal police forces. Municipal police forces share jurisdiction with provincial police forces within the boundaries of their municipality.

Under Canada's constitution, the administration of justice within a province is the responsibility of provincial governments. The provincial governments administer justice through departments of the Attorney General. The department of the Attorney General employs full-time lawyers at judicial centers throughout the province for purposes of prosecuting criminal offenders. In addition, the federal government employs lawyers as prosecutors through the federal Department of Justice, for purpose of prosecuting offenders under federal statutes other than the Criminal Code. Examples of such federal statutes are the Narcotic Control Act and anticombines legislation. Some urban areas also employ counsel as prosecutors, for purpose of prosecuting those offenders charged by their municipal police forces under the Criminal Code or under local regulatory legislation.

All offenders are entitled to defense counsel if they request representation. An offender who cannot afford counsel may be appointed counsel at the Court of Appeal level (section 611), or he may approach provincial legal aid offices, which provide free legal services to those who cannot afford to employ counsel. Both provincial and federal governments are involved in setting up and staffing the system of criminal courts in Canada. The provincial governments appoint provincial judges or magistrates, who sit as the lowest level of criminal court and as the court with whom the offender first has contact when entering his plea or being remanded in custody. At the next level are district or county court judges, appointed by the federal government. District court and county court judges sit as appeal courts from the magistrates' level and as courts of first instance for those Criminal Code offenses allowing an election by the accused as to his manner of trial. The highest level of court is the Court of Queen's Bench, composed of a judge and jury. Queen's Bench judges are appointed by the federal government.

At the appeal level, district or county court judges, as well as Queen's Bench judges, sit as appeal courts from the magistrates' courts. Above these judges sit the provincial Courts of Appeal and the Supreme Court of Canada. Both of these courts have appellate jurisdiction only. The judges of these courts are appointed by the federal government. The Supreme Court of Canada is the court of last resort for criminal appeals as well as civil appeals.

II. SUBSTANTIVE CRIMINAL LAW

GENERAL PRINCIPLES OF RESPONSIBILITY

Section 8 of the Criminal Code provides that no person shall be convicted of an offense at common law. The effect of this provision is that all acts that are not prohibited or made offenses by a statute of the Canadian Parliament, or other level of government, are lawful. The philosophical base of this concept is to be found in Canada's background of British legal institutions, Magna Carta, and the rule of law.

Under sections 449 and 450 of the Criminal Code, the powers of arrest for ordinary citizens and peace officers are defined. Lawful arrests must be made in strict compliance with these sections. Section 454 states that all arrested persons are required to be taken before a justice within 24 hours, or where a justice is unavailable within that period, as soon as possible, to be dealt with according to law. It is not permitted to arrest a person and detain him under normal circumstances without charging him and taking him before a justice. Any arrest or detention considered to be unlawful may be tested by habeas corpus. This writ requires that the detained person be brought before a court and that his confinement be justified according to law.

Under a federal statute (the War Measures Act), the federal Cabinet, acting as the executive branch of the federal government, is empowered to declare martial law in a national emergency, thereby suspending the civil liberties of Canada's citizens. This legislation has only been used once in peacetime since it was enacted, during the October Crisis of 1970 in the Province of Quebec. The legislation was implemented at that time to curtail terrorist activities within that province.

Changes in the criminal law are usually only interpreted as being retroactive in Canada if the change in the law favors the accused. If the law is made more strict between the time of the offense and the time of the accused's trial, then there is a presumption that the law as it existed at the date of the offense applies. If the law is made less strict during this period, then the presumption is that the new law applies to the accused.

There are two grades of criminal offenses in Canada. The less serious criminal offenses are called "summary conviction offenses." Under section 722 of the Criminal Code, summary conviction offenses carry a maximum sentence of six months in prison and/or a fine of $500. All summary conviction offenses are within the exclusive jurisdiction of provincial court judges or magistrates.

The more serious criminal offenses are called "indictable offenses." The maximum punishment for indictable offenses is life imprisonment. Section 483 provides that certain of the least serious indictable offenses shall be triable only by a magistrate. Section 427 requires that the most serious indictable offenses listed therein are within the exclusive jurisdiction of a judge of the Court of Queen's Bench sitting with a jury. All other indictable offenses allow the accused an election as to his mode of trial: trial by magistrate, trial by a district or county court judge sitting alone, or trial by a Queen's Bench judge and jury (section 484(2)). Many criminal offenses are called "dual offenses." Where an accused is charged with a dual offense, the prosecutor is allowed an election whether the accused will be prosecuted in a summary manner or by indictment. First offenses will usually be prosecuted in a summary manner; aggravated first offenses or repeated offenses will generally be prosecuted by indictment. The discretion with regard to the mode of procedure is left entirely with the Crown prosecutor acting as the agent of the provincial attorney general.

Section 12 provides that no person shall be convicted of an offense under the code while he or she is under the age of 7. Section 13 states that no person between the ages of 7 and 14 shall be convicted of a criminal offense unless that person is competent to know the nature and consequences of his conduct and to appreciate that it was wrong. The accused's age at the date of the offense, not at the date of the trial, is the relevant age for purposes of these sections. Criminal offenders under 16 are classified as juvenile delinquents. Juveniles are dealt with in separate courts which use an informal procedure and are not subject to adult punishments, such as imprisonment or fines, except in exceptional circumstances. A juvenile's criminal record is not considered when he first comes before the adult courts after his sixteenth birthday.

The Criminal Code provides that corporations are in the same position as a natural person for the purposes of criminal prosecution for any act the corporation is capable of doing (section 2). The mental element for the offense will be found in the mind of the corporation's agent, who was the controlling mind of the corporation for purposes of the prohibited acts or omissions. The Criminal Code provides procedures for the prosecuting of corporations (sections 486, 548, 735(3)). Section 647 of the Code states that corporations are subject only to fines. For summary offenses, the maximum fine is $1,000. No maximum fine is provided for indictable offenses committed by a corporation. In most cases, the individual who has acted as the corporation's agent for purposes of doing the criminal acts will also be liable to prosecution and imprisonment as an individual.

Every criminal offense in Canada requires a mental element or intent *(mens rea)* on the part of the accused. Where the offense requires a specific intent, that intent must be proved by the Crown. Where no specific intent is required by the code, the accused must be proved to have had the general intent to do the acts which constitute the alleged offense. There are no offenses of strict liability in the Criminal Code. For all criminal offenses, the specific intent required by the section, or at least a general intent to do the prohibited act or omission, must be proved by the prosecution. Accordingly, all criminal offenses in Canada require a *mens rea,* thereby allowing a defense of mistake of fact. Section 19 states that mistake of law, as such, can never be a defense to a criminal charge in Canada. However, there are offenses in the code such as theft, where a mistake of law may give an accused a color of right, thereby negating the required specific intent.

There are regulatory offenses in Canada that are not criminal offenses which are strict liability offenses. For some of these minor regulatory offenses mistakes of law may be a defense.

That special class of criminal offense involving criminal negligence also requires a mental element, just as all other criminal offenses do. The intention in the case of criminal negligence will be supplied by the accused's recklessness with foresight.

Section 24(1) of the Criminal Code defines a criminal attempt to be any act done as part of a series of acts intended to result in the commission of an offense. Section 24(2) indicates that the question of when an accused's act ceases to be mere preparation and becomes part of the offense is a question of law. The section also provides that a person may be guilty of an attempt to commit the offense, although he could not have committed the offense in fact (for example, attempting to rob a man with no money). The law generally requires that for an act to constitute an attempt, the actual transaction must have commenced which, if not interrupted, would have ended in the commission of the crime. The accused must have entered upon a course of conduct for the purpose of immediately accomplishing his criminal object. There are numerous offenses under the Criminal Code where the attempt is one manner of committing the substantive offense (such as treason, section 46; corrupting judicial officers, section 108; obstructing justice, section 127).

Under section 421, any person attempting to commit an indictable offense punishable by life in prison is liable to 14 years' imprisonment. Any person found guilty of attempting to commit an indictable offense punishable by 14 years' imprisonment or less is liable to one-half of the maximum punishment prescribed by the code for that offense. Attempts to commit summary offenses are punishable equally with the substantive offense.

Under the Criminal Code, everyone is a party to an offense who actually commits the offense, or who does any act or omission for purposes of aiding another to commit the offense (section 21). The parties must have formed a common intention or design to do the acts which constitute the offense. All parties to an offense may be charged as principals and face the same punishment as the principal offender. In addition, by section 21(2), anyone who shares a common intention to commit an unlawful act is made a party to any other offense committed by any of the parties to the first offense, which he knew or ought to have known would be the probable result of carrying out the shared intention.

In Canada it is an offense to counsel another person to commit an offense (section 22). Anyone who does so is made a party to that offense by this section, and is also made a party to all other offenses which the person counseled committed and which the counselor knew or ought to have known would likely be committed in consequence of the counseling. If the offense is an indictable offense and is not in fact committed by the person counseled, then the counselor is still guilty of an attempt (he would be deemed a party to an attempt to commit the offense counseled, [section 422(a)]). If the offense counseled was a summary offense and the offense is not committed, then the counselor is guilty of an offense punishable on summary conviction (section 422(b)). Note that there need be no causal connection proved between the counselling and the commission of the offense.

Section 23(1) of the Code provides that anyone who knows that a person has been a party of an offense and assists him in escaping is an accessory after the fact. Section 23(2) exempts spouses from the operation of this rule.

Section 421 provides that accessories after the fact face a maximum punishment of 14 years' imprisonment where the principal offense was an indictable offense punishable by life imprisonment. For principal offenses punishable by 14 years' imprisonment or less, the accessory faces a maximum sentence equal to one-half of the punishment to which the principal offender was liable. In order for a person to be convicted as an accessory after the fact, the principal offender must first be convicted of the principal offense. If the principal offense is not proved, any party charged as an accessory must be discharged.

The essence of criminal conspiracy under the Criminal Code is an agreement between two or more persons to affect an unlawful purpose or to affect a lawful purpose by unlawful means. All conspiracies in Canada are indictable offenses (section 423). Special provisions are contained in the code (section 425) which exempt trade unions from the conspiracy sections, unless acts done pursuant to any agreement are expressly punishable by law. What is an unlawful purpose under this section is defined in the case law as including criminal acts, malicious or fraudulent torts, agreements to breach a contract under circumstances peculiarly injurious to the public, and agreements to do acts outrageously immoral or extremely injurious to the public. There may be a conspiracy under the code even if the offense agreed to be committed is not committed in fact.

Section 7(3) of the code states that all common law defenses are retained unless they have been altered by or are inconsistent with the Criminal Code or any other federal statute. In addition, certain specific defenses are expressly provided for in the code; for example, the defense of insanity in section 16 and the limited defense of duress or compulsion in section 17. The Criminal Code also provides exemptions and provisos in the definitions of various offenses which will give an accused a defense, if established by the accused on a balance of probabilities (section 730(2)); that is, those offenses which must be done without lawful excuse or without lawful authority. The code further provides for the special pleas of autrefois acquit, autrefois convict and pardon (section 535). Autrefois acquit and autrefois convict are available defenses whether the previous verdict was rendered inside or outside Canada (section 6(4)). The common law defenses retained by the Criminal Code include the defenses of self-defense, necessity, consent, drunkenness, provocation, entrapment, double punishment, *res judicata,* and inconsistent verdicts. The common law defense of self-defense has been codified by the Criminal Code in sections 34 and 35. These sections basically provide that anyone is justified in using as much force as he reasonably but subjectively believes necessary to prevent his being killed or seriously injured.

The defense of necessity may be applied by a court wherever it is established that it was necessary to break the law in order to avoid harm more serious than the commission of the offense.

The defense of consent is limited by the Criminal Code. Section 14 states that consent to death is excluded from any defenses that might be open to one inflicting death. Consent is also not a defense to a charge of statutory rape or indecent assault where the victim is under the age of 14 (section 140), or to a charge of abducting a female under the age of 16 (section 249).

The defense of drunkenness is a good defense to all criminal charges requiring a specific intent if the accused's drunken condition causes him not to have the required intent. Theoretically, there is an argument that drunkenness should be a good defense wherever the accused is thereby caused to lack the intent required by the code, be that intent specific (knowingly) or general (just the intention to do the prohibited act). However, there is a tendency for Canadian courts to disallow a defense of drunkenness to a charge requiring only a general intent wherever the accused's acts resulting in the drunkenness were willful.

The defense of provocation is codified in Canada in the Criminal Code. Section 36 defines provocation as including blows, words, or gestures. Under section 215(1), it is provided that provocation may reduce the offense of murder to manslaughter. Section 215(2) states that any wrongful act or insult of such a nature as to deprive an ordinary person of the power of self-control is provocation for purposes of section 215(1), if the accused reacted immediately and before there was time for his passion to cool.

Entrapment has not been widely recognized in Canada as a valid defense. However, in cases of severe police misconduct it is suggested that Canadian courts may exercise their inherent jurisdiction to stay proceedings.

Section 11 of the Criminal Code provides that where an act or omission of an accused is punishable under more than one federal statute, unless a contrary intention appears, the accused is not liable to be punished more than once for the same offense. In addition, recent developments in the case law have clarified the common law prohibition against double punishment. These cases provide that an accused is not liable to two criminal convictions where more than one criminal offense is constituted by one transaction or act of the accused.

The common law defense of *res judicata* prevents a conviction wherever a previous trial necessarily determined an issue or issues which would determine the second trial in favor of the accused. This common law defense is accepted in practice in Canada.

In addition to those defenses contained within the Criminal Code and those common law defenses described above, the Canadian Bill of Rights is capable of providing a defense to a criminal charge. Any section of the code or any other federal act which cannot be read without conflicting with the

Bill of Rights must be read subject to the Bill of Rights. In addition, the Bill of Rights contains guarantees of civil liberties and fair procedure which operate in favor of an accused. However, it should be noted that Canadian courts have been loath to strike down federal legislation merely because it may conflict with the Bill of Rights.

PENAL MEASURES

Sentencing of criminal offenders in Canada is within the discretion of trial judges, except where the few minimum and/or maximum sentences are prescribed by the Criminal Code. In such a case, the judge then exercises a discretion, within the prescribed limits. Under the Criminal Code, there is provision for the appeal of a sentence passed on an indictable offense, to the provincial Court of Appeal, with leave of that court (section 603). Section 748 states that an accused, or the Crown, may appeal a sentence received on a summary conviction offense to a district or county court judge. No further appeal to the Court of Appeal is permitted unless the sentencing judge has erred in law in sentencing the offender (whether a sentence is merely excessive is not a question of law).

In terms of general philosophy, it is considered necessary that a judge, in sentencing an accused, consider whether the sentence imposed is appropriate for punishing the offender, deterring the offender, as well as potential offenders, rehabilitating the offender and isolating him from society where it is necessary to do so for the protection of the community. It is generally agreed that imprisonment is the sentence of last resort, because of the severity of such a sentence and because of the adverse effects of imprisonment upon the accused.

The most lenient sentence that may be imposed under the Criminal Code is an absolute discharge (section 622.1) An absolute or conditional discharge is available to an accused wherever he is charged with an offense for which no minimum punishment is required and the maximum punishment to which he is liable is less than 14 years' imprisonment. Absolute or conditional discharges will be given if it appears to the judge that such a disposition is in the accused's best interest and is not contrary to the public interest.

If the offender is ordered discharged absolutely, he is immediately freed and no criminal conviction is recorded. If the offender is ordered discharged upon conditions, then he is immediately released on probation. If the offender meets the conditions imposed by the court, at the expiration of his probation period no criminal record is kept of the offense. However, the fact that the accused was ordered discharged is recorded for the court's information.

Examples of conditions which may be imposed on an accused under a probation order include good conduct, reporting to a probation officer or counselor, a residence requirement, a requirement that the accused perform community service work, or a requirement that the accused make restitution or compensate his victim.

For offenses where probation is not considered appropriate, fines may be levied. The maximum fine for a summary offense is $500. No maximum fine is provided for indictable offenses.

The maximum term of imprisonment provided under the Criminal Code for summary offenses is six months. Maximum terms of imprisonment for indictable offenses range from two years to life imprisonment, depending on the seriousness of the offense. Maximum terms for specific offenses in the Criminal Code are two years: section 72, fighting duels, five years; section 132, escaping prison, ten years; or life imprisonment for rape, murder, treason, and other serious offenses. The code also provides for other types of custodial penal measures, such as indeterminate detention of those found to be habitual criminals or dangerous sexual offenders (sections 688 and 689). A habitual criminal is defined as anyone who has, since age 18, been convicted of at least three independent indictable offenses on which he was liable to five years' imprisonment or more.

Reliable statistical data are not available in Canada on a sufficiently precise basis to analyze the distribution of penal measures in detail. However, according to those statistics available, incarceration as a penal measure is declining in Canada. In the past decade, Canada has had a relatively high rate of prison use in comparison to some other Western nations. This rate now seems to be decreasing, while fines, probation, and suspended sentences are increasing in terms of their proportion of the total imposition of penal measures.

Juvenile criminal offenders are dealt with separately from adult offenders under the Juvenile Delinquents Act, R.S.C. 1970, c.J-3. Juvenile offenders are defined as all offenders under the age of 16, or whatever higher age limit is set by the provincial government within whose boundaries the offender is being tried. Under this act, provision is made for special courts for the handling of juveniles. Special penal measures are provided for juveniles as well, including placing the offender in a foster home or a training school. Section 441 prohibits the publicizing of a juvenile's trial in the interests of protecting the offender and his family.

Where an accused is found to have been criminally insane (section 16) at the time of the offense, he will be acquitted of the offense and detained at the pleasure of the provincial representative of the Queen, the lieutenant governor (section 542). Where an accused is thought by the court to be mentally disordered at the time of his trial, he may be remanded in custody for 30 days for psychiatric observation (section 532(2)). If the accused is found to be unfit to stand trial, the court shall order him detained, again at the pleasure of the lieutenant governor. Pursuant to section 545, the lieutenant governor may detain the accused absolutely or upon conditions wherever release appears in the accused's best interest and is not contrary to the interests of society. This discretion is usually based on the recommendations of a review committee which considers the mental health of the person on a biannual basis.

A number of programs are being developed in Canada with some emphasis on juvenile offenders which provide alternatives to prosecution, conviction, and penal sanctions. Young first offenders who admit their guilt may be diverted to community projects or to compensating the victim of a property crime. Similarly, there has developed a consensus in Canada that convicted persons ought not to be imprisoned merely because they are unable to pay a fine. Poverty alone should not lead to imprisonment. Work programs have been substituted for those who cannot pay fines. Offenders work off the sum of the fine by engaging in community service work, often under the supervision of a probation officer or volunteer agency.

There continues a residual discretion exercisable by peace officers, prosecutors, and the courts at all stages of the criminal process. The police officer diverts those offenders from the criminal justice process who, in his opinion, do not constitute a threat or who have not engaged in a serious offense or who are first offenders. The discretion exercised by prosecutors to stay proceedings or withdraw or reduce charges has been the subject of some discussion in Canada because of the lack of guidelines or appropriate criteria for this informal decision-making.

The National Parole Board has been in operation in Canada for 18 years. The board was created in 1959 by the federal Parliament as an independent authority whose purpose would be to facilitate the release of imprisoned criminal offenders into society. Under section 8 of the Parole Act, the board is empowered to release any offender serving a sentence at large in society, under whatever conditions are thought necessary to ensure that the offender will lead a law-abiding life. The board may release an offender on full parole or on day parole only. Under Canada's parole system, the board informs each offender of his parole eligibility date. It is then left to the offender to apply for parole shortly before he becomes eligible. The granting of parole is not irrevocable. The board can require the offender to be returned to prison wherever such a course will be in society's or the offender's best interests.

Section 669 of the Criminal Code states that any accused sentenced to life imprisonment for treason or for first-degree murder will not be eligible for parole for 25 years. Second-degree murder carries a mandatory penalty of life imprisonment without parole eligibility for at least 10 years, or any greater number of years up to 25 years, substituted by the court (section 671). All other offenses prima facie leave the offender eligible for parole upon completing the normal portion of his sentence, as required by the regulations made under the Parole Act by the federal Cabinet (section 8).

III. CRIMINAL PROCEDURE

The criminal process in Canada is an adversary process. All prosecutions are carried on in the name of the Queen by government prosecutors. The federal Department of Justice, provincial Departments of the Attorney General, and most larger municipal governments employ counsel as agents for purposes of prosecuting criminal offenses. Generally, they are full-time prosecutors. Private counsel may appear as prosecutors when the case load so requires.

The criminal law of Canada has followed, for the most part, the common law and rules of evidence as developed in England. The final burden to prove each ingredient of the offense beyond a reasonable doubt always remains on the Crown. The accused is presumed innocent until proven guilty (section 5(1)).

One common law exception to the above-stated rule regarding the burden of proof in a criminal case involves the defense of insanity, which must be established by the accused on a balance of probabilities or a preponderance of evidence. Section 16(4) expressly states this rule and makes it a part of the statute law of Canada. There are numerous other examples in the Criminal Code and in other federal statutes of express statutory variation of the general rule through the provision of reverse onus clauses. For example, section 237(1)(a) of the Code provides that a person found in the driver's seat of an automobile shall be deemed to have the care and control of the vehicle, unless the accused establishes that he did not enter the vehicle for the purpose of setting it in motion. As a further example, under section 8 of the Narcotic Control Act, R.S.C. 1970, c. N-1, it is provided that an accused charged with possession of a narcotic for the purposes of trafficking, upon the Crown proving the element of possession, must disprove that he had possession for the purposes of trafficking.

According to a recent discussion of the Supreme Court of Canada, the burden of proof imposed on an accused under a reverse onus clause is always the lesser burden of proof, on a balance of probabilities or a preponderance of evidence. In addition to specific reverse onus clauses, section 730 provides that proof of all exceptions, exemptions, and provisos in the Criminal Code, contained within the definitions of offenses therein, rests upon the accused by a balance of probabilities.

PHASE OF CRIMINAL PROCEEDINGS

All phases of criminal procedure, from arrest to conviction or acquittal, are governed by the Criminal Code. Powers of arrest under the Criminal Code are contained in sections 449 and 450. Section 449 makes provision for the arrest of an accused without warrant by a private citizen wherever a suspect is found committing an indictable offense or appears on reasonable and probable grounds to have committed a criminal offense and is escaping from and freshly pursued by persons with lawful authority to arrest him. Section 450(1) provides that a peace officer may arrest without warrant any suspect whom he finds committing a criminal offense, or whom he believes on reasonable and probable grounds has just committed, or is about to commit, an indictable offense or for whom he believes on reasonable and probable grounds that a warrant is in force within that territorial jurisdiction. The powers of a peace officer to arrest without warrant under section 450(1) are expressly limited by section 450(2) for certain less serious offenses, wherever the officer does not have reasonable and probable grounds to believe that the public interest requires the arrest of the accused.

Criminal proceedings in Canada are commenced by the swearing of an information for summary matters (section 723) or an indictment for indictable offenses (section 455). The information must be sworn within six months of the date of the alleged offense for summary offenses (section 721(2)). Time does not run against the Crown on indictable offenses. In general terms, the accused, if arrested, must be taken before a justice within 24 hours or as soon as possible (section 454). If the accused is not arrested and was issued an appearance notice, then he must appear before the court at the time and place indicated therein or a warrant will be issued by the presiding judge or magistrate for his arrest pursuant to section 453.4 of the code. For all criminal offenses, an accused's first appearance will be before a provincial court judge or magistrate.

If the offense charged is a summary conviction offense or a dual offense upon which the Crown elects to proceed by way of summary conviction or an indictable offense contained in section 483 and is not an offense contained in section 427, the accused's plea may be taken by the magistrate on the accused's first appearance before him and a trial will be held before the magistrate. If the offense charged is an indictable offense or a dual offense upon which the Crown elects to proceed by way of indictment, and the offense is not in section 427 or section 483, the accused will be asked to elect his mode of trial before the magistrate upon his first appearance (section 464). If the accused elects to be tried by a magistrate, the accused's plea will be taken and a trial will be held by the magistrate. If the accused elects trial by judge without a jury or elects trial by judge and jury, the magistrate will proceed to hold a preliminary inquiry. At the preliminary inquiry, the Crown will be required to demonstrate a prima facie case against the accused. If the Crown produces sufficient evidence, the accused will be committed for trial in the court of his election (section 464(4)). At the trial of the accused, the Crown will be required to prove every element of the offense charged beyond a reasonable doubt, in order to establish the guilt of the accused.

RIGHTS OF AN ACCUSED

At common law, the accused was entitled to make a full defense to the charges brought against him. Section 737.1 codifies this rule. If the accused wishes to be represented by counsel, it is his right to employ a defense lawyer. The accused or his counsel will be allowed to cross-examine all Crown witnesses.

No admission against interest, made by the accused to a person in authority, will be allowed to be put in evidence against the accused, unless the Crown first proves during a *voir dire* (a trial within a trial) that the statement made by the accused was made voluntarily. A voluntary statement is defined as one made without fear of threat or promise of favor.

The accused has a right not to take the witness stand and give evidence on his own behalf. Neither the court nor the prosecutor can comment on the accused's failure to testify (Canada Evidence Act, R.S.C. 1970, c. E-10, s. 4(5)).

For most offenses, if the accused has been arrested and kept in custody before his first appearance before a magistrate, or if the accused has been at liberty prior to his first appearance, the Crown must show cause why the accused should not be released on his own undertaking to reappear, or the accused will be ordered released by that magistrate pending any further appearances before the court (section 457). If necessary, the magistrate may remand the accused in custody until the show cause hearing can be held (section 457.1). The accused cannot be remanded under this section for more than three clear days without his consent. The Crown and the accused are allowed one appeal from a detention order to a Queen's Bench or district court judge (section 457.5).

Under certain circumstances, the onus on a show cause hearing is reversed (section 457(5.1)) and the accused, upon first appearing, will be detained in custody unless he shows cause why he should be released. These circumstances include being charged with any one of several of the more serious offenses in the Criminal Code or in the Narcotic Control Act; being a non-Canadian resident charged with an indictable offense; being charged with murder or conspiracy to commit murder; or being charged with any offense relating to failing to appear which was committed while the accused was at large on bail awaiting trial on another charge.

An accused may appeal by right from a conviction, or against sentence on a summary conviction offense (section 748(a)). The Crown or the informant may appeal against sentence, or from an order dismissing an information (section 748(b)). There are two methods of appeal: An appeal on the record from a summary court is heard by a district or county court judge (section 755); alternatively, an appellant may require the court below to state a case and then proceed to appeal on the grounds of error of law or excess of jurisdiction (section 762). Appeals by way of stated case are heard by the superior court of criminal jurisdiction in the province (the Court of Queen's Bench). If upon application of the accused, the informant, or the Crown, the appellant feels that the interests of justice would be better served by holding a trial *de novo*, or a new trial, then the appeal may be heard in such manner (section 755(4)).

For indictable offenses, the accused (section 603) or the Crown (section 605) may appeal to the Court of Appeal of the province by right on a question of law alone, may appeal on a question of mixed fact and law if the trial judge or Court of Appeal gives leave, or may appeal on any other ground which the Court of Appeal consents to hear. Secondary appeals of summary offenses are heard by the Court of Appeal of the province on the same grounds as have been outlined above regarding indictable appeals. A further appeal from the Court of Appeal of summary and indictable offenses may be heard by the Supreme Court of Canada with the leave of that court.

PRETRIAL DETENTION

Under the Criminal Code, pretrial detention is discouraged. Section 455.3(4) requires that an accused who has been arrested be released by the magistrate after being issued a summons, unless it appears that the public interest requires that the accused be taken into custody. In addition, section 450(2) requires peace officers to issue appearance notices rather than take a suspect into custody, unless it appears on reasonable and probable grounds that the need to identify the accused, preserve evidence, or protect society requires an arrest. After the accused has been arrested, section 453 requires that the peace officer in charge of a lock-up release the accused upon serving him with a summons or appearance notice requiring his appearance in court, unless the offense involved is one of those serious indictable offenses listed in section 427, or unless he has the same reasonable and probable grounds listed above from section 450(2) to believe that the detention of the accused is necessary.

SPECIAL MODES OF CRIMINAL PROCEEDINGS

The implementation of the War Measures Act in 1970, during peacetime and on two other occasions during wartime, invoke special provisions permitting detention of a longer duration prior to trial and broad arrest provisions.

LAY PARTICIPATION IN CRIMINAL PROCEEDINGS

Anyone may lay an information and commence criminal proceedings who has reasonable and probable grounds for believing a person has been guilty of a crime.

Section 449 of the Criminal Code outlines the powers of arrest which are given private citizens, as they have been discussed above.

A private citizen may represent an accused or appear on his behalf on a summary conviction offense, with the court's consent (section 735(2)). As well, an accused may conduct his own defense throughout his trial, whether the procedure is summary or indictable (section 737(2)).

Laypersons serve on criminal juries (The Jury Act, R.R.S. 1965, c. 79, s. 4).

SPECIAL PROCEDURES FOR JUVENILES

Criminal procedure for juvenile offenders in Canada is governed by an act of the federal Parliament of Canada, the Juvenile Delinquents Act (R.S.C. 1970, c. J-3). This act covers all criminal offenders under the age of 16 or whatever age is prescribed by the province in which the offender is tried. Age limits in Canadian provinces vary from 16 to 18 years.

Section 3(2) of the act indicates that juvenile offenders are to be dealt with in a separate juvenile court created by the province—not as criminals, but rather as persons requiring help, guidance, and supervision. Trial procedure under the act is adopted from the procedures prescribed for summary trials in the Criminal Code (section 5(1)). Section 17 further provides that proceedings shall be as informal as the interests of justice will permit.

Under section 9 special provision is made for juveniles over 14 who have committed an indictable offense. This section empowers the juvenile court to order that the juvenile stand trial as an adult in the criminal courts.

Section 10 of the Juvenile Delinquents Act requires that notice of the hearing of a charge in juvenile court be served on the offender's parent, guardian, or upon a relative. Section 37 of the act permits an appeal to a Supreme Court judge with leave of the judge if he considers that the appeal is essential to the public interest or the due administration of justice. Procedure on appeal is adopted from those provisions of the Criminal Code providing for the appeal of convictions or acquittals on indictable offenses.

IV. EXECUTION OF PENAL MEASURES (CORRECTIONS)

The basic principles of criminal sentencing in Canada are governed by the common law. They are the rehabilitation of the offender, retribution, deterrence of the offender and others from repeating his offense, and the protection of society. It is the task of the judges to balance these interests in their discretion so that the accused's and society's interests are served. Each case depends upon its own facts. Imprisonment is theoretically the punishment of last resort in Canada, because it is recognized that a sentence of imprisonment militates seriously against the rehabilitation of the accused while increasing deterrent and retributive elements. In general, imprisonment is reserved for those cases where society must be protected from a dangerous offender, where no other punishment will adequately condemn the harm done, or where the accused has not been deterred by lesser sentences.

USE AND IMPLEMENTATION OF THE DEATH PENALTY

The death penalty was abolished in Canada in 1976. No criminal executions have taken place in Canada since 1962.

EXECUTION OF DEPRIVATION OF LIBERTY AND
OTHER CUSTODIAL MEASURES

The operation of penal institutions is shared by the federal and provincial governments. A system of federal penitentiaries is administered by the federal government. The provinces operate provincial jails, reformatories, training schools, and the like. Offenders sentenced to two years' imprisonment or more are sentenced to federal penitentiaries (section 659 of the Criminal Code). Sentences of less than two years are served in provincial jails.

Federal penitentiaries are administered by a commissioner of penitentiaries under the Department of the Solicitor General of Canada. Provincial jails are administered by the Corrections Branch of the provincial Department of Health and Welfare or Social Services.

Those offenders sentenced to federal penitentiaries are classified according to the gravity of their conduct and personal characteristics and sent to maximum security institutions is currently being established by the federal maximum security institutions is currently being established by the fedeal government for the psychological rehabilitation of dangerous sexual offenders, habitual criminals, and criminally insane offenders, who are considered dangerous.

Juvenile offenders are institutionalized as a separate class. Section 26 of the Juvenile Delinquents Act provides that no juveniles shall be incarcerated in any penitentiary, jail, or police station or other place where adults may be imprisoned. The policy of this provision is to prevent the further criminalization of the juvenile through contact with adult criminals.

Canadian penal institutions basically fall into the classifications of federal penitentiaries and provincial correctional centers. Federal penitentiaries are located across the country and are generally maximum or medium security institutions. Most offenders are sentenced to provincial correctional centers.

Federal penitentiaries and provincial correctional centers provide training or educational opportunities for offenders as well as some type of work within the prison. In addition, many provincial correctional centers have an industrial or farm annex where the least dangerous offenders are allowed to work under more moderate supervision.

In addition to the formal penal institutions, there are halfway houses that provide a place of residence for inmates who are out on parole and are trying to adjust to the transition from institutionalization to life in society.

Men and women are imprisoned at separate institutions in Canada under both the federal and provincial systems. For juvenile offenders there are numerous types of custodial institutions, including detention homes, training schools, and foster homes.

The rights of offenders are severely limited during imprisonment. Certain minimal rights are preserved, however, such as the offender's right to the statutory remission of one-quarter of his sentence and his right to apply for parole as soon as he is eligible. Recent judicial decisions have not acceded to argument for increased prisoners' rights in terms of natural justice within the institution in the determination of internal penalties by custodial staff.

EXECUTION OF NONCUSTODIAL MEASURES

The most utilized noncustodial penal measures are fines, suspended sentences, and probation. The proportion of total dispositions which result in fines and probation, rather than deprivation of liberty, has increased in the last few years.

Section 646(1) of the Criminal Code provides that where the accused has committed an indictable offense by which he is liable to imprisonment for five years or less he may be fined in addition to, or in lieu of, any other punishment that is authorized. Section 646(2) states that where the accused is convicted of an indictable offense punishable by imprisonment for more than five years he may be fined in addition to, but not in lieu of, any other punishment that is authorized. Subsection (3) permits the judge to impose a term of imprisonment in default of payment of the fine. Section 651(1) states that the proceeds of any fine, penalty, or forfeiture are to be payable to Her Majesty in right of the province, and shall be paid by the offender to the treasurer of that province. Section 655 of the Criminal Code gives the judge authority to make an order requiring that a criminal offender who has committed an indictable offense shall restore any property obtained by the commission of that offense to the person entitled to it, if at the time of the trial the property is before the court.

Section 662 of the Criminal Code authorizes the absolute or conditional discharge of an accused wherever it is the judge's opinion that the best interests of the accused will be served by discharging him without any damage to the interests of society. Under a conditional discharge, the judge can require that the accused report to probation officers; can limit those activities the accused may enjoy; require that the accused take certain courses of action, such as finding and maintaining suitable employment; and generally require that the accused comply with such other reasonable conditions as the court considers desirable for securing the good conduct of the accused and for preventing a repetition, by him, of the same offense or any other offense (section 663(2)).

PART II

CIVIL LAW SYSTEMS

Civil law, also referred to as continental law or Romano-Germanic law, developed in Europe and is primarily centered there, although through colonial expansion and adoption it has spread to most large areas of the world. The Federal Republic of Germany, Sweden, and Japan are the criminal justice systems described in this part. Sweden and West Germany are representative of the systems found throughout Western Europe. Japan may be viewed as a mixture of civil law with regard to substantive criminal law yet with elements of the common law in the field of criminal procedure. The Japanese criminal justice system was greatly influenced by the occupation following World War II when an attempt was made to inculcate American legal concepts.

Compared with other parts of the developed world, Western Europe has advanced further toward the concept of rehabilitation of offenders and the use of noncustodial measures. The day-fine, work release, relatively short terms of incarceration, and elimination of the death penalty have been incorporated into the criminal justice systems of Sweden and the Federal Republic of Germany as means to achieve these goals. The problems of political terrorism and criminality among guest workers have affected European countries during the past decade, and steps have been taken to deal with these situations.

In each of the chapters students should make comparisons among the countries and especially between the two European countries and Japan. To what extent are there characteristics that are held in common?

4

FEDERAL REPUBLIC OF GERMANY

Joachim Herrmann

I. GENERAL INFORMATION

The Federal Republic of Germany originated after World War II when the German Reich was divided into a western part—the Federal Republic—and an eastern part—the German Democratic Republic. The City of Berlin, which lies in the eastern section, is an independent entity under the control of the Four Powers who were victorious in 1945.

The Federal Republic is a country in the center of Europe at the frontier between the western and eastern worlds. In the East it is bordered by the German Democratic Republic and Czechoslovakia, in the West by France and the Benelux States. In the North-South direction it stretches from the North Sea, Denmark, and the Baltic Sea to the Alps, Austria, and Switzerland.

The Federal Republic has a population of approximately 61.5 million. It covers an area of some 96,000 square miles. The population of the Federal Republic, which is one-third of the American, lives in a territory that is only three percent of the United States in area.

In addition to the 61.5 million Germans, about four million "guestworkers," foreigners, mostly from South European countries, live in the Federal Republic. Officially they reside in West Germany on a temporary basis, but a considerable number have stayed for many years. They and their families have started to blend into West German society.

Class distinctions, which in former times played an important role in German life, were greatly reduced after World War II. Education is never the main factor of upward mobility, though on the whole there is still less social mobility in the Federal Republic than in the United States.

The political order of the Federal Republic is based on the Constitution of 1949, which provides for a democratic and social federal state under the rule of law. The Constitution includes a bill of rights which affords a comprehensive protection of human rights and which plays an important role in public life. The ten West German States—Laender—exercise much less political power than do the states in the United States. Communities and counties are mainly administrative units with limited autonomy.

The Federal Republic is a highly industrialized state that, since its founding, has gone through periods of rapid economic growth. In terms of gross national product, it is ranked third after the United States and Japan. The output of industrial goods is much higher than the domestic market can absorb. Therefore, West Germany is heavily dependent on exports of its goods such as machinery and electrical equipment, motor vehicles, chemicals, and precision tools.

West German economic life follows the principle of "social market economy," which provides for economic freedom and, at the same time, for a fair distribution of profits among the people. The income of the West German worker is, by and large, comparable to that of his American counterpart. He works 40 hours per week. His fringe benefits, such as social insurance, annual vacations, and vacation bonuses, are extensive.

GENERAL DESCRIPTION OF THE LEGAL SYSTEM

Since the Federal Republic of Germany is part of the civil law, law is primarily codified. Many of its codes date back to the times of the German Reich. The Penal Code became effective in 1871, the Code of Criminal Procedure in 1879. Over the years both have undergone numerous changes and thorough revisions.

When talking about peculiarities of Civil Law one cannot overlook that today the United States—a common law country—also relies on codes and statutes rather than solely on precedents. Yet, different from most legislative acts in the United States, codes and statutes that are typical of a civil law system tend to be carefully integrated bodies of general principles arranged in a highly systematized manner and phrased in abstract language. These characteristics call for liberal rather than narrow interpretation. Traditionally, West German lawyers engage in a great deal of liberal statutory construction. They emphasize abstractions rather than particulars and concrete cases.

In the Federal Republic, and other civil law systems, court decisions are not taken as sources of law but only used in interpreting the legal text. The common law doctrine, that precedent is binding, is unknown in West Germany. Judges of lower courts, however, quite readily follow prior decisions of higher courts, since they know that otherwise they are likely to be reversed on appeal.

West Germany is a federal state, but, unlike in the United States, almost all criminal, procedural, and private law is subject to federal legislation. On the other hand, all courts are state courts except the highest appellate courts and the Federal Constitutional Court, which hears only cases involving questions of federal constitutional law. Thus federal law is regularly applied by the state courts. This does not mean, however, that federal law is applied differently in each state. The general willingness of state courts to maintain the law in the same way, as well as the wide reviewing powers of the highest federal appellate courts, have proved effective in maintaining the uniformity of the law.

AMOUNT, STRUCTURE, AND DYNAMICS OF CRIMINALITY

Crime rates have been rising in the Federal Republic since its founding. For example, in 1963 about 1.7 million offenses were known to the police; this figure increased to some 3.1 million in 1976. Road traffic offenses are not included in this count. Crime rates per 100,000 population were 2,914 in 1963 and 4,980 in 1976. This amounts to a 70 percent increase within 13 years, or an annual increase of about 5.3 percent.

The category of violent crimes (e.g., willful killing, rape, robbery and aggravated assault) makes up about 2.5 percent of the cases that become known to the police. Figures of violent crimes are substantially smaller in the Federal Republic than in the United States. Table 4.1 gives crime rates per 100,000 in 1976. The comparison is somewhat distorted, since West German figures include complaints of crimes that police investigations later disclosed had not been committed.

The category of larceny, aggravated larceny, and burglary amounts to about two-thirds of all offenses. This contradicts the idea that economic prosperity and high personal income reduce crimes against property.

TABLE 4.1

	Federal Republic	United States
willful killing not including attempt	1.4	8.8
rape	11.3	26.4
robbery	31.6	195.8
aggravated assault	81.0	228.7

Since World War II criminality of juveniles and adolescents has risen faster than offense rates of adults. In 1976 more than 25 percent of the identified offenders were between 14 and 21 years of age. Seven percent were even younger than 14. About one-third of all male persons have been convicted at least once before they reach the age of 25.

The crime rate of guestworkers is somewhat higher than that of the West German citizens. Yet, most guestworkers are male and belong to an age group with a generally high crime rate.

SCOPE OF CRIMINAL LAW

General statements about the scope of criminal law are difficult to make. An example may illustrate this.

American criminal law requires a high degree of negligence for criminal responsibility, while in West Germany ordinary negligence is sufficient. It would be a mistake, however, to believe that because of this difference criminal law is more lenient in the United States than in the Federal Republic. American legislatures frequently have enacted strict liability statutes that impose criminal responsibility for conduct unaccompanied by fault. In addition, payment of damages may have a punitive function in American law. Both strict responsibility and punitive damages do not exist in West German law.

During the last ten years the criminal law of the Federal Republic has undergone far-reaching changes. On the one hand, new provisions were added to the Penal Code to cope with newly arising crime problems, such as new forms of terrorism, kidnapping, and highjacking, as well as the steady increase in white-collar crime.

On the other hand, there was a strong movement toward decriminalization, which was accomplished in two ways. First, offenses against morality, such as adultery, bestiality, and homosexuality among consenting adults, were stricken from the Penal Code. Abortion was considerably liberalized. Second, petty misdemeanors (violations of traffic laws as well as of business and trade regulations) were relabeled petty infractions and removed from the criminal process. The sanctions provided for petty infractions are regulatory fines instead of the harsher penalties of the Penal Code involving moral blame. The prosecution of petty infractions and the imposition of sanctions are the province of administrative authorities, primarily the police. The judiciary becomes involved only if an accused files a complaint against an administrative order imposing a regulatory fine.

STRUCTURE AND FUNCTIONING OF LAW ENFORCEMENT AGENCIES

Judges in the Federal Republic of Germany are career judges who enter the judiciary as soon as they have finished their legal education. After a probationary period of three or four years they are appointed for life. The best judges are promoted to higher office—for example, to an appellate court.

There is a uniform court system with two tiers of trial courts for criminal cases in each state. Local courts having jurisdiction over less serious cases sit with either a single professional judge or with a panel of one or sometimes two professional judges and two lay judges. District courts hearing serious cases are composed of panels of three professional judges and two lay judges.

Appeals *de novo* from local courts are heard by district courts. In addition there are state appellate courts and the High Federal Court of Appeals that hear appeals for error. Constitutional issues may be raised before the Federal Constitutional Court. Petitions contending that the European Convention for the Protection of Human Rights and Fundamental Freedoms have been violated may be brought before the European Commission of Human Rights and the European Court of Human Rights. Thus international institutions have jurisdiction to review domestic cases.

West German prosecutors also work in a career system. Some of the states provide for transfers between the prosecutor's office and the judiciary in order to make prosecutors familiar with the judge's business, and vice versa.

The prosecutor's office is hierarchically organized on a statewide basis, with an attorney general at the top who is responsible to the minister of justice. Whatever the single prosecutor does is supervised by his superiors. This results in considerable uniformity of law enforcement.

As everywhere, the police serve two purposes: to maintain law and order and to detect and investigate crime. As regards the latter function, they work together with the prosecutor, though police officers are not his subordinates.

West German attorneys, before being admitted to the bar, have to go through the same legal education as judges and prosecutors. Any practicing attorney may defend any criminal case. There is no special criminal bar, though a few attorneys have specialized in defending criminal cases.

II. SUBSTANTIVE CRIMINAL LAW

GENERAL PRINCIPLES OF RESPONSIBILITY

The Constitution of the Federal Republic provides that no one shall be punished for anything that is not expressly forbidden by law. Since in civil law countries all criminal law is contained in the penal code and statutes, the problem of common law crimes does not exist.

Problems arise, however, with regard to the interpretation of penal provisions. Following civil law tradition, the West German Penal Code defines offenses in more general and abstract terms than typical American criminal codes. The common law method of strict construction of penal provisions would be incompatible with the general and abstract definitions. Therefore, West German judges construe penal provisions liberally in order not to defeat the intention of the legislature. On the other hand, judges are not permitted to resort to interpretation by "analogy" and apply penal provisions to conduct not proscribed by them.

Often it is not easy to distinguish between liberal interpretation and illegal analogy. Generally, West German judges do not hesitate to broaden the definition of an offense if they consider it necessary in the interests of justice. For instance, in the provision on dangerous assault, "by means of a weapon" was interpreted to include the throwing of hydrochloric acid in the victim's face and ordering a dog to attack. In the definition of robbery, "by force" was construed to include nonviolent narcotization of the victim.

A void-for-vagueness doctrine exists in West German criminal law. It plays a minor role, however, because general and abstract definitions of the penal code tend to make penal provisions less precise.

A provision forbidding retroactive application of criminal law is embodied in the West German Constitution. Like in the United States, there is some controversy among West German lawyers whether the ex post facto prohibition applies also to laws of procedure and to judicial decisions. Generally, the view is taken that both may be changed retroactively, but in recent years it was suggested that exceptions should be made to protect the interests of the accused.

GRADES OF OFFENSES

The West German Penal Code places criminal offenses into two categories: felonies punishable by imprisonment for at least one year and misdemeanors punishable by imprisonment for a shorter minimum period or a fine. The category of misdemeanors is broad and includes many crimes that would be considered felonies under American law, such as larceny, fraud, extortion, abortion, and negligent homicide.

The classification serves practical purposes. For example, only a conspiracy to commit a felony is a crime. Jurisdiction of local courts and district courts depends mainly on the classification of offenses. Only an accused who is convicted of a felony may be disqualified from holding public office or from practicing as an attorney.

AGE OF CRIMINAL RESPONSIBILITY

Juveniles of less than 14 years of age are not criminally responsible at all. There is an irrebuttable presumption of their criminal incapacity. Offenses they have committed are dealt with by guardianship courts.

Juveniles between 14 and 18 are criminally responsible if they are sufficiently mature to appreciate the unlawfulness of the offense they have committed and to conform their conduct to such appreciation. Sanctions provided for juveniles are educational and disciplinary measures. Punishment is to be inflicted only as a last resort.

Adolescents between the age of 18 and 21 are fully responsible. If the adolescent has a juvenile personality or if the offense he has committed was typical of a juvenile, one of the special sanctions provided for juveniles will be imposed; otherwise the adolescent will be punished like an adult.

CRIMINAL RESPONSIBILITY OF CORPORATIONS

Since West German criminal law is based on the principle that punishment presupposes personal guilt, criminal responsibility of corporations does not exist. Officers and agents of a corporation are individually responsible for what they have done in its behalf. Their individual guilt is to be the basis for fixing punishment. When imposing punishment upon an officer or agent, the court may, however, order the corporation to forfeit the profits from the illegal enterprise. Thus, from a practical point of view, West German law may not be very different from that of the United States, where corporations are held criminally responsible.

THE MENTAL ELEMENT; STRICT RESPONSIBILITY; MISTAKE OF FACT AND LAW

All criminal laws have to face the difficulty of defining various mental elements of criminal conduct that in some way reflect actual states of mind and that, at the same time, can be used as manageable tools for attributing criminal responsibility. West German criminal law tries to solve this problem by distinguishing two main categories of culpability: intention and negligence. Intention is subdivided into three kinds. An offender acts intentionally when he desires that his conduct causes the consequence he envisages, when he knows that the consequence will result from his conduct, or when he considers such consequence possible and does not mind it.

Differing from American tradition, ordinary negligence is a sufficient basis for criminal responsibility in West German law. Only some modern statutes limit responsibility to gross negligence. Recklessness is unknown as a separate category of responsibility.

West German criminal law does not distinguish between conscious negligence and inadvertent negligence. From a psychological point of view, it certainly makes a difference whether or not an offender is aware of a risk he creates. Yet, in practice it is often impossible to find out the offender's actual state of mind. In addition, one must keep in mind that conscious negligence is not necessarily a more serious form of culpability than inadvertence. A person who trusts his own competence to such an extent that he is not aware of the great risk he creates may deserve as much blame as the one who foresees the possibility of a damage he may cause but tries to avoid it.

The distinction between conscious negligence and intention generally is drawn in the following way: An offender acts with conscious negligence when he foresees that a certain consequence will possibly result from his conduct but trusts that he will not effectuate it. He acts intentionally when he foresees a possible consequence but does not mind it.

As mentioned above, strict responsibility is unknown. Responsibility without fault would be irreconcilable with the principle that punishment presupposes guilt. It may be argued that West German criminal law does not need to rely on strict responsibility because the concept of ordinary negligence is broad enough to cover all conduct deserving punishment.

West German criminal law recognizes in roughly the same way as American law that a mistake of fact negates the mental element and thus excludes criminal responsibility. As regards mistakes of law, however, both laws are in sharp contrast. While in the United States a mistake of law is generally no excuse, West German law distinguishes between unavoidable and avoidable mistake of law. The Penal Code provides: "If the offender in committing the act lacks the appreciation that he is acting unlawfully, he acts without guilt provided the mistake was unavoidable to him. If he could have avoided the mistake, the punishment may be mitigated." The practical impact of the concept that an unavoidable mistake of law serves as an excuse is, however, comparatively limited. In cases involving traditional criminal law, West German courts usually hold mistakes of law to be avoidable, since anyone knows or could know the central prohibitions of the law. Only when public or economic welfare offenses are concerned do courts to some extent consider a mistake unavoidable.

PREPARATION—ATTEMPT; COMPLICITY (CONSPIRACY)

Attempts to commit a felony are always punishable; attempts to commit a misdemeanor only if expressly provided for. Punishment may be mitigated in cases of an attempt. Mitigation is not obligatory because the missing damage may be counterbalanced by the gravity of the offender's conduct.

The Penal Code defines "attempt" as an act by which the offender, according to his plan, directly begins to carry out the intended crime. The requirements of the offender's plan and of the direct beginning are devised to distinguish attempt from preparation. Courts, however, often have tended to include preparatory acts in the concept of attempt.

The impossibility of committing an attempted offense excludes or mitigates punishment only if, because of gross misjudgment of the law of causation, the offender fails to realize that the intended crime could not possibly be completed. An example would be a woman who tries to procure an abortion by drinking camomile tea.

Unlike in most American jurisdictions, voluntary abandonment is a defense in West German law. Exemption from punishment is based on different considerations: The offender, so to speak, has rehabilitated himself; he should be encouraged to desist from committing the planned crime; he deserves leniency.

Parties to a crime are divided into three categories: principals, instigators, and accessories. Principals are offenders who commit the crime in person, through another, or together with another principal. The instigator intentionally incites another to commit an intentional crime. He is punished in the same manner as the principal. Accessories are persons who intentionally aid a principal before or while he is committing the crime. Punishment of the accessory is to be mitigated.

Because of this mitigation there is considerable controversy as to how to distinguish between accessories and principals. Courts ordinarily take a subjective approach by asking whether the offender intended to act as a principal or as an accessory. Legal writers have criticized this approach for relying on an utterly vague criterion. They suggest asking who was in charge of committing the offense and of what importance was the individual contribution.

Accessories after the fact are punished for crimes which are distinct from the crime they aid.

Conspiracy is a crime only if two or more persons agree to commit a felony. In addition, the Penal Code proscribes the forming of and joining in societies whose purpose or activities are directed toward committing crimes or acts of terrorism.

DEFENSES (INSANITY, SELF-DEFENSE, ETC.)

While American lawyers tend to treat criminal law problems in a procedural context, West Germans follow the civil law tradition and clearly differentiate between substantive law and procedural law. They do not talk about "defenses" but rather about justification and excuse. Defenses, especially affirmative defenses, that first place a burden of producing some evidence and sometimes even a burden of persuasion on the defendant would be irreconcilable with the presumption of innocence, which in West German law requires the state to carry these burdens without any exceptions.

Justification and excuse are concepts that are strictly separated in West German criminal law. An act that violates the literal terms of the criminal law is justified when it serves to protect a superior interest—for example, in cases of self-defense—or when protection of an interest is waived—as in cases of consent. An act may be illegal but the offender may not deserve personal blame, since he acted under extraordinary psychological pressure, as in a case of duress.

The concept of necessity may help to explain the difference between justification and excuse because West German criminal law distinguishes between "justifying necessity" and "excusing necessity." If, for example, the cashier of a supermarket who is held up at gunpoint hands the robber a sum of money, he acts in a state of "justifying necessity": The loss of his life which was in imminent danger would have been a greater harm than the loss of the money. If, however, after a shipwreck two sailors are reaching for the only life jacket and the stronger one pushes the other man away in order to save his own life, he acts under extreme psychological pressure and thus in a state of "excusing necessity."

The distinction between justification and excuse is of considerable practical importance. If, for example, an insane person points a gun and threatens to kill, the person is excused and thus not guilty of attempted homicide. His attack on the intended victim is, however, unlawful and therefore the intended victim is justified in wounding or even killing in self-defense.

As regards self-defense there are two striking differences between West German and American law. First, American criminal law distinguishes between defense of persons, dwellings, and other property as well as between the use of deadly and nondeadly force. The West German Penal Code defines self-defense in a very brief way as "the defense which is necessary to avert an immediate and unlawful attack from oneself or from another." This again may be taken as a typical example of the civil law method of legislation. It also may be argued that in an emergency situation the attacked person should not be hampered in his defense by detailed and complex provisions.

Second, the West German concept of self-defense does not require some kind of proportionality between the interests to be protected against the aggressor and the damage caused by the defense. The limits of justified defense are determined solely by the severity of the attack. Self-defense is based on the idea that law does not have to yield to lawlessness. Thus, deadly force may be applied even to defend property in case of simple theft. A more modern view, however, tends to restrict self-defense when the aggressor is a young, drunk, or insane person; when the attack is not carried out intentionally; or when the interest to be protected is disproportionately less valuable than the interest damaged by the defense.

To define insanity the West German Penal Code relies on psychological and biological criteria. The offender must be "incapable of appreciating the unlawfulness of his act or of acting in accordance with such appreciation." This incapacity must be the result of "a morbid emotional disturbance, a serious disturbance of consciousness, mental deficiency, or a serious emotional deviancy." This definition comes close to modern American law on insanity. The West German clause of "serious emotional deviancy" is interpreted to include extreme cases of psychopathy and neurosis.

West German law recognizes incapacity because of insanity and also diminished capacity. In the latter case punishment may be mitigated.

PENAL MEASURES

To understand the West German philosophy of penal measures one has to keep in mind that it distinguishes between two types of sanctions: penalties, and measures of rehabilitation and safety.

Penalties are considered means of retribution for the offender's guilt, but they also serve rehabilitation and deterrence. The Penal Code provides: "The offender's guilt shall be the basis for fixing punishment. The expected effects of punishment on the future life of the offender in society shall be taken into consideration." It remains an open question, however, what sentence, in a given case, will be required for retribution and for rehabilitation and how these heterogeneous objectives can be reconciled with each other.

Measures of rehabilitation and safety, such as commitment to a psychiatric hospital or revocation of a driver's license, serve solely preventive purposes. Their aim is to treat the offender with therapeutic and pedagogic means and to protect the public. Therefore, measures are imposed that are independent of the offender's guilt. For example, a defendant who is found not guilty by reason of insanity can be committed to a psychiatric hospital.

West German penal policy is guided by four main principles. The principle that guilt is to be the basis of punishment limits the penalizing power of the legislature as well as of the courts and thus helps to avoid penalties that would be out of proportion to the gravity of the offense. The indeterminate prison sentence, a sanction that is often used in the United States, is considered irreconcilable with this principle.

The principle of legality that prohibits punishment without a statutory basis has been dealt with above. It further is interpreted to require sentencing by the judge. Since the judge has evaluated the defendant's guilt, he, rather than a parole board, is considered the proper authority to determine the length of a sentence and to decide questions involving parole or revocation of a suspended sentence.

A third principle guiding West German penal policy is the protection of human dignity. It forbids cruel and inhuman punishment and serves to limit criminal law in order to protect individual freedom and the development of a pluralistic society.

The principle of social justice requires that the criminal not be expelled from society but rather given help favoring his rehabilitation. This principle, above all, must guide the execution of penal measures.

KINDS OF PENAL MEASURES

Capital punishment has been abolished by the West German Constitution. It may not even be inflicted under military law or in times of war or revolution. Criminal lawyers and criminologists argue that it would be irreconcilable with human dignity and that it cannot be regarded a better deterrent than life imprisonment.

The Penal Code prescribes a uniform type of imprisonment. Penal servitude was abolished in 1970, since it stigmatized the offender and thus impeded his rehabilitation. Imprisonment may be for a fixed term with a maximum of 15 years or for life. Life imprisonment, which is mandatory in cases of murder and genocide, means that the prisoner normally must serve between 15 and 25 years before he may be pardoned. In recent times, life imprisonment was criticized as destructive of the prisoner's personality, but the Federal Constitutional Court held it constitutional.

There is general agreement in the Federal Republic that short-term imprisonment is more harmful than useful. It is too short for rehabilitation but long enough to alienate prisoners from their families and jobs. Therefore, short-term imprisonment to a great extent has been replaced by fines. According to the Penal Code, a prison sentence of less than six months may be imposed only "if special circumstances concerning the offense or the personality of the offender render confinement indispensable to influence the offender or to protect the legal order."

The West German equivalent to probation in American law is the suspension of a prison term for a fixed period, placement of the defendant under the supervision of a probation officer, and issuance of probation directives. The upper limit for sentences that may be suspended is two years.

Since the combined problem of crime and poverty does not exist in the Federal Republic in the same measure as in the United States, fines play an important role in the West German law of sanctions. In the past West German courts have imposed fines in about 83 percent of all cases. Fines are fixed according to a day-fine scheme that was imported from Sweden. First, the court determines the number of day-fines proportionate to the defendant's guilt and takes into consideration aspects of rehabilitation and deterrence. Second, the amount of a single day-fine is specified in proportion to the defendant's financial situation. The amount should equal his average net daily income. For example, a defendant is sentenced to 20 day-fines; a day-fine is set at 50 West German marks.

As mentioned above, the Penal Code provides not only for penalties but also for measures of rehabilitation and safety. While guilt serves as a limitation of punishment, measures of rehabilitation and safety are limited by the principle of proportionality.

The following measures involve a deprivation of liberty: protective custody, commitment to a psychiatric hospital, commitment to an institution for withdrawal treatment, and commitment to an institution of social therapy. Institutions of social therapy are for dangerous habitual offenders with major personality dysfunctions, dangerous sexual offenders, young adults with a record of serious offenses who show a disposition to become habitual offenders, and persons with mental problems. Since there are not yet enough institutions of social therapy, the legislature has postponed commitment to such an institution until 1985. So far, a few of these institutions run on a trial basis.

The following measures do not involve a deprivation of liberty: revocation of driver's license, prohibition against practicing a profession, and probationary surveillance. Revocation of driver's license plays by far the most important role.

DISTRIBUTION OF PENAL MEASURES IN PRACTICE

As a consequence of the reform of the Penal Code over the last 10 years there is a strong movement away from prison sentences toward suspended sentences with probation and fines. Short-term imprisonment especially has decreased considerably. Table 4.2 does not include traffic offenses or juvenile and adolescent offenders who were sentenced according to juvenile law.

SPECIAL TREATMENT OF JUVENILES, RECIDIVISTS, AND OTHER OFFENDERS

If a juvenile, or an adolescent who is to be ranked as a juvenile, has committed a crime, educational or disciplinary measures such as warnings, directives, correctional education, or short-period detention may be imposed. For serious crimes the juvenile or adolescent may be punished by imprisonment in a prison for juveniles.

No increased sentences are provided for recidivists: the statutory maximum sentences are considered high enough. The Penal Code sets the minimum term at six months for third convictions when the defendant already has been imprisoned for at least three months and "fails to heed the warning of the prior sentences." Thus habitual offenders who tend to commit more or less insignificant crimes may be sentenced to a prison term that is not too short for therapeutic and pedagogic efforts.

TABLE 4.2

Year	Total of Sentenced Offenders	Percentage of Fines	Percentage of Prison Sentences Not Suspended	Percentage of Suspended Prison Sentences
1967	558 384	62	25	13
1969	530 947	70	16	14
1970	553 692	84	7	9
1974	599 368	82	7	11
1976	592 154	83	6	11

PAROLE

A prisoner must be paroled after having served two-thirds of his term if he consents and if he is not likely to commit new offenses. In exceptional cases parole may be granted after half the term has been served. No parole is provided for life imprisonment.

DIVERSION FROM THE CRIMINAL JUSTICE SYSTEM

So far, diversion plays only a minor role in the West German criminal justice system. Prosecution of misdemeanor cases may be suspended by the prosecutor with the court's consent, if the guilt of the offender is minor and if the offender agrees to make restitution, to contribute to the public treasury or a charity, or to perform some other act in the public interest. After the offender has complied with the condition set by the prosecutor, the case is finally closed.

III. CRIMINAL PROCEDURE

GENERAL PRINCIPLES

Some principles of criminal procedure in the Federal Republic are similar to those in the United States. For example, in both countries formal accusations to the courts are made by prosecutors. In the Federal Republic some crimes can be prosecuted only after the victim has filed a motion for prosecution. In cases involving a breach of domestic peace, an insult, or other offenses directed against predominantly personal interests, the victim may press a private charge.

The trial must be public. The principles of orality and immediacy require that witnesses who have observed the alleged crime must be examined at the trial. The examination may not be replaced by reading the record of a previous examination or of a written declaration. The accused has a right to be heard by the court and to confront the witnesses against him.

The accused is presumed to be innocent until the court is convinced of his guilt. As pointed out above, West German law never places a burden of producing evidence or a burden of persuasion on the accused. In courts sitting with more than one judge, a two-thirds majority is necessary to find the accused guilty. After a decision has become final, the principle of *res judicata* forbids a retrial for the same offense.

Other principles of West German procedure demonstrate major differences from the American criminal justice system.

According to the principle of compulsory prosecution, the West German prosecutor is required—except in certain situations specified in the Code of Criminal Procedure—to prosecute all charges for which there is sufficient evidence. Equal enforcement of the criminal law and protection against prosecutorial arbitrariness are predominant values.

The West German trial follows in inquisitorial principle. It is not the parties but the judge who calls and interrogates the witnesses and who decides upon the order in which the evidence is taken. The distinction between examination-in-chief and cross-examination is unknown. Questions to test the reliability of a witness and the accuracy of his statements are put by the judge in the course of his comprehensive interrogation. The judicial inquiry into the facts also includes the questioning of the accused at the beginning of the trial.

In advance of the trial the judge studies the file of the case that was assembled by the police and the prosecutor and that was given him with the written accusation. Without being thoroughly informed about the facts as they appear in the file of the case the judge could not effectively interrogate the witnesses and the defendant.

Prosecutor and defense counsel play comparatively minor roles at the trial. After the judge has finished the examination of a witness, or of the accused, they may ask additional questions. They also may move that the judge take further evidence. Defense counsel in West German criminal procedure has a right to pretrial inspection of the prosecutor's file. Experience has proved that pretrial inspection does not lead to a tainting of the evidence nor to fabricating defenses.

Following civil law tradition, West German courts do not exclude hearsay evidence. Exclusion of evidence would be considered irreconcilable with the trial judge's duty to find the facts. At the same time, professional judges are trusted that they can properly evaluate the probative value of hearsay evidence.

PHASES OF CRIMINAL PROCEEDINGS

Three phases may be distinguished in West German criminal proceedings: proceedings before trial, the trial, and appellate proceedings. Proceedings before trial are the province of the prosecutor and the police. According to the law, the prosecutor is in charge of the investigative proceedings. In fact, however, it is the police that in almost all cases carry out investigations. The prosecutor's function ordinarily is reduced to deciding whether a formal charge is to be filed with the court.

Preliminary judicial investigation by an investigating judge was abolished in 1975 because it tended to duplicate investigations already done by the police and the prosecutor and thus caused unnecessary delay. A procedure comparable to preliminary examination in the United States does not exist in West Germany. The accused must be given a chance to answer the charge prior to his trial, but this need not be done by a judicial officer. Also, a grand jury is unknown in the Federal Republic.

The trial begins with the judicial interrogation of the accused as to his personal circumstances. Thereupon the prosecutor reads the accusation. The presiding judge advises the accused that he may decline to speak about the case. If the accused is willing to speak, he is interrogated by the presiding judge. To hear the accused at the beginning of the trial is considered a privilege, since he is offered an opportunity to present his version of the case before other evidence is taken.

After the accused has been heard, the presiding judge calls and interrogates the witnesses. The other professional judges, the lay judges, the prosecutor, the accused, and the defense counsel may put additional questions. The presiding judge also reads documents and other written matter serving as evidence. After the interrogation of each witness, as well as after the reading of each piece of written matter, the presiding judge asks the accused whether he wishes to comment. The prosecutor and the defense counsel also have a right to comment.

After all evidence is taken, the prosecutor and the defense counsel present their closing arguments. The accused is entitled to the last word.

Thereupon the judges retire to deliberate and decide on innocence or guilt and if the accused is found guilty on a sentence. Separate sentencing procedures are unknown in the Federal Republic. Evidence necessary for sentencing is gathered in the course of the trial.

As opposed to American law, the prosecutor and the defense have equal rights to appeal. This means that the prosecutor may appeal from an acquittal. Since he is under a duty to see that justice is done, he even may, and sometimes does, appeal in favor of the accused.

RIGHTS OF AN ACCUSED

Defense counsel is admitted at the trial as well as during the proceedings before trial. In cases involving serious crimes or an accused with mental problems, participation of defense counsel at the trial is obligatory. If in these cases the accused fails to appoint a counsel of his own choice, the court will appoint one for him. The accused's right to self-determination is considered less decisive than the protection of his procedural rights and the accuracy of fact-finding. Both are better guaranteed when the accused is represented by counsel.

Before an accused is interrogated by a police officer, a prosecutor, or a judge in the course of pretrial investigations he must be advised that he need not answer questions; that he may, even before the examination, consult with an attorney of his choice, and that he may move for the taking of particular evidence. The similarity of West German law to the Miranda warnings is obvious. Yet, no lawyer is appointed if the accused is interrogated before trial, nor is a lawyer the accused has chosen entitled to attend the interrogation.

A search warrant is not necessary if getting the warrant would cause unreasonable delay. Since police and prosecutors usually manage to induce citizens to consent to search or seizure, warrants are not often used.

Illegally obtained evidence is in principle admissible in West German courts. Exclusionary rules are recognized only in a few instances—for example, when a statement is obtained by coercion, fatigue, hypnosis, or similar forbidden methods. Exclusionary rules are considered neither an efficient means nor necessary to deter police misconduct. The West German police, hierarchically organized on state level, is efficiently controlled through inner-office supervision.

ARREST, BAIL, AND PRETRIAL DETENTION

A judge may issue an arrest warrant if a person is suspected of an offense and if he is likely to flee, to tamper with the evidence, or to commit certain further offenses which are limited in the Code of Criminal Procedure. Prosecutors and police officers may arrest without a warrant, if applying for a warrant would cause unreasonable delay. Even a private citizen can arrest without a warrant if a person who is caught "red-handed" is likely to flee or if he cannot be identified.

An arrested person is to be brought before a judge without delay. The judge may release him if he agrees to periodically report to the police, remain within his residence, not contact certain persons, or furnish bond. In practice, conditional release is granted in only a small percentage of cases, since an arrest warrant is issued only if there is danger that the accused will flee, tamper with the evidence, or commit certain further offenses.

An accused who is detained prior to his trial may, at any time, move for a judicial hearing to determine whether the arrest warrant should be vacated or its execution be suspended. The period of pretrial detention should normally be limited to six months, but it is extended in a considerable number of cases.

SPECIAL MODES OF CRIMINAL PROCEEDINGS

The guilty plea is unknown in West German criminal procedure. It is generally argued that a guilty plea would be irreconcilable with the duty of the judge to ascertain the facts of the case. On the other hand, the criminal justice system of the Federal Republic cannot afford a trial for every case. The Code of Criminal Procedure provides for a less formal, written procedure to process the bulk of less serious cases. In cases involving misdemeanors the prosecutor may, instead of taking the case to trial, apply to the judge for a "penal order." The prosecutor prepares the draft of the proposed penal order. The judge decides whether to issue the order solely on the basis of the prosecutor's draft and file of the case. Usually, the judge's review of the proposed order and of the file is perfunctory. To some extent, the penal order is comparable to the guilty plea in American procedure. It is a written offer by the judge to the accused to accept the prosecutor's charge and admit his guilt.

LAY PARTICIPATION IN CRIMINAL PROCEEDINGS

In former times two types of courts with lay participation existed in the German criminal justice system: jury courts and mixed courts where lay judges sat together with the professional judges in a single panel. In German jury courts the functions of the judges and the jury were different from what they typically are in the United States. Jurors were asked not to decide on the issue of guilt as such but only on single questions of fact. Since jurors did not always comply with this restriction, they were looked upon with suspicion. General distrust of the jury was one of the main reasons it was abolished in 1924.

The mixed system of lay judges and professional judges still operates today. As was pointed out, lay judges sit together with professional judges in local courts and in district courts. They deliberate and decide together on guilt, punishment, and procedural questions. It goes without saying that professional judges exercise great influence during the common deliberations.

Since decisions on guilt and punishment require a two-thirds majority, the two lay judges who in local courts sit with a single professional judge can outvote him and find the accused guilty over his objection. If the two lay judges who in district courts sit with three professional judges vote for acquittal, the accused cannot be found guilty. In practice, however, it rarely happens that lay judges affect the determination of guilt. Likewise, their influence on sentencing is to be considered very moderate.

SPECIAL PROCEDURES FOR JUVENILES

Cases involving juveniles and adolescents are heard by juvenile courts, which are special branches of the criminal courts. Depending on the seriousness of the case, juvenile courts sit with a single judge, with a professional judge and two lay judges, or with three professional judges and two lay judges. Professional judges and lay judges as well as prosecutors should be qualified as educators.

Since education is the predominant consideration, proceedings against juveniles and adolescents follow their own rules. Prosecutor and judge cooperate with the local youth authorities, which supervise the offender and prepare a report on his personality. The public is excluded from trials against juveniles. The judge may summon the juvenile's parents to attend his trial.

IV. EXECUTION OF PENAL MEASURE (CORRECTIONS)

AIMS AND BASIC PRINCIPLES OF THE EXECUTION OF PENAL MEASURES

According to the Code on the Execution of Prison Sentences and of Measures Involving a Deprivation of Liberty, imprisonment in the first place should serve rehabilitation. As explained in the chapter on the philosophy of penal measures, retribution is the basis for fixing punishment. This is not a contradiction of the rehabilitative purpose of imprisonment, for different aims may be followed in meting out punishment and in the execution of a prison sentence.

The extent to which the rehabilitative ideal is achieved in practice is difficult to evaluate. So far any optimism seems to be unfounded. On the other hand, the new American attitude that rehabilitation does not work is not endorsed in the Federal Republic. It is argued instead that carefully planned treatment in prisons may improve possibilities for rehabilitation.

EXECUTION OF DEPRIVATION OF LIBERTY AND OTHER CUSTODIAL MEASURES

Penal institutions are administered by prison authorities on the state level under the supervision of the state ministries of justice. The Code on the Execution of Prison Sentences provides that expert advice has to be solicited for the administration of prison labor, social help, professional training, health care, and other treatment of inmates.

Supervision over prison authorities is exercised by special courts that are organized on the district court level in districts that have penal institutions. These courts hear inmate complaints against prison authorities. In addition, they hear cases dealing with the execution of penal sanctions, such as revocation of probation or parole.

The prosecutor supervises the legal formalities of the execution of penal sanctions. He sets the date when the offender has to begin serving his prison term or when he has to pay a fine. He is, however, not authorized to interfere with the administration of penal institutions.

Ordinarily, offenders are classified according to age, sex, type of offense, length of sentence, and prior convictions. Different types of offenders are assigned to different penal institutions. Prison experts have criticized this classification system because it is not primarily based on individual treatment. In addition, offenders with prior convictions who turn out to be high recidivist risks may be unnecessarily stigmatized.

When entering a penal institution, inmates who have to serve a term of more than one year are assigned to an observation unit for a detailed classification procedure. Their personality is examined and a treatment plan is worked out to cover the following: placement in a closed, an open, or a half-open institution; assignment to a special residential unit or to a treatment group; assignment to work, professional training, and continued education; special privileges, such as supervised or unsupervised work outside the institution; and preparations for release.

Formerly, each inmate at the beginning of his sentence had to serve some months with hardly any privileges. This retributive phase of imprisonment was abolished long ago, since it was considered irreconcilable with the rehabilitative ideal.

It was pointed out above that the West German Penal Code prescribes a uniform type of imprisonment to aid rehabilitation. At the same time, the rehabilitation goal requires different types of penal institutions. Therefore, a considerable variety of institutions exist in the Federal Republic. Closed institutions are distinguished from half-open institutions where security measures are reduced or virtually nonexistent. Closed institutions by far outnumber the other types.

Many penal institutions are still located in old-fashioned, large, star-shaped buildings designed to isolate inmates and improve control. These antiquated buildings seriously hamper rehabilitative efforts. Today, modern institutions for rehabilitative treatment mostly are built in pavilion style and designed for between 200 and 300 inmates. Some penal institutions are especially equipped for professional training and continuing education. Separate institutions exist for juveniles.

Psychiatric hospitals and institutions for withdrawal treatment are outside the administration of penal institutions. Institutions of social therapy are ranked penal institutions but are under the management of physicians. No separate institutions of protective custody exist. Since only a few recidivists are sentenced to protective custody, they are committed to top security prisons.

Inmates are obliged to work and are paid a few marks per day. An increase of payments is provided for by the Code on the Execution of Prison Sentences, but the effective date of the relevant provision was postponed by the legislature for financial reasons. To encourage professional training, inmates in training programs are paid as if they were working.

Disciplinary measures to control inmates are limited to those listed in the Code on the Execution of Prison Sentences. They include warnings, denial of entertainment such as television or sports programs, visitor limitations, or placement in solitary confinement for up to four weeks.

The Code on the Execution of Prison Sentences also makes detailed provision for a variety of privileges and rights of inmates, such as mail, telephone calls, visitors, and permission to leave the institution for up to 21 days per year.

In the past, decisions concerning inmates were left to the uncontrolled discretion of prison authorities. Today inmates are entitled to file complaints whenever they believe their rights have been violated. Complaints are heard by the courts that supervise prisons. The inmate's right to formal complaint is considered essential to the rule of law, though prison authorities sometimes argue that inmates take irrelevant cases to court and impede prison administration. Yet, an allegedly irrelevant case may be important, if looked upon from an inmate's point of view. To him it will make a difference whether his complaint is decided upon by prison authorities or by a court.

5

SWEDEN

Alvar Nelson

I. GENERAL INFORMATION

Sweden is situated in the northern part of Europe and has land-frontiers with Norway and Finland and sea-boundaries with Denmark, West and East Germany, Poland, and the USSR. The total area is approximately 175,000 square miles, of which less than one-tenth consists of cultivated land. Sweden has a population of approximately 8,200,000 (52 persons per square mile), which is rather unevenly distributed. During and after the two world wars immigration has been considerable. The former Nordic ethnic unity is gradually disappearing as a result of the influx of 600,000 immigrants, refugees and, after World War II, guestworkers.

Sweden is a kingdom, although the royal power has been gradually diminishing and the king is now primarily a symbol of national unity. The political power has been taken over by *Riksdagen* (the parliament) and *Regeringen* (the government). The Parliament is responsible for legislation and economy while the government is responsible for administration. The political parties form two blocks of almost equal strength: the bourgeois and the socialist. Although in principle apolitical, the main organizations of the employees—in particular the Confederation of Trade Unions and the Central Organization of Salaried Employees—take part in the debate on nearly all political matters.

The Swedish economy is mainly based on industrial production and on the export of iron and wood products. The living standard is among the highest in Europe. Living costs are high due to the high living standard, the climate, and the taxes. On the other hand, social, educational, vocational, and health benefits are unsurpassed in the world.

SURVEY OF THE LEGAL SYSTEM

The Swedish legal system is based on meticulous legislation, independent courts, and public control of the administration. Although the system in principle is derived from the early Middle Ages, it has been reviewed, revised, and improved over time in order to protect the citizens and other residents from arbitrary and unjust actions by the rulers, once the king and the army, now the politicians and the civil servants. The present Constitution of 1974 gives the legislative power to the Parliament alone and empowers the government to issue ordinances within that legislation. Additional directives are issued by the central administration boards. The county and municipal authorities, however, have gained partial independence with regard to health and social services, public schools, and vocational training centers.

All the ordinary courts hear both civil and criminal cases; with rare exception, sessions are open to the public. Judges and justices are irrevocably appointed by the government. Lay assessors, serving in the local courts and the courts of appeal, are elected by the municipal and county councils, respectively. Administrative matters were once handled by the civil servants but are now, to an increasingly greater extent, heard by administrative courts. Thus the county administrative court decides in matters concerning mandatory treatment of children and young persons and of alcoholics.

Public control is exercised not only by the man in the street and the mass media but also by the lay members of the administrative boards and the lay assessors in the courts. Moreover, the Parliament Ombudsmen supervise all parts of the administration. All documents in the courts as well as in the central and local administration in principle are available to everyone.

STRUCTURE AND FUNCTIONING OF THE LAW ENFORCEMENT AGENCIES

The Ministry of Justice has a staff of 160 persons and is divided into 11 units, of which 6 work within the field of criminal justice: Prison, Probation and Parole; Courts; Police; Mercy; Procedure; Penal Law and Law and Order Regulations. The Ministry considers applications for Mercy (pardons) and prepares the Government Bills on Criminal Justice to be presented to Parliament.

The Central Administration of Criminal Justice under the ministry is entrusted to five independent boards and two offices: the Council for Crime Prevention; the National Police Board, the Chief Prosecutor and his Office; the Courts' Administration Board, the Central and Local Boards for Probation and Parole; the Attorney-General and his office; and, finally, the National Prison and Probation Board. There are lay members on all the boards, with the exception of the Offices of the Chief Prosecutor and the Attorney-General.

The Police (including the National Security Police) have a total staff of 19,000 persons, divided into 23 regions, which are subdivided into 118 local districts. Modern equipment and an efficient computer system have been added since 1965, when the municipal police forces were transferred to the national organization under the Ministry of Justice. The police have a strictly limited authority to omit reports to the prosecutor on petty offenses provided the offender is advised or admonished. They are also empowered to impose fines for breaches of regulations.

Prosecution is almost entirely undertaken by the public prosecutors. There is a total staff of 1,400 persons. The head of the prosecution function is the chief prosecutor who is also, by virtue of his office, prosecutor at the Supreme Court. The state prosecutors are in charge of 24 regions, which are subdivided into 86 districts, each having several district and assistant prosecutors. There are four additional state prosecutors for special tasks (mainly economic crimes). All prosecutors are professionally trained. The prosecutors have the authority to impose day-fines for minor offenses and to remit prosecution for certain groups of offenses in general, without limitations for youthful offenders and to a restricted extent for patients under care in institutions for inebriates.

All the courts hear both civil and criminal cases. The total staff exceeds 4,000 persons working in the 100 district courts, the six courts of appeal, and the Supreme Court. In the district court petty offenses are tried by a professional judge alone (in 1976, 18,000 cases) while the more serious cases are heard by a professional judge and five lay assessors (in 1976, 71,000 cases). In the court of appeal criminal cases are heard by three justices and two lay assessors. Only 6,000 cases were appealed in 1976. Criminal cases can be brought to the Supreme Court only with the consent of the court or upon the request of the chief prosecutor. Three justices hear applications for review (in 1976, 838 applications were heard) and review is granted if at least one of the justices agrees (in 1976, 51 cases were granted).

The judges and justices are appointed by the government on purely professional merits and retain their jobs until retirement. Lay assessors are elected by the municipal and county councils on proposal from the political parties. They are paid $40 per day in service. They vote individually and the joint opinion of four of them outweighs the judge's. This happens from time to time, generally to the favor of the accused or convicted.

The Prison and Probation Administration has a total staff of 5,500 persons, of whom 350 work at the central administration, 4,350 in the penal institutions, and 800 with probation and aftercare. Probation and aftercare work is directed by the central and local boards, and supervision of the clients is to a large extent carried out by 9,000 voluntary (lay) supervisors.

The country is divided into 13 regions. There are 23 national and 50 local penal institutions with a total capacity of 4,200 (2,300 in closed institutions and 1,900 in open) and a few halfway houses. Pretrial detention institutions are also administered by the prison service. Probation and aftercare are the core of the correctional system and incarceration is used only as a deterrent or last resort. Today there are four times as many people under supervision as there are in prison.

The Crime Prevention Council was established in 1974 to coordinate responses to crime and to conduct research on crime problems. The council has published approximately 20 reports, has given economic support to conferences, and has provided economic support for research outside the council. Efforts to reduce crime are also made by the National Police Board throughout the country as well as in specific regions or districts.

SCOPE OF CRIMINAL LAW

When the Penal Code of 1864 was being prepared, the leading principles were that the code could only include infringements of human rights (innate or gained) and be restricted to intentional acts. Neither principle was fully observed, as the code punished cruelty to animals as well as causing another's death through carelessness. Although the present Penal Code of 1962 (PC) follows the same lines, the arrangement of its content has been completely changed. It is divided into three parts:

(1) General provisions concerning the definitions of offenses and sanctions (Chapter 1) and the applicability of Swedish penal law (Chapter 2).
(2) specific offenses (Chapters 3-22) and the provisions regarding preparation, attempt, conspiracy, and complicity (Chapter 23) and on self-defense and other acts of necessity (Chapter 24). The specific offenses are distributed within four categories:
　(a) offenses against persons (Chapters 3-7);
　(b) offenses against property (Chapters 8-12);
　(c) offenses against the public (Chapters 13-15); and
　(d) offenses against the state (Chapters 16-22).
(3) The sanctions (Chapters 25-36) and provisions regarding central and local boards (Chapter 37) and provisions regarding the administration of criminal justice (Chapter 38).

The statistics for 1976 show that of 84,943 persons sentenced by the courts, 36,412 (43%) were convicted of offenses against PC. Of the 29,196 persons sentenced to heavier penalty than fines, 21,196 (73%) had offended PC. This shows that PC today covers a minority of all offenders coming before the courts but the vast majority of those found guilty of serious offenses. It should be pointed out, however, that 36,486 persons had obtained prosecution remission and 381,575 had consented to pay administratively imposed fines.

Outside PC there are many statutes and innumerable ordinances with provisions concerning offenses against their regulations. Only few of the most important are mentioned here:

(1) the Road Traffic Offenses Act of 1951, where drunken driving is the most important offense (11,379 persons convicted, of whom 3,921 were sentenced to imprisonment),
(2) the Product of Smuggling Act of 1960,
(3) the Narcotic Drugs Penal Act of 1968,
(4) the Revenue Offense Act of 1971.

Within the category offenses against the person, considerable technical changes were made in the legislation. With regard to offenses against life and health, the complicated old-fashioned provisions were simplified. Among the sexual offenses, adultery and prostitution were decriminalized in 1918, and bestiality in 1937. Homosexual act were partially decriminalized in 1944 and totally in 1978; and incest, with the exception of carnal knowledge of parents-children and brother-sister, in 1973. Within offenses against property, the provisions for receiving stolen goods, extortion, and usury were broadened. Among offenses against the public and the state important innovations occurred. The Military Penal Code was abolished and some offenses were transferred to PC (Chapters 21 and 22). Offenses committed in office by public servants were restricted in PC and further restricted in 1975, but broadened with regard to bribery in 1977. The punishment for public drunkenness was abolished in 1976.

As can be seen, modern offenses are to a large extent kept outside PC partly due to technical problems but mainly due to an inability to incorporate them within the old systematics.

Decriminalization is the slogan of today, but very little has happened. When the punishment for public drunkenness was abolished, a statute on temporary care was introduced. The provision on disorderly conduct (Chapter 16, Section 16) is still in force but rarely used due to a statute limiting temporary detention to at most six hours. Persons committing petty offenses (such as shoplifting) are rarely brought to the courts but rather are either remitted or administratively fined and in both cases registered.

In the last few years efforts have been made to reduce the mass of petty offenses through the use of surcharges instead of fines. Infringement of local parking regulations is thus no longer an offense but simply an act leading to surcharge in accordance with a statute. A similar solution can be found in the use of public transport without a ticket. The same legislative technique applies to minor mistakes in income-tax reports and the like. Surcharge is applied without regard to *mens rea*.

Today, criminal policy with regard to criminalization-decriminalization is characterized on the one hand by attempts to find a new value system as basis for legislation and on the other by attempts to coordinate administrative regulations (for example, on consumers' protection and protection of the environment) with central penal legislation where criminal sanctions seem to be applicable and appropriate.

PHILOSOPHY OF PENAL MEASURES

In comparison with the continent, Sweden has based its penal reforms more upon pragmatism than on philosophy. Nevertheless, it would be fair to mention that during the last two centuries the constant aim has been to combine humanity with efficiency. The manner in which this has been carried out can be seen in the approach to different types of penal sanctions.

(1) Death penalty. This punishment was rarely used in the nineteenth century, and the last execution took place in 1910. The death penalty was abolished in 1928 for peacetime offenses and in 1973 for wartime offenses. The Constitution of 1974 bans the death penalty (Chapter 2, Section 4).

(2) Incarceration. The present prison system dates back to 1825, when the central administration of the prisons was established. PC of 1864 knew penal servitude (for life or from three months to ten years) and imprisonment (from one month to two years or according to a scale as penalty in default of paying fines). These two types of incarceration were amalgamated into one, referred to as imprisonment, by PC of 1962.

> *(a) Imprisonment for life* is used only in exceptional cases (16 persons sentenced since 1965). Imprisonment for one year or more is uncommon (1,185 persons in 1977; of them, only 149 for three years or more). In earlier times, fines were frequently converted to imprisonment in default of payment, but now this penalty is used only in exceptional cases (20 persons in 1977) and will be completely abolished. Conditional release was introduced on a small scale in 1906 and gradually expanded in 1943 and by PC to be used for all prisoners serving more than four months.
>
> *(b) Youth imprisonment* was introduced in 1935 (in force 1938) and will not be abolished.
>
> *(c) Preventive detention* (for mentally disturbed offenders) and internment (for recidivists) were two sanctions introduced in 1927 and expanded in 1937 (in force 1946). They were combined by PC into internment, a sanction rarely used. The Ministry of Justice is now considering abolishing the sanction.

Youth imprisonment and internment always include the provision that the first part of the sentence be served in prison and the latter part under supervision outside the institution.

(3) Probation. Different forms for probation and conditional sentence were introduced in 1906 and expanded in 1918 and 1939 (in force 1944). PC makes clear a distinction between conditional sentence and probation:

> *(a) Conditional sentence with a trial period of two years and without supervision.* It may be combined with day-fines. This sanction has lately been used increasingly (in 1966, 2,836 persons; in 1976, 5,231 persons).

(b) *Probation with a trial period of three years and regular supervision for two years.* Probation may be combined with day-fines. Institutional care (in a prison) may be ordered for a period of one to two months.

(4) Fines. The introduction of day-fines in 1931 made fines a sanction not only for petty offenses but also for many other offenses for which supervision or incarceration was considered inexpedient. Today monetary fines are regularly used as a penalty imposed by the police, while day-fines are imposed by the prosecutors or the courts.

(5) Surrender for special care. This sanction is new in PC. With regard to youthful offenders, preceding provisions were given in a statute from 1952 (in force 1954). In 1977, the National Council for Crime Prevention published a report with ideas and proposals concerning a new penal system. The report begins with a statement that PC of 1962 is, to a large extent, built on the idea that the purpose of punishment is to treat and adapt the individual offender to society. For that reason the choice of punishment and its assessment is often determined according to the offender's need for treatment, and therefore he is sentenced to mandatory care within a prison or under supervision. Thus the connection between offense and punishment is lost and injustice caused. The council claims that the new penal system should be based on justice, proportionality, and humanity. The code should bluntly state that punishment is meant to be and is an inconvenience which should be graded according to the gravity of the offense. Social service, care, and treatment should be provided for independently of the penalty. Since many offenders are socially maladjusted, special efforts are needed to help them.

The council's report argues in favor of a still more extensive use of fines and conditional sentences. Probation should be fortified by more intense supervision for a shorter period. Incarceration should be restricted to one sanction, imprisonment, and be used only for those offenses where the offender really merits the most severe punishment.

The report has wrongly been characterized as neo-classical. It is meant only to create a realistic approach to the role of punishment in modern society.

II. SUBSTANTIVE CRIMINAL LAW

THE PRINCIPLE OF LEGALITY

Sweden observed the rules: no crime, no punishment without law. An explicit provision based on this principle, however, was not given until the present Constitution of 1974, according to which no penal sanction or legal consequence could be imposed for an act that was not unlawful when committed, and no more serious sanction could be imposed for a punishable act than the sanction stipulated at that time. This implies that penal provision can never be retroactive.

In regard to the assessment of punishment, one could scarcely carry the principle of legality so far as to claim that punishment should be enforced in the same way against every offender. The power given to the police and to the prosecutor to drop a case, as well as the liberty of the court to choose the appropriate sanction in a particular case with regard to the offender's personal characteristics and situation, show the boundaries for the principle of equality before the law.

GRADES OF OFFENSES

According to the Penal Code, all violations for which punishment is stated are called offenses regardless of the gravity of the act. An offense is any act for which punishment is stated; the penalty may be a monetary fine or imprisonment for life. The differences are to be found in provisions for the administration of criminal justice. The police have a discretionary power not to report petty offenses to the prosecutor. The prosecutors are empowered to remit prosecution for less serious offenses.

AGE OF CRIMINAL RESPONSIBILITY

Since 1864, the age of criminal responsibility has been 15 years. While the Penal Code of 1964 had adopted the ideology of responsibility, the present penal code has abandoned it and replaced it with restrictions concerning the use of different sanctions. As no sanction is applicable to anyone for an offense committed before reaching 15 years of age, no prosecution is undertaken. The police may report him to his parents or to the social board for appropriate measures.

CRIMINAL RESPONSIBILITY FOR CORPORATIONS

The criminal justice system in Sweden is based entirely on individual responsibility not only for the one who has committed the act but also for anyone who has furthered it by advice or deed. Thus, a corporation as such cannot be found guilty of an offense. However, the responsible decision makers do have individual responsibility. In recent years there has been discussion regarding the introduction of some form of responsibility for corporations and similar juridical entities for certain types of offenses—such as those against environment—but no final decision as yet has been made.

MENS REA

A violation does not constitute an offense unless individual guilt exists at the moment of the act. No definition of guilt is given in PC, although intention or negligence is mentioned in PC as well as in many other penal regulations. The conceptual definition of *mens rea* has been left to jurisprudence and the practice of the courts. The legislative method in PC has been to assume that intention is required unless the contrary is specifically stated. However, where special penal regulations are involved outside PC, negligence is often considered sufficient.

Swedish jurisprudence recognizes intention in three forms: direct intention if the consequence of the act is desired; indirect intention if the consequence is necessary but not desired; eventual intention if the offender realized the possibility of the consequences and still undertook the act with the risk that the consequence might occur.

The concept of negligence in Swedish criminal law includes both conscious (advertent) and unconscious negligence but does not create criminal liability unless the negligence reaches higher degrees of carelessness, foolishness, or thoughtlessness than in the law of torts.

Within PC intention is the general requirement for an offense, although it is sometimes limited to purpose (direct intention). For some acts negligence is enough to constitute an offense, such as causing another's death. Outside PC negligence is often sufficient—for example, dangerous driving.

Swedish criminal law has never accepted strict responsibility. However, in several statutes there are presumptions according to which the accused is liable for omitting to control acts committed by other persons. For example, an innkeeper for not having had such control of his staff that violations of the liquor regulations were prevented.

Where intention is required for criminal responsibility, mistake of fact excludes liability if the fact is an essential part of the offense. In regard to mistake of law, the practice of the courts has leaned toward a reluctance to accept such a mistake unless the mistake is due to

(a) improper publication of the statute;
(b) ambiguity of the statute; and
(c) erroneous information from an authority.

To believe that the act is right from a religious or moral standpoint does not constitute a defense. The legislators have tried to avoid conflicts between the interests of society and the conscience of the individual by offering alternatives (such as civilian work instead of armed service) or by abstaining from constructions leading to an offense (for example, by accepting participation in a strike organized by a union).

ATTEMPT, PREPARATION, CONSPIRACY, AND COMPLICITY

With regard to attempt and preparation, Swedish criminal law has chosen a different approach than most continental systems. Attempt and preparation are only punishable where express provision is made and where special requirements for attempt or preparation are met. The same applies to conspiracy.

Although PC in conformity with common usage makes distinctions among the actor, the instigator, and the accessory, all offenses in PC are punishable for all three categories, each according to the offender's intention or carelessness. Outside PC the same principle is applied *ex analogia* for serious offenses (such as drunken driving). The penalty for an accessory can be set below the punishment stated for the offense.

RULES OF EXCEPTION

In Swedish jurisprudence a distinction is usually made between cases where the object to be protected is missing and cases where the act is justifiable by reference or other interests. Exceptions amount to defenses either by express provision or by court decisions.

(1) Attack on one's own interests. A person can abuse his body or his health, or even attempt to take his own life as long as he does not thereby incapacitate himself for completion of a public obligation (for example, military service). He can devastate his property as long as no creditor's right is injured or the act does not prejudice another's right or involve jeopardy to another's life or health or destruction of another's property.

(2) Consent. It is sometimes expressly required that the act be committed without consent. Usually the courts decide the extent to which lack of consent may be an essential part of the offense. They have taken a cautious approach toward implied consent.

(3) Obedience of orders. Exclusion of responsibility takes place only if an offense which a person commits was performed in the execution of an order from a person to whom he owes obedience, and only in cases where he had to comply with the order.

(4) Lawful authority. When a person in the course of his official duty (a policeman on duty, a serviceman on sentry duty, and the like) meets with violence or the threat of violence, he is permitted to exercise such force as can be regarded as justifiable in view of the circumstances in order to accomplish his task. Any person who comes to his assistance has the same right to use force as the person he assists.

(5) Self-defense. Self-defense against an attack upon one's person or property has traditionally been considered permissible but is now considerably restricted in PC.

(6) Acts of necessity. A provision regarding freedom from responsibility is given in PC.

A person who uses more force than required when exercising lawful authority or acting in self-defense or in situations of necessity is, in principle, responsible for the excess force used but can be freed from responsibility or subjected to a lesser penalty.

KINDS OF PENAL MEASURES

Part Three of PC regulates the application of the various sanctions and the form they may take. There are also provisions for forfeiture of property. Other legal consequences of crime (such as loss of driving license and forfeiture of inheritance) are regulated elsewhere. The sanctions are fines, imprisonment, conditional sentence, probation, youth imprisonment, internment, and surrender for special care.

When fines are imposed for more serious offenses, day-fines are used. The number of day-fines imposed varies to a maximum of 120 with the gravity of the offense. Each has a value of $50 to $100, depending on the economic situation of the offender. For petty offenses and breaches of regulations fines take the form of a fixed sum, maximum $100, and are known as monetary fines. A few types of offenses lead to fines calculated on another basis and are referred to as standardized fines. The vast majority of fines are imposed by the police or the prosecutor.

For imprisonment the latitude in sentencing ranges from one month to ten years or life. The court makes the assessment within the terms set forth for the offense (for theft, at most ten years). The convict is usually released on parole (conditional release) after having served two-thirds of the sentence (at least four months). Under certain conditions release may follow after half of the sentence has been served. The very few persons who are sentenced to life imprisonment may, by grant of pardon (mercy), have their sentences converted to a fixed period of imprisonment and are released on the same conditions as others.

If an offense is punishable by imprisonment, the court may give a conditional sentence for an occasional offender. This implies that no further sanction will be imposed provided the convicted person does not commit any other offense within two years (trial period). The sentence is not combined with supervision or any special instructions but may be combined with day-fines if this measure is considered necessary for the correction of the offender or to maintain general obedience to the law.

Probation may be applied where an offense is punishable by imprisonment. Probation implies that no further sanction will be imposed if the convicted person does not commit any other offense within three years (trial period). During the first year the probationer is under supervision and has to obey instructions that may be given concerning residence, work, and treatment. As in the case of conditional sentences, probation may be combined with day-fines. If the probationer is over 18 years of age, it may be decided that the order should include institutional care for at least one but not more than two months. This decision is either made by the court at the initial sentencing or by the Supervision Board within the trial period. The courts sometimes use the institution order as additional sanction upon reconviction of a probationer for a new offense.

Youthful offenders (mainly in the 18-20-year age group) may be imprisoned for a period that is not determined in advance but is decided administratively depending on the offender's progress. The first part of the sentence is served in a prison (in most cases 10-12 months) and the second part under supervision at liberty. Readmission to the prison is frequently ordered by the courts or by the Youth Imprisonment Board.

If an adult offender has committed an offense punishable by imprisonment for two years or more and is a recidivist, he may be sentenced to internment if the court finds it necessary in order to prevent further serious criminality on his part. The court determines a minimum period of incarceration which varies according to the individual case from one to 12 years. After the period in prison the convict serves the rest of the sentence in liberty under supervision. The Internment Board determines when the sentence is fully served. The majority of the convicts are mentally disturbed. Readmission due to new offenses or disorderly behavior is frequently ordered by the courts or by the Internment Board.

Surrender for special care is a sanction that may be imposed on offenders in need of care and treatment outside the criminal justice system in accordance with social and medical welfare statutes:

(a) care and treatment under the Child Welfare Act of 1960 (the sanction may be combined with day-fines);
(b) mandatory care and treatment in an institution for inebriates under the Temperance Act of 1954 (the sanction is mainly used for petty offenses);
(c) mandatory care under the Insanity Act of 1966 or the Debility Act of 1967 (this sanction may in exceptional cases be used even when the mental disturbance has occurred after the offense was committed);
(d) open psychiatric care for cases where such care is deemed appropriate and mandatory care is not considered necessary.

These sanctions correspond to a great extent to decisions rendered by the prosecutor in similar situations. Nevertheless, many cases are brought before the court.

SOME CATEGORIES OF OFFENDERS

Under this heading information is given concerning different categories of offenders: youthful offenders, mentally deviant offenders, addict offenders, persistent offenders, female offenders, and non-Swedish offenders.

Since 1865 the age of criminal responsibility has been 15 years. According to PC, even children can commit offenses, but an offender may be not sentenced to any sanction within the criminal justice system for an offense committed before he has reached 15 years of age. Depending on the gravity of the offense, the police may hand him over to his parents or report the case to the Social Welfare Board. It is then up to the board of find appropriate measures for the child within the Child Welfare Act of 1960.

Offenders aged 15-17 fall in principle under the Social Welfare system. However, the prosecutor is given a decisive role. He may drop the case and merely notify the young offender about his decision. In cases where the prosecutor finds social welfare measures appropriate, prosecution is remitted in accordance with the Young Offenders Act of 1964. Fines may be imposed administratively. The remaining cases are brought before the court. If the court finds the young offender guilty, the choice of sanctions is restricted with regard to probation, imprisonment, and youth imprisonment. Probation can be used only as an alternative to surrender for social welfare if probation is deemed more appropriate. Probation may be combined with fines but not with deprivation of liberty. Imprisonment may be used only in exceptional cases, for a specified term but never for life. Youth imprisonment may be imposed if it is obviously a more suitable sanction than any other. Milder punishment than that which is provided for the offense may be imposed.

There are few limitations with regard to sanction for offenses committed by youthful offenders after 18 years of age: Imprisonment may be imposed on offenders in the age 18-20 only when deprivation of liberty is particularly called for in deference to public law obedience or when imprisonment is found to be more appropriate than another sanction. Youth imprisonment is generally intended only for offenders in the said age group but may be used up to the age of 23 if it is deemed obviously more appropriate than another sanction.

While rejecting the concept of criminal responsibility based on the offender's maturity and mental health, the legislators in Sweden have made such personal disqualifications prerequisites for the use of all or of some sanctions. Although such limitations can easily be given with regard to the age factor, problems arise in defining the borderline between mental health and illness. Psychiatry has now established generally accepted criteria for insanity and debility, but there is still uncertainty concerning abnormality (especially psychopathy) and temporary insanity. In addition, psychiatrists have difficulty deciding whether the mental defect already existed at the time of the offense, while the courts have difficulty determining whether the offense was committed under the influence of such mental conditions.

The Penal Code limits the sanctions imposed on offenders who committed crimes under the influence of insanity, debility, or higher degrees of abnormality to surrender for special care, fines (if they serve the purpose of deterrence), and probation, if such a sanction is considered more appropriate. Such an offender should never be sent to a correctional institution, probation may never be combined with institutional care, and fines cannot be converted to imprisonment. If none of these sanctions is found appropriate, the offender shall be convicted but shall be free of sanctions.

For those offenders who are suffering from psychopathy of a lesser degree, all sanctions are applicable. A milder punishment than that provided for the offense may, however, be imposed for an offense committed under the influence of such mental abnormality.

In order to avoid suffering by the mentally deviant offenders and unnecessary court proceedings, the prosecutors are empowered to remit prosecution of such offenders given the conditions that it is obvious that the offense was committed under influence of insanity, debility, or a higher degree of abnormality and that provision (not necessarily mandatory) is made for institutional care.

The decisions and convictions concerning mentally deviant offenders are based on medical reports, ordered by a court. These reports are of two types: a brief report by a doctor (in most cases a psychiatrist) and an exhaustive report by a psychiatrist connected with a clinic or station within the state forensic organization. In rare instances the offender himself requests a doctor to make a statement. The court may ask the Council for Forensic Psychiatry to give its opinion on a doubtful report. (In 1976 the council came to a different conclusion than the doctor in 18 of 92 examined reports.)

OFFENDERS WITH ALCOHOL OR DRUG PROBLEMS

Research has confirmed that drunkenness and alcoholism are very important factors in the crime pattern of Sweden. For this reason, drunkenness in a public place was made a penal code offense punishable by monetary fines in 1864. The offender was seized by the police and placed in the arrest house for a few hours to sober up before he signed an agreement to pay the fines ordered by the court (or in later years, the prosecutor). The fines were rarely paid and as a result were converted to imprisonment. It was not until 1916 that society began to take responsibility for the inebriates on the basis of the Temperance Act of 1913. The local communities and the counties were empowered to control alcohol consumption and to take care of the alcoholics through supervision or controlled care. The present Temperance Act of 1954 follows the same lines as the older statutes. By that act prosecutors became empowered to remit prosecution for minor offenses committed by persons under controlled care. The effect of the preventive and mandatory measures was limited and often a failure.

In 1976, 22,034 persons were subject to various measures of the Temperance Act. Of this number, 8,170 were admitted to institutions, 4,232 to private institutions, and 3,938 were put under care in public institutions. Only 527 men and 37 women were received in accordance with an order for mandatory care.

Since 1977, drunkenness in a public place is not an offense. However, persons who are found unable to take care of themselves are brought to arrest houses or hospitals for treatment and social assistance.

Since 1960 the use of narcotics has become an increasingly serious social problem inducing many persons to crime in order to obtain money for drugs on the black market. This has caused an increase in the crime rate, especially for robbery and burglary. Numerous persons become involved in the illegal traffic of drugs and stolen goods. To the public, drug addicts seem to be a greater threat to society than inebriates. Nevertheless, alcoholism is still a more widespread and destructive factor than drug addiction. The state liquor shops collect larger sums in taxes than those used for the total criminal justice system (police, prosecution, courts, and prison and probation administration).

The prison and probation administration has estimated that in 1976 15 percent of the probationers and 28 percent of the inmates were drug addicts. No estimates have been published with regard to the proportion of alcoholics.

Available statistics for 1975 prove that mental hospitals and clinics have taken over care and treatment of the majority of inebriates and drug addicts. There were 1,150 patients with the diagnosis alcohol psychosis, 15,441 with the diagnosis alcoholism and 1,660 with the diagnosis or narcomania. Mandatory care for a short period is frequent. From a social point of view, the aftercare within the mental care system is insufficient.

DANGEROUS AND PERSISTENT OFFENDERS

Until the end of World War II Sweden had very few offenders who had committed dangerous offenses or had been a serious threat to the prison staff. Many of those who had committed serious offenses—for example, homicide or rape—were certified insane and put into mental hospitals for mandatory care. The rest served long sentences without conflicts with the staff. The rather peaceful atmosphere in the institutions seemed to depend on their small size and the authority of the staff.

Today the situation is different. Bank and post office robberies are frequent, terrorism has come to Sweden, as well as smuggling and the sale of hard drugs. Police and prosecutors have concentrated their efforts to fight crime that is dangerous to society and they have been fairly successful. However, riots occur in the penal institutions, and the narcotic traffic does not stop outside the prison walls. The authority of the prison staff is declining and staff members are uncertain about their roles. Prisons have become more difficult for inmates and staff. Although this situation has not called for maximum security prisons, sections of existing closed institutions have been fortified in order to meet the demands from the public and the staff. An increasing number of inmates are requesting isolation for their own security, and restrictions have been ordered concerning furloughs for certain groups of offenders.

The traditional division of offenders into first-time offenders, recidivists, and persistent offenders does not fit into the system of Swedish criminal justice. It is easy to follow the persistent offenders through their careers, beginning with the child welfare system long before reaching criminal age, finding them some years later loaded with prosecution remissions prior to their first appearance in court, then sentenced to probation several times and sentenced again to youth imprisonment with recalls, and at length sentenced to imprisonment and finally to internment with several recalls. This pattern seems frustrating, but at the same time it is deceptive. The machinery of the criminal justice system sorts many more out of the system at every step, and those who do follow the line to the bitter end (internment) are certainly persistent but often rather harmless.

FEMALE OFFENDERS

Although women are in majority in the total population, they are a small and often neglected group among offenders. Female criminality is less frequent and less serious than male criminality. They constitute 11.4 percent of the prosecution remissions and 12.4 percent of all sentences. The proportion of female offenders differs from offense to offense: homicide, 12 percent; theft, 9.4 percent; petty theft, 30.1 percent; robbery, 6.9 percent; unauthorized use of a motor vehicle, 2.4 percent; arson, 11.3 percent; careless driving, 13.6 percent; driving under the influence, 9.6 percent; and narcotic offenses, 14.6 percent. During 1976 the prison and probation administration received 12.9 percent female probationers and the penal institutions only 2 percent. It should be added that the average length of prison sentence is considerably shorter for women. Of those sentenced to two years imprisonment or more, only 15 were women.

OFFENDERS FROM ABROAD

The increase of immigration by refugees and guestworkers in conjunction with the swelling stream of foreigners coming over the borders for shorter visits has caused an upward trend in the crime rate along with a corresponding increase in pressure on the criminal justice agencies. The variations in cultural patterns and the multitude of spoken languages have increased the difficulties for the staff in handling cases where aliens are involved.

The Nordic countries allow their citizens to pass the frontier to another Nordic state without a passport and to take a job without residence and work permits. Due to the economic situation in their own country, many Finnish citizens live and work in Sweden. Other immigrants try to stay in Sweden with or without required permits. Most guestworkers are men in their active years living away from their families. During the present period of economic depression the public is less tolerant toward aliens, especially those who cause trouble. Only a few realize that the national prosperity was created to a considerable extent by the inflow of foreign manpower.

In 1976, Sweden had 8,236,179 Swedish inhabitants and 418,016 alien residents, registered in the local community where they lived. Of those, 187,528 came from Finland, 40,513 from Yugoslavia, 7,663 from Great Britain, 2,565 from Poland, 10,240 from Turkey, and 5,967 from the United States. Although the registered foreigners were 4.8 percent of the total population, their part in crime was almost twice as high.

According to the 1976 statistics presented by the prison administration 1,939 foreigners (19.6 percent) out of 9,901 persons (in 1961, 687 out of 10,040) were admitted to the Swedish prisons to serve a sentence. The foreign female inmates were 47 (23.9 percent) out of 197 female prisoners. For 708 of the 1,939 foreigners the sentence was combined with expulsion after the execution of the sentence.

DIVERSION FROM THE CRIMINAL JUSTICE SYSTEM

Diversion has never been clearly recognized in the Swedish criminal justice system. The ideology has been that all cases should be brought to the court and all offenders be punished. Even today Swedish procedure is based on the concept of an absolute duty to institute public prosecution in all such cases. This principle has been replaced in many areas by a relative duty giving prosecutors the power to exercise discretion under conditions stipulated in the legislation. Sometimes the criminality is viewed as being so trivial that prosecution would be unnecessary or cause more trouble than would be merited. In other instances the criminality is so widespread that it would be impossible to prosecute every case. There are also instances where legal proceedings would result in the interruption of care, education, or upbringing already in progress, or where social or medical care seem more urgent than the imposition of a sentence.

Furthermore, the Penal Code empowers the prosecution to exercise discretion on conditions specified for particular offenses after an examination is sometimes based on complaint of the injured party, sometimes on what is called the general standpoint, mostly with regard to general observance of law.

III. CRIMINAL PROCEDURE

Criminal procedure in Sweden can be summarized as follows: A preliminary investigation is undertaken by the police or the prosecutor. Inquiries are made concerning the person who reasonably may be suspected of the offense. Any person may be examined who is thought to possess information of importance to the investigation. The suspect is entitled to have his defense counsel and a witness commissioned by the investigation authority present at the examinations. He and his counsel may put questions to the examined person. If the suspect has no private defense counsel, the court designates a member of the bar association to assist him in the capacity of public defense counsel, upon request if the court finds it expedient for the protection of his rights. All decisions concerning pretrial detention and measures taken to secure evidence are made by the court. Seizure, however, may take place without court order if it is not possible to wait for such an order. As soon as prosecution has been decided upon, the accused or his defense counsel receives a copy of the record or notes of the investigation upon request. All cases are heard by an ordinary court. If penalties are administratively imposed but not accepted by the offender, the case may be reviewed by the court. The courts are presided over by judges who have been appointed by the government strictly on professional merit. Lay assessors are a part of the district court and the court of appeal in all criminal cases, except in those where the maximum penalty is a fine. The accused is presumed to be innocent until he is found guilty and the conviction has obtained legal force. The procedure is adversary, and the court is bound to follow the description of the act as presented in the summons. The accused is protected against double jeopardy. The procedure is in principle free of charge for the offender. A public defense counsel is paid in advance from public funds. Other costs are paid by the offender himself. Most offenders' costs are covered in accordance with the 1972 Legal Aid Act. If the offender is incapable of understanding Swedish or if his speech or hearing is seriously damaged, the court may designate an interpreter to assist the court. The costs are paid from public funds. The judgment of the court is given in writing and specifies the reasoning in support of the judgment, including a statement of what has been proved, the conviction, and the sentence. All criminal cases may be appealed from the district court to a court of appeal. The judgment of the court of appeal is generally final.

PHASES OF CRIMINAL PROCEEDINGS

Most criminal cases begin with the police investigation. Its purpose is to ascertain whether an offense has been committed and, if so, who the offender might be. The police officer in charge of the investigation keeps the prosecutor continually informed about the progress of his work. In order to obtain evidence the police examine any person who is thought to possess relevant information and request anyone found at the scene of the offense to accompany them to the police station where the person may be kept for up to six hours.

There are three stages involved in the treatment of a suspect person.

(1) Apprehension. Any policeman may apprehend a person when there is

cause for arrest. Anyone may apprehend a person who has committed an offense punishable by imprisonment, if the suspect is caught in the act of committing the offense or running away from the scene.

(2) Arrest. The investigating authority (police or prosecutor) may issue a warrant of arrest for a suspect person. The suspect must be released within 24 hours unless detention is initiated by the prosecutor.

(3) Detention must be ordered by the court within four days. It is then up to the court to decide when the suspect shall be released. The detention order details the offense of which the detained person is suspected and states the cause for the detention.

In 1976, 26,135 persons were arrested and 8,341 applications for detention orders were issued. Any period exceeding 24 hours during which a person has been arrested or detained leads to a corresponding reduction of the penalty to which he is sentenced. If acquitted, he may claim compensation.

The prerequisites for arrest and detention, travel prohibition, and provisional attachment, as well as for seizure, are carefully regulated. Bail is unknown in Swedish law.

Persons who are detained in accordance with court order are generally kept in a remand prison under the prison administration. Their cases have priority in the courts. The detention period varies, but two-thirds of the cases are heard within one month. Offenders under 18 are rarely detained.

When the investigation has proceeded to a point at which a person is reasonably suspected of the offense, he is informed of the suspicion. He and his defense counsel are provided with the opportunity to be informed of what has taken place at the investigation. Prosecution may not continue until they have been given such an opportunity. After the conclusion of the investigation, the prosecutor must decide whether or not to process the case to trial. Plea-bargaining is not used.

Prior to the trial the prosecutor or the accused may ask for a personal case study. The court may not order such a study to be carried out unless the accused has pleaded guilty or the court is satisfied that the evidence against him is reasonably strong. No person may be sentenced to imprisonment for six months or more, conditional sentence, probation, youth imprisonment, internment, or surrendered for special care unless a personal case study is undertaken or equivalent information is made available to the court. The study is carried out by a competent person, selected by the chief probation officer. The court may also order that a medical examination of the accused be conducted. Even stronger restrictions limit the court from ordering a forensic psychiatric examination of the accused. Such a report concerns the offender's mental state when the crime was committed and the conditions under which he may be surrendered for mandatory care under the Insanity Act or the Debility Act.

At the main hearing the prosecutor states his charge and the accused is asked whether he admits the offense or not. The plea of guilty or not guilty is not used in the same way as in England or the United States. To the astonishment of many foreign visitors, the accused rarely denies the act as such but he or his defense counsel frequently raises objections to the legal implications of it. These objections may concern a defense or the applicability of the provisions upon which the charge is based. Cross-examination as it is known abroad is not practiced. After the pleadings of the prosecutor and the accused have been completed, the court must decide on guilt and sanction. The verdict is usually given the same day, but in complicated cases it may be postponed for a couple of weeks. The verdict is given in writing and includes information concerning steps for appeal.

When the sentence is pronounced the accused and the prosecutor are asked whether they accept the judgment. A declaration from the sentenced person can be given at any time before the elapse of the term for appeal. The execution of the sanction commences when an affirmative declaration is given. Such a declaration is irrevocable. The court may decide that a sentence to probation with institutional care or to youth imprisonment shall take effect even though it has not acquired legal force.

In principle, the execution of the sentence takes place when it has acquired legal force or an affirmative declaration of acceptance has been given. An order of summary punishment by fines consented to by the suspect has the same effect as a conclusive sentence. If the offender is detained in a remand prison after being sentenced to imprisonment, youth imprisonment, or internment he is immediately transferred to serve his sentence.

From the time of the Middle Ages the king had the prerogative of mercy and used it frequently either in the form of total pardon or more often of commutation of the sentence. Today mercy is granted by the government following a recommendation from the Minister of Justice. An application for mercy may be made by the offender or by anyone else. It is reviewed in the Ministry of Justice and supplemented by relevant information before being considered by the minister. Applications for mercy to some extent have become an alternative to appeal in regard to the assessment of the punishment. The procedure is quick and free. Before pardon is granted the application has to be reviewed by the Supreme Court (three justices). In 1976, the government rendered decisions on 1,820 applications, of which 375 led to pardon or commutation. In the majority of the cases the decisions were in accordance with the opinion of the Supreme Court. Almost all favorably decided cases concerned commutation of the sentence to a milder sentence or postponement of the execution of the sentence. Pardon is also used in favor of the applicant when the offense he had committed is subsequently changed or repealed. Thus, in 1977, over 500 conscientious objectors were granted pardon.

IV. EXECUTION OF PENAL MEASURES
(CORRECTIONS)

Criminal justice in Sweden is based on humanity, fairness, and efficiency. Efficiency is achieved by means of selection, training, and further education of the staff within the criminal justice agencies and by registration of the clients with regard to their personality, social situation, criminal record, and served sentences. Fairness is built into the total criminal justice system and is under the control of the Ministry of Justice, the central authorities, the ombudsman, and the mass media. The humanitarian tradition is kept alive by current public debate and the resistance of the politicians and the civil servants to demands for harsher methods in fighting crime through the use of more severe measures against offenders.

There is no statement in PC of the philosophy on which it is based, but it is clear from the views expressed during its preparation that it has as its foundation the idea of prevention and not retaliation. It is stipulated that in the choice of sanction in the individual case the court shall, without ignoring the need for general deterrence, keep in mind that the sanction should serve to foster the offender's adaptation to society (Chapter 1, Section 7).

FINES

The execution of fines is regulated in the statutes of 1964 and supplementary ordinances. Imprisonment in default of payment is carefully restricted and may be ordered only by the courts. It is now under consideration to abolish the conversion of fines to deprivation of liberty.

PROBATION

Probation is based on the idea of supervision of the offender in liberty. The supervision includes control and support by a lay supervisor or social worker (in all, approximately 9,000 persons, mainly laymen) under the guidance of the local probation officer and his office (in 1978 there were approximately 50 chief probation officers in the entire country) and under the control of the local probation and parole board (in 1978, about 55 boards). As the control is based on cooperation of the offender with the supervisor, failing to cooperate may lead to intervention by the board through the use of disciplinary and constructive measures. Thus, in 1976, the boards decided to warn 69 probationers, to take 439 into temporary custody, and to issue special directives for 85 probationers with regard to residence and lodging, use of leisure time, disposal of wages, participation in education or vocational training, or submittance to medical care. The boards requested the prosecution to raise with the court the question of treatment in a penal institution for six probationers and of revocation of the probation in combination with a new sentence for 14 probationers.

The supervision is usually restricted to the two first years of the trial period and may be terminated prior to that. The board may also decide to resume the supervision during the trial period. In the beginning of 1977, 11,732 male and 1,606 female probationers were under supervision. The supervisor is elected by the court or the board. The remuneration of the laymen is restricted to $20 per month plus recovery of expenses.

The prison administration consists of the central administration, located in Norrköping, and 13 regions, each headed by a governor. A governor has the responsibility for all institutional and noninstitutional care (local and remand prisons, probation and parole) within his region. The prisons are divided into two groups: national and local prisons. There are now 22 national prisons with a total capacity of 1,659 in closed institutions and 553 in open institutions. The 52 local prisons have a capacity of 707 in closed institutions and 1,189 in open institutions. They are divided among the regions in order to obtain the possibility to place the inmates near their homes. In addition, there are 21 remand prisons with 1,207 places for persons detained prior to trial. Three central boards, the Internment Board, the Youth Imprisonment Board, and the Board of Corrections, have important tasks within their spheres. The Board of Corrections decides about release of inmates serving a sentence of imprisonment for more than one year. It is at the same time an appellate board with regard to some decisions made by the local probation and parole boards. The Internment Board and the Youth Imprisonment Board are concerned with aftercare and have an advisory position in relation to the courts.

Sweden never fully adopted the principles for classification of offenders and at present there are very few provisions concerning placement of the inmates according to age, sex, risk for escapes, previous convictions, dangerousness, or mental deviance. However, division of the prisons into national and regional, closed and open institutions allows a certain margin for variations. With regard to security arrangements, some prisons are more likely to care for dangerous offenders or offenders likely to escape. However, there are no maximum security institutions per se.

Inmates who are sentenced to imprisonment for more than one year, to youth imprisonment, or to internment are generally placed in the national institutions but are often transferred to local prisons in preparation for their release. To some extent, the national prisons accept shorttimers and inmates who do not fit into the local prisons.

TREATMENT AND CARE

The basic ideas behind the present correctional system can be summarized as follows:

(1) a minimum of intervention; noninstitutional care is the principle form of correctional care;

(2) institutional care should be closely related and coordinated with noninstitutional care;

(3) institutional care should be carried out near the offender's home unless the public safety requires otherwise;

(4) outward-oriented activity—society's service organs (such as social service, medical and dental service, the educational and vocational training facilities, and the leisure-time activities) should be used to the greatest possible extent.

The guideline for correctional care is that it should make full use of the services that are offered by the community to all inhabitants and should restrict and supplement them only when it is necessary in regard to the purpose of punishment. The probation and aftercare service offered to offenders is restricted to use as a supplement to ordinary social service while at the same time serving as a control instrument.

The objectives of correctional care in institutions are (1) to promote the inmate's adjustment to society and (2) to counteract the injurious effects of deprivation of freedom. A treatment plan is established for every inmate and includes preparation for life outside the institution as well as work and studies within the institution.

During his stay in the institution, the inmate is placed on a time schedule that includes 40 hours of work or studies per week. Since the average period for inmates sentenced to imprisonment is very short (in 1976, just over 100 days), vocational training is mainly restricted to longtimers and to offenders sentenced to youth imprisonment or internment. For the majority of the clientele it is usually work training—that is, training to participate in a work routine in a factory or at outdoor work. The educational program is primarily directed toward basic school subjects and social subjects and social adaptation. The teaching program as well as the training program are carried out by the local and county authorities or in collaboration with them.

Many countries use grades, marks, and rewards as instruments to maintain peace and order in their institutions and further the prison work. This is no longer accepted in Sweden. The methods of "whip and carrot" which were formerly appreciated by many have been abolished. In earlier times the prisoner's conduct during his stay in the institution and his mental attitude at the time of parole were taken into consideration by the probation and parole board. However, today the board has only to consider the effects of continued deprivation of liberty and the chances for the prisoner's adaptation to society with regard to the circumstances in which he would find himself upon release.

Prisoners' rights are carefully regulated by statutes. The inmate is entitled to freedom of worship and to uncontrolled written communication with Swedish authorities and members of the bar association. Control of other correspondence and of telephone calls is restricted and shall in principle be known to the inmate. Prison visits are generally allowed and rarely controlled.

EXTRAMURAL ACTIVITIES

Many inmates in local and some in national institutions are granted "town passes" for participation in schooling (including university studies), vocational training, and leisure activities, such as in study groups or sports associations. Some of the inmates are accompanied by staff members while on these "passes."

An inmate may be granted permission to leave the institution for a brief period (short furlough) in order to facilitate his adjustment to society and maintain his contact with his family. As preparation for release inmates may also be given the opportunity to remain outside the institution for a longer period (release furlough) prior to the date of release in order to make arrangements for working and living. Altogether 42,663 furloughs were granted in 1976. Of these, 8 percent were abused by late returns and 3 percent due to other misconduct, such as misuse of alcohol or drugs or criminal activities.

In the case of some offenders sentenced to institutional care, such care may prove detrimental to their readaptation. In such instances the court is empowered to place these inmates in a school with a boarding establishment, a treatment home for addicts, a suitable private home, or in military service. In 1976, 407 inmates were given this opportunity, some within a few days after their admission to a prison. Approximately 30 percent of them misused the privilege.

DISCIPLINARY MEASURES WITHIN THE INSTITUTIONAL CARE

The relative freedom given to the inmates has in many respects made prison life more tolerable in comparison with earlier regimes. Nevertheless, many inmates, particularly longtimers and recidivists, point out that the incapacitation of prisoners still remains due to the time schedule and types of prison activities and to their total submittance to the discretion of the staff. Prison strikes are not uncommon and some riots have occurred. However, the small size of the institutions in conjunction with the large staff has diminished these effects. Escapes from prisons in 1976 amounted to 1,980.

The statutory provisions for breaches of prison discipline (not including offenses) are rather limited. Interruption of the term of imprisonment due to abuse of furlough or escape leads to a prolongation of the time to be served by the number of days of unlawful absence. The purely disciplinary measures are a warning (in 1976, 3,679 cases), and prolongation of the time to be served is limited to a period of at most ten days (in 1976, 828 cases). Such prolongation may be repeated for new breaches but may never exceed 45 days in total. Other disciplinary measures used are restrictions in regard to extramural activities, delay of furlough, and transfer to another prison. In 1976, such transfers occurred in 2,126 cases, most frequently due to escape or abuse of furlough.

INTERNATIONAL COLLABORATION IN EXECUTION OF PUNISHMENTS

For the last quarter of a century collaboration has taken place within the Nordic countries with regard to the execution of sentences to fines, probation, and institutional punishments according to a Swedish statute of 1963. Within the Council of Europe a convention on the international validity of criminal judgments was adopted and open to accession from 1972. This led Sweden to draft a statute on this subject, which has been in force since 1972 with a subsequent ordinance passed in 1977.

6

JAPAN

Kenichi Nakayama

I. GENERAL INFORMATION

Japan consists of four main islands and thousands of smaller islands and islets. The archipelago, lying off the eastern coast of the Asian continent, stretches in an arc 3,800 kilometers long. It covers an area of 377,435 square kilometers, which is about one-twenty-fifth that of the United States, one and a half times a big as that of the United Kingdom.

Between 1872 and 1975, the population of Japan more than tripled, from 34,800,000 to 111,934,000. Now Japan ranks sixth in the world in terms of population, and its population density of 297 persons per square kilometers places it among the most densely populated nations in the world.

The new constitution, which was promulgated just after World War II in 1946, differs in many important respects from the Meiji Constitution of 1889. Some of its key provisions are these: The Emperor is a symbol of the states, and sovereign power now rests with the people; Japan renounces war and the threat of force to settle international disputes; fundamental human rights are guaranteed as eternal and inviolable; the bicameral Diet consisting of the House of Representatives and the House of Councillors is the highest organ of state power and is elected by the people; executive power is vested in the Cabinet, which is collectively responsible to the Diet; and local self-government is established on an extensive scale. Besides the ruling Liberal party, there are at present four major opposition parties. Although the former conservative party long held an absolute majority in the Diet, its influence has recently weakened and now is equalled by the progressives.

The contemporary legal system of Japan is similar to that of continental Europe. After World War II, Anglo-American law exerted a strong influence on its present shape. Additionally, the old Japanese traditions are still very strong. Despite contradictory experiences, Japanese law has been systematically classified and differentiated according to the model of traditional Roman law. The Constitution ranks first, then public and private law are differentiated. Another classification is also observed in the form of substantive and procedural law. Criminal law is one of the public, substantive, and judicial laws.

Japan has adopted, like almost all European countries, the statutory law principle. In criminal law this principle has been carried through without exception: Only statutory law, neither custom nor judicial decisions, is the source of criminal law. In practice, judicial decisions play an important role in the legal system. Although their primary purpose is to decide cases, the principles or theories behind the decisions create precedents for future cases with identical or similar facts. Supreme Court decisions have binding force over ensuing decisions, including those of lower courts. But, strictly speaking, they are not recognized as a source of law under the Japanese legal system.

AMOUNT, STRUCTURE, AND DYNAMICS OF CRIMINALITY

For the last 100 years, the number of persons arrested annually by the police for Penal Code offenses on the whole has risen, as has the nation's population. Some fluctuations of criminality are worth mentioning. The figure of registered crimes rose in 1890, when inflated rice prices led to riots and Japan's immature capitalist system suffered its first panic. A rather steady increase followed, amid fluctuations. A long economic depression in 1919 brought about a continued increase in crime. The worldwide depression of the 1930s, with a high rate of unemployment, resulted in the unprecedented growth of criminality. It reached its peak in 1934 but abated thereafter, probably due to economic recovery, international tensions, and war. These events, in turn, strengthened society's morale.

Just after the war, in 1946, the figure almost doubled that of the previous year. It increased steadily until 1950, but then declined until 1956. This may be attributed to the economic and social recovery from the postwar devastation. The number of recorded crimes started to rise again in 1957, mainly due to the increase in traffic offenses. The highest crime rate of the past 100 years was recorded in 1970. It then underwent a steady decline until 1974. From 1975 the figure has been on the increase, probably due to the recent economic depression.

SCOPE OF CRIMINAL LAW

The Penal Code covers crimes and criminal punishments. The catalog of Penal Code offenses is fairly stable and fixed in regard to traditional crimes such as homicide, theft, and rape. But sometimes the ambit of criminal sanctions changes drastically by some alteration of the existing social and political order. It is very characteristic that just after World War II the Penal Code dropped such crimes as those against the Emperor, espionage, adultery, and the like. Recently introduced into the Penal Code are such offenses as intimidation of witness and possession of immovable property. The Revised Draft Code of 1974 is definitely inclined toward further criminalization: It proposed adding about 20 new crimes to the present Penal Code.

Besides the Penal Code, special laws regulate various offenses such as hijackings. A separate body of law is the law of violations dealing with minor breaches of the legal order. There are also many special laws of administrative character which carry punishments.

The Penal Code applies primarily to the crimes committed within Japan. Only in exceptional cases may it be applied to crimes committed abroad in order to protect the national interest. If the offender has already served, either in whole or in part, the punishment pronounced abroad, the execution of punishment in Japan must be reduced or remitted.

STRUCTURE AND FUNCTIONING OF LAW ENFORCEMENT AGENCIES

The police organization now belongs directly to the Prime Minister's Office. Before the war, it belonged to the Ministry of Internal Affairs, which is no longer in existence. Moreover, to secure the political independence of the police, the National Police Public Safety Commission was created. The National Police Agency comes under its control.

The Public Prosecutor's Office belongs to the Ministry of Justice. The office consists of the Supreme, high, district, and local levels in accordance with court hierarchy. Public prosecutors, who are accountable to the minister of justice, institute prosecution of criminal cases, request the proper application of law by courts, and supervise the execution of judgments. The minister of justice exercises general supervision and control over their activities.

Defense attorneys are not public officials, but, because of the public nature of their responsibilities, they are regulated by law. They are organized in collectives of lawyers, possessing wide autonomy in their activities.

According to the Court Organization Law (1947), the five courts are Supreme Court, high courts, district courts, family courts, and summary courts. The Supreme Court, with 15 judges, is the highest court in Japan and has appellate jurisdiction only. High courts are located in eight major cities and as a rule hear appeals filed against judgments of the lower courts.

District courts hear cases primarily of original jurisdiction. Family courts exclusively handle domestic and juvenile cases. Summary courts have the power to try minor civil and criminal cases by summary procedure, where the claims and punishments are relatively limited.

Judicial power is vested exclusively in a Supreme Court and other courts established by law, and the Executive has no final judicial power. The court organization is completely separated from the Ministry of Justice, and the authority of judicial administration is also given to the Supreme Court. The Constitution has empowered the courts to determine the constitutionality of any law, order, regulation, or official act, and has also guaranteed the independence of judges, who are bound only by the Constitution and the laws.

II. SUBSTANTIVE CRIMINAL LAW

GENERAL PRINCIPLES OF RESPONSIBILITY

In the present Penal Code of Japan there is no specific provision proclaiming the principle of "No crime, no punishment without law." However, the Constitution says no person shall be deprived of life or liberty, nor shall any other criminal penalty be imposed, except according to law. The Constitution furthermore forbids double jeopardy and says criminal laws shall not be imposed retroactively. Specifically, no person shall be held criminally responsible for an act that was lawful at the time of its commission. According to the Penal Code, when a punishment is changed by law after the commission of a crime, the lesser punishment is to be applied. Charges must be dropped when the punishment has been abolished by a law or ordinance subsequent to commission of the offense. In theory, it is also recognized that customary law is not the source of criminal law and that absolutely indeterminate punishments are prohibited. Interpretation by analogy is also not accepted, although in practice the boundary between analogy and acceptable extensive interpretation is sometimes difficult to fix with precision.

The Penal Code has no such formal gradation of offenses into felonies and misdemeanors, although the code of 1882 had such gradation. Violations—that is, minor breaches of the legal order—are regulated almost fully by the Law of Violation of 1948. They are now subject only to penal detention or minor fines. Punishments provided for Penal Code offenses are much more diversified.

According to the Penal Code, the age of criminal responsibility is 14 years and under no circumstances may anyone younger be held criminally responsible. Under the Juvenile Law, 16 is the age of regular prosecution. Anyone who is younger may be sentenced to educational measures by the family court. Until a juvenile is 20 years old he may be criminally prose-cuted or educational measures may be applied to him by the family court.

The Penal Code has no classification of offenders, in particular by fre-quency of conviction. The code provides that repeated convictions are treated the same way as the second conviction—with aggravated punish-ment. A new provision of the Revised Draft of the Penal Code has introduced a category of habitual recidivists upon whom an indeterminate sentence might be imposed. This idea has been strongly criticized by scholars.

It has long been accepted that only individuals may be criminally respon-sible. For a long time the concept of criminal responsibility of corporations was rejected by scholars and practitioners. Recently, however, more opin-ions in favor of criminal responsibility of corporations are heard. Some special administrative-type laws already provide for the imposition of fines on corporations. Nevertheless, the punishment of the corporation is still exceptional. Caution regarding this matter seems well recommended.

The Penal Code recognizes the importance of the mental element of crimes. Intent and negligence are two basic forms of *mens rea*. An act committed without criminal intent is not criminal except as otherwise spe-cially provided by law. This exception has been interpreted to introduce crimes due to negligence. This means, consequently, that the principle "No crime, no punishment without *mens rea*" has been fully implemented. Un-fortunately, there exist some exceptions to this rule. For example, some special administrative-type laws provide for punishment of negligent crimes despite the fact that the laws are silent on this issue. Some deviations from the principle of guilt can also be seen in the case of the crime aggravated by the result. In practice, even negligence is not required regarding the result aggravating responsibility. The Revised Draft of the Penal Code in this instance is clearly progressive: It tries to improve the situation by saying that if it is impossible to foresee such result, aggravated punishment cannot be imposed.

Theory and practice recognize the mistake of fact as a defense. An offender may be held responsible for an intentional offense only if he was aware of all definitional elements of the offense. (The mistake regarding the existence of self-defense is regarded in practice as the mistake of fact, excluding intent.)

Ignorance of the law is not considered a defense. Knowledge that the act is prohibited is not a necessary element of intent. Ignorance of law may not exclude but only mitigate criminal responsibility for intentional offense. The Revised Draft of the Penal Code also in this instance is advancing: If lack of awareness of the law is excusable, the responsibility is excluded. This solution has been supported by scholars.

Preparation is punishable only in a few serious crimes, such as insurrec-tion, arson, homicide, and robbery.

Attempt is punishable more often in about 20 crimes. In addition to those mentioned above, the following may be listed: rape, abortion, theft, and extortion. The punishment for attempt may be mitigated. This optional, not mandatory, mitigation of punishment for attempt has been said to reflect the subjective approach to criminal responsibility favored by the code.

Attempt has been defined by the code as the commencement of the execution of the offense. This objective element differentiates attempt from mere preparation. In practice, the boundaries of attempt have been drawn rather narrowly.

So-called impossible attempt is not provided for in the present code, but theory and practice regard the ineffective attempt unpunishable within narrow limits.

According to the Penal Code, if one stops the criminal act voluntarily in the course of its commission, the punishment is reduced or remitted.

Complicity is divided into three forms: coprincipals who act jointly in the commission of crime, instigator of another's crime, and accessory to a crime. The punishment of instigator and principal is equal, while that of accessory is reduced. Each of the coprincipals acts, as a rule, for himself, but court practice has long recognized another category of coprincipals where two or more persons conspire to commit a crime and any one conspirator commits the crime pursuant to the common design. Despite strong theoretical criticism, this concept of conspirator-principals is fixed in court practice. The Revised Draft Code has certified it legislatively.

Insanity is one of the defenses. According to the Penal Code, the act of an insane person is not punishable, and in case of diminished responsibility punishment is reduced. Theory and practice say insanity exists when the perpetrator lacks the mental capacity to evaluate his conduct properly or to act in accordance with such evaluation. In the case of diminished responsibility this capacity is seriously limited. Japanese courts are rather reluctant to accept the defense of insanity, fearing that dangerous persons are released without any effective measure of control.

The Revised Draft Code introduced a new clause about self-induced insanity. The defense of insanity will not be available to a person who, with intent or negligence, has induced himself to the state of insanity and committed the act prohibited by law. This will mainly apply to criminal acts committed while intoxicated.

Self-defense and averting imminent dire necessity are also defenses. They are both urgent, spontaneous acts. Self-defense is characterized as a kind of defense-rights against unjust, illegal attack, while in the dire necessity one aims at shifting the danger onto another's shoulders. Therefore, especially in the latter case, injury should not exceed harm which was sought to be averted.

PENAL MEASURES

The Penal Code of Japan, despite its age (1907), has been sufficiently modernized to meet the growing demands of contemporary penal policy. The code is characterized by simple and abstract descriptions of crimes and by a great variety of penal measures at the judge's disposal to leave ample room for judicial discretion. The code allows for modern criminological means of social defense and individualized treatment of offenders. As long ago as 1907, the widely framed suspended sentence with supervision during the trial period as well as parole with relatively early possibility of release were introduced. Both institutions are motivated by the spirit of special prevention and rehabilitation of offenders. At the same time, it cannot be denied that the spirit of general prevention and retribution is deeply rooted in the penal policy. Its function is conservative, aiming at the irrational threat of severe punishment in the interest of securing public order. It must not be overlooked that this classical approach has resulted in reasonable limitation of criminal responsibility and punishment within the spirit of legality.

According to the Penal Code, the kinds of penal measures are as follows: death, imprisonment with labor, imprisonment without labor, fine, penal detention, minor fine, and confiscation as a supplemental punishment.

The death penalty is still maintained as the most severe punishment for several crimes, such as insurrection, arson, sabotage of trains, homicide, and death through robbery. The Revised Draft Code does not abolish the death penalty but diminishes the number of capital crimes. In practice, the death penalty is imposed only in the case of aggravated homicide or homicide with robbery.

Imprisonment with labor is the typical punishment and is either life term or limited term. The limited term of imprisonment is to be not less than one month nor more than 15 years, but under special aggravating or mitigating circumstances the term may be extended to 20 years or reduced to less than one month. Even life term is in fact not limitless, as one can be paroled after ten years.

Imprisonment without labor is provided for in such instances as political, official, and negligent crimes. These offenders are not obliged to work but may work upon petition. In practice, they do exercise this right. Recently, arguments have rejected the work distinction and asked for unification of imprisonment. The Revised Draft Code still maintains this distinction.

Penal detention is a short-term (1-30 days) deprivation of liberty in a penal detention house and is limited to a few offenses, such as insult and public indecency. It is provided often by the Code of Violations. Probably this form of punishment will disappear.

Fines (4,000 yen or $20 and up) and minor fines (up to 4,00 yen) are the monetary punishments. Those who cannot pay are detained in a work house for one day to two years. In case of minor fines, the period of detention is up to 30 days.

According to the statistical data gathered by the prosecutor's office, distribution of penal measures applied by courts in Japan in 1976 is as follows: death, 2 (0 percent); imprisonment with labor, 69,702 (2.9 percent); imprisonment without labor, 6,008 (0.2 percent); fine, 2,339,579 (95.8 percent); penal detention, 102 (0 percent); minor fine, 23,469 (1.5 percent). However, as far as the Penal Code offenses are concerned, the situation is quite different: imprisonment ranks first, while fines account for only about five percent.

One of the special correctional measures other than original punishment is educational measures for juveniles, mainly probation and committal to Juvenile Training School. The latter is a custodial measure; it is not considered punishment and is to be applied for the protection and education of the juveniles. When a juvenile is to be sentenced to original punishments, special treatments are provided by law. For example, the death penalty must not be applied on a juvenile under 18; life-term imprisonment is replaced by a limited term; a juvenile is given an indeterminate sentence; no juvenile is to be sentenced to confinement in a work house due to nonpayment of a fine.

The provisions of the present Penal Code about recidivism are simple. Punishment for a second offense shall not exceed twice the maximum term of imprisonment with labor provided for the crime committed. Third or subsequent conviction is treated in the same way as the second. The Revised Draft Code introduced a category of habitual recidivists. An indeterminate sentence may be imposed with the minimum term of one year on the recidivist.

The Penal Code has no provision for security measures concerning insane, drug, and alcohol offenders. These have been treated partly as administrative problems, sometimes on the level of mental health law. The Revised Draft Code has tried to introduce a system of security measures as a kind of judicial treatment of these offenders. Two kinds of security measures were proposed: curative measures for mentally disordered offenders and abstinence measures for addicts. These measures were meant not only to protect society but also to treat the offenders. But many lawyers doubt the effectiveness of these measures and claim that the only real effect would be long and unfixed terms of isolation of these offenders from society. Those laywers say the country's social and medical policy must be improved first. The issue of security measures is one of the problems hotly debated in Japan on the reform of criminal law.

As far as the present law is concerned, there is no judicial measure of pre- and postdelictual character.

Probation under the Japanese system takes the form of suspension of execution of sentence. According to the Penal Code, suspension of execution of sentence—with or without probationary supervision—may be applied to a person who was sentenced for not more than three years or a fine of not more than 200,000 yen ($1,000), providing he has not been previously sentenced to imprisonment or that five years have passed since last sentence. It should be noted that in adult probation no presentence report prepared by the investigator is required; in the case of a juvenile such a report is absolutely necessary. The sentence is suspended for a trial period (from one to five years). If an offender is convicted of another crime during this period, the suspension may (in some cases must) be revoked and the sentence executed. In 1976, 60.3 percent of the sentences were suspended regarding imprisonment with labor and 84.3 percent regarding imprisonment without labor. Of all suspensions, 17.1 percent were with supervision; 10.5 percent of suspensions were revoked. A shortage of probation officers is said to be a principal defect of the Japanese probation system.

Those serving the penalty of imprisonment may be paroled and put on probation by the parole board after they have served one-third of the sentence for limited term or ten years of a life sentence. The board must be of the opinion that the convict has been genuinely rehabilitated. If a parolee violates the conditions of the parole, he may be sent back to prison to serve the remaining part of his sentence. In 1976, 10.4 percent of all applications for parole were rejected. Of the prisoners released from prison, 54.4 percent were released on parole. About 80 percent of the parolees were discharged from prisons after having served more than 80 percent of their sentences, so the probation periods for parolees are generally very short (the majority are for two months). Of the parolees, 5.8 percent were revoked.

III. CRIMINAL PROCEDURE

GENERAL PRINCIPLES

The procedure followed in criminal cases is the same throughout Japan. There is only one territorial jurisdiction and it is on a national level. The Code of Penal Procedure (1948) and the Rules of Penal Procedure (1949) are the main sources of law governing criminal procedure.

Historically, the Japanese law of criminal procedure is a mixture of European and Anglo-American law. After Meiji Restoration, the Japanese Code of Criminal Procedure was enacted, first on the basis of French law (1890), and then on that of German law (1922). The new Code of Penal Procedure (1948) was adopted under the influence of American law, although, in its general scheme, there still remain traces of the old law.

The present Code of Penal Procedure declares that the purpose of criminal procedure is to clarify the facts in criminal cases and to implement criminal laws fairly and speedily. At the same time, public welfare and security must be maintained and fundamental human rights observed. The principal task, therefore, is to establish the facts of the case. According to the Constitution, this process must be fair, speedy, and performed in the manner provided by law, in particular with preservation of all the accused's rights guaranteed by the Constitution and other laws.

Another objective is that innocent persons must not be punished. The underlying principle is the presumption of innocence. The new Constitution provided for basic human rights in criminal procedure, including the guarantee of due process and the prohibition against double jeopardy.

The present law adopted to a great extent the adversary principle as it has been thoroughly applied in the Anglo-American legal system. Proceedings are usually conducted in the form of attack and defense by the parties, and the principle of officially guided proceedings has come to be auxiliary.

PHASES OF CRIMINAL PROCEEDINGS

Criminal proceedings consist of the following phases: investigation, prosecution, trial, appeal, and, finally, extraordinary remedies.

The principal investigating agencies are the police and public prosecutors. The public prosecutor, if he is convinced of the guilt of the suspect, may file an information with the court to open his prosecution and has the discretion to suspend prosecution.

Public trial consists of such stages as the introductory procedure, opening statement, introduction of evidence, closing argument, and judgment. The party may appeal to a high court or, under certain conditions, further to the Supreme Court. A decision of the Supreme Court, or that of a high court from which no appeal is made, is final. However, even the final judgment can be revised by means of extraordinary proceedings. The first is an extraordinary *de novo* proceeding for the benefit of the defendant, requested by a prosecutor or the defendant, and the second is an extraordinary appeal to the Supreme Court, requested by the prosecutor-general and couched in terms of the violation of law. These proceedings are very rare, but currently the gate to an extraordinary *de novo* proceeding seems to be opening a bit wider.

RIGHTS OF THE ACCUSED

The Constitution has detailed provisions for defendants' rights. The main rights of a suspect as well as an accused are that no person shall be arrested except upon warrant issued by a competent judicial officer unless caught in the act. No person shall be detained without being at once informed of the charge against him and without the immediate privilege of counsel. Each search or seizure shall be made upon separate warrant issued for adequate cause by a competent judicial officer. Torture by any public officer and cruel punishments are absolutely forbidden. In all criminal cases the accused shall enjoy the right to a speedy and public trial by an impartial tribunal. He shall have the assistance of competent counsel, who shall, if the accused is unable to secure him by his own efforts, be assigned to his use by the state. No person shall be compelled to testify against himself, and a confession made under compulsion, torture, or threat shall not be admitted in evidence. The Code of Penal Procedure also guarantees an accused under detention the right to request release on bail, although under certain circumstances granting of bail depends on the discretion of the court. Needless to say, he has the right to appeal to a higher court.

The problem is, of course, how and to what extent these rights and principles are realized in the practice of criminal procedure. The interest of maintaining public order and finding the true facts of cases sometimes run counter to the realization of these rights.

PRETRIAL DETENTION

An arrested suspect must be taken by police to a public prosecutor within 48 hours. The public prosecutor must inform him immediately of the charges against him and of his right to counsel, and if the detention of the suspect is necessary and supported by reasonable grounds, the prosecutor must, within 24 hours, request a judge to issue a warrant for detention.

When the judge is asked to issue a warrant for detention, the judge interrogates the suspect and gives him an opportunity for explanation and examines the evidence submitted by the prosecutor. This procedure is closed to the public, but if a warrant is issued, the suspect may request the judge to disclose the grounds for detention in open court.

The period of detention is 10 days as a rule but may be extended to 20 days. Public prosecutors are requested to carry out their investigations within this period and to decide whether or not there is sufficient evidence to prosecute the detained suspects. If they are convinced of the guilt of the suspects, they may file an information with the court to open their prosecution.

SPECIAL MODES OF CRIMINAL PROCEEDINGS

Public prosecutors may institute relatively informal criminal actions in the summary courts (without public hearing) for minor crimes, provided that the defendant makes no objection. However, sentences over 200,000 yen ($1,000) cannot be imposed and the defendant may always demand a formal trial if not satisfied with the sentence.

The Traffic Violation Fine System is a special procedure under which an offender receives a notice from the police requiring the payment of a fine. If he pays the fine, the matter is over. If he fails to do so, the case is dealt with under regular criminal procedures.

LAY PARTICIPATION IN CRIMINAL PROCEEDINGS

Japan has no such system as a grand jury. Since 1948, however, the Prosecution Investigation Committee, or Inquest of Prosecution, consists of lay people chosen by lot who investigate and control the discretionary power of the public prosecutors. They are an advisory body to the prosecutor. As far as the layman's participation in court proceedings is concerned, the Jury Trial Law (1923) was suspended in 1943. Even prior to its suspension the right to jury trial was only seldom exercised. There has been a tendency to trust the professional judge, and in most cases the judge has been less strict than the jury.

SPECIAL PROCEEDINGS FOR JUVENILES

Inquiry and hearings by the family court for juveniles under 20 are carried out on a diagnostic and therapeutic basis. The court is staffed with presentence investigators who are social workers. The family court may sentence only to educative measures, not punishments. If the court finds it reasonable to impose punitive measures, the case may be referred to the public prosecutor, who prosecutes the juveniles over 16 years old in an ordinary court.

IV. EXECUTION OF PENAL MEASURES (CORRECTIONS)

AIMS AND BASIC PRINCIPLES

The present Penal Code and the Prison Law (1908) do not spell out the aims and basic principles of penal measures. However, it has been claimed that in practice the principle of rehabilitation through individualized treatment is dominant. Although there still remains some thought of retribution, there seems to be no question of the principle of rehabilitation. The Revised Draft of the Penal Code (1974) referred to this very principle, emphasizing that the goal of penal measures should be rehabilitation in accordance with the individuality of offenders.

USE AND IMPLEMENTATION OF DEATH PENALTY

The death penalty is executed under an order from the minister of justice within six months from the day the death sentence becomes final, with an extension of time if the defendant appeals. If a person convicted to death is insane, or a woman convicted to death is pregnant, the execution is stayed by order of the minister of justice until the defendant is deemed sane or the pregnancy is concluded. Death is by hanging at a prison in the presence of a public prosecutor, his assistant officer, and a director of the prison, or his representatives, who attest to the execution.

EXECUTION OF DEPRIVATION OF LIBERTY

Penal administration and the treatment of prisoners are regulated by the Prison Law (1908), the Prison Law Enforcement Regulations (1908), the Ordinance for Prisoners' Progressive Treatment (1933), the Prisoners' Classification Regulations (1972), and other directives of the Ministry of Justice. The basic Prison Law is dated. Attempts to reform it started in 1967 and are still under way.

Penal administration is under the authority of the Correction Bureau of the Ministry of Justice since Meiji Restoration, although from 1874 to 1903 it was under the authority of the Ministry of Internal Affairs. The Correction Bureau is now responsible for the administration not only of prisons, houses of detention, and juvenile prisons but also of juvenile training schools, juvenile classification homes, and women's guidance homes.

Control and supervision are shared by eight regional correction headquarters, which are the intermediary supervisory organizations for the respective penal institutions.

Treatment of convicted prisoners is based on the classification and progressive system. The classification system introduced in 1949 has been substantially revised by the new Prisoners' Classification Regulations (1972). A specially equipped and staffed institution was established as classification center in each of eight correction regions, where the examination for classification takes about two months. Under the regulations, there are two prisoner groups: one for custodial considerations (sex, nationality, age, prison term, degree of criminal inclination, mental or physical defect) and the other for treatment considerations (types of treatment required, such as training, schooling, therapy, and protection). Prisoners are assigned to suitable penal institutions in accordance with this classification, and the concrete treatment program is organized on the basis of classification.

The progressive system is conducted under the Ordinance for Prisoners' Progressive Treatment (1933). The system has four grades starting with the lowest, or fourth, grade for newcomers. In principle, those who are placed in the fourth and third grades are confined in community cells and those in second and first grades are in individual cells at night. In the highest grades they enjoy extensive self-government and privileges.

Japan has 56 prisons, 9 juvenile prisons, 3 medical prisons, 7 detention houses, 62 juvenile training schools, 51 juvenile classification homes, and 3 women's guidance homes. Besides the traditional type of closed prisons, there are many open institutions. A new mode of open institutional treatment has been tried in every correctional region since 1961, and at present there are over 50 labor camps attached to prisons throughout Japan, 15 of which are open-type "living in" camps. There are also open institutions for traffic offenders.

The rights and duties of inmates of the penal institutions are determined by Prison Law. Labor is compulsory for prisoners sentenced to imprisonment with labor. Those sentenced to imprisonment without labor and penal detention may be employed on their own applications. Token wages are paid for prison labor, but not enough to stimulate prisoners to work. Vocational training is offered to those who might be rehabilitated easily as well as to youth and juvenile offenders. Such training is offered in addition to regular labor and includes the repair of automobiles, barbering, dressmaking, and the like. School education is given four hours a day to juveniles and other inmates who need such education. For juveniles and adult inmates, correspondence courses are encouraged.

Basically, convicted prisoners receive food, clothing, and medical care, while unconvicted inmates may purchase their own food if they so desire. An interview between a prisoner and a visitor is conducted in the presence of a prison official, except in the case of an interview between an unconvicted prisoner and his attorney. All mail to and from prisoners is censored. To prevent escape, violence, and suicide, restraining instruments, such as straight jackets, handcuffs, and arresting ropes, are used, but no chains. Revolvers, gasguns, and police sticks are used, but no swords.

Outstanding prisoner conduct is rewarded, and any inmate who violates prison rules is liable to disciplinary punishment, such as reprimand, suspension of privileges or physical exercise, reduction of food, or minor or major solitary confinement. Punishment is not regulated by the law, and reformers are proposing to introduce the guarantee of due process as well as to eliminate the measures of reduction of food and major solitary confinement. Under present law, inmates are entitled to submit petitions or complaints to either the minister of justice or to inspecting officers, but there is no regulation which obligates the authorities to answer promptly.

PART III

SOCIALIST LAW SYSTEMS

In this final portion are found descriptions of criminal justice in three socialist countries—the Union of Soviet Socialist Republics, the Polish People's Republic, and the German Democratic Republic. These European socialist systems exhibit a level of apparent diversity that some may explain as being related to national characteristics, while others may suggest that even though they profess a common ideology, their criminal justice systems reflect the different paths of historical development in each country. In the USSR the Revolution of 1917 seems to have caused a prompt rejection of the prerevolutionary system, and by 1919 a new statement of principles to guide the administration of justice is found in the Leading Principles of Criminal Law in the Russian Soviet Federative Socialist Republic. This statement argues that the proletariat should not adopt the ready-made bourgeois state machinery to its own aims, but abolish it and create its own system of justice. However, in those Eastern European countries that became socialist following World War II, there has been a greater tendency to maintain elements of the prior continental legal system.

When trying to understand these countries the nonsocialist must realize that he is trying to study not only another legal system but one based on a totally opposite ideology. To understand properly socialist criminal justice, one must become well acquainted with a set of basic philosophical ideas of Marxist-Leninist thought. But it is also to recognize, as some scholars point out, that there are elements of the civil law tradition that are apparent in the socialist system of criminal justice. As pointed out in the introduction, some scholars continue to believe that there is not a separate legal family of socialist law. Finally, it is important to recognize that, to some extent, there are differences among the countries under review. When reading the chapters one must ask the question as to whether the particular phenomenon can be explained by the fact that we are dealing with the socialist family of law or simply because the individual element is part of the particular national heritage.

7

UNION OF SOVIET SOCIALIST REPUBLICS

Valery M. Savitsky and Valery P. Shupilov

I. GENERAL INFORMATION

The Union of Soviet Socialist Republics is a federal, multi-national state formed through the self-determination and voluntary association of 15 equal Soviet Socialist Republics. The diverse population, which exceeded 260 million in 1977, speaks more than 20 major languages and numerous minor languages. The territory of the USSR (the largest country in the world) is almost three times the size of the United States. For example, when a new day begins in Vladivostock it is "yesterday evening" for the people in Leningrad.

Union Republics take part in decision-making in the Supreme Soviet and its Presidium (Executive Council), the Government of the USSR, and other bodies of the Union of Soviet Socialist Republics in matters that come within its jurisdiction.

Each Union Republic is responsible for comprehensive economic and social development in its territory. The Union Republics facilitate the exercise of power of the USSR in its territory and implement the decisions of the highest bodies of national authority and administration.

Each Union Republic has its own constitution and legislation. Federal jurisdiction insures uniformity of legislative norms and establishment of the fundamentals of all legislation.

The leading and guiding force of Soviet society and the nucleus of its political system, including state and civic organizations, is the Communist Party of the Soviet Union (CPSU). The CPSU exists for the people and serves the people.

The Communist Party, armed with Marxism-Leninism, determines the general perspectives of the development of society and the course of internal and foreign policy of the USSR; directs the great constructive work of the Soviet people; and imparts a planned, systematic, and theoretically substantiated character to the struggle for the victory of communism. Party directives, however, have no force of law. All party organizations function within the framework of the Constitution.

The highest body of national authority is the Supreme Soviet, which is empowered to deal with all matters within the jurisdiction of the Union as defined by the Constitution. The exclusive prerogatives of the Supreme Soviet include the adoption of and amendments to the Constitution, admission of new Republics, endorsement of the formation of new Autonomous Republics and Autonomous Regions, approval of national plans for economic and social development, adoption of the budget of the USSR and of reports on their execution and the creation of national bodies accountable to it.

Laws of the Union are enacted by the Supreme Soviet or by a nationwide vote ordered by it. The Supreme Soviet consists of two chambers: the Soviet of the Union and the Soviet of Nationalities. The chambers have equal rights. Deputies to the Supreme Soviet are elected on the basis of universal, equal, and direct suffrage by secret ballot for a five-year term of office.

GENERAL DESCRIPTION OF THE LEGAL SYSTEM

The criminal justice system of the USSR, including the imposition and execution of punishment, is regulated by the Fundamentals of Legislation on the Judicial System of the USSR and Autonomous Republics, Fundamentals of Criminal Legislation of the USSR and the Union Republics, Fundamentals on Criminal Procedure of the USSR and Union Republics adopted by the Supreme Soviet on December 25, 1958, and Fundamentals of Corrective Labor Legislation of the USSR and Union Republics adopted on July 11, 1969.

Each Union Republic has adopted its own criminal law, criminal procedure, and corrective-labor codes based upon the Fundamental acts. The codes reflect national, geographic, and other characteristics of each Republic.

Judicial decisions do not have the power of precedent and must be pronounced in strict conformity with the legislation in force. In practice, lower courts pay close attention to the rulings of higher courts, particularly to the Supreme Court of the USSR.

AMOUNT, STRUCTURE, AND DYNAMICS OF CRIMINALITY

Crime in the USSR has undergone considerable alteration during more than 60 years of Soviet power. Reflecting the acute class struggle that took place in the country during and beyond the Great October Revolution, the Civil War period of 1917-1920 was characterized by a high level of dangerous counter-revolutionary crimes. This period was also characterized by a considerable growth of crimes against persons and property.

The growth of crime slowed by 1924 and then crime began to decline. Two and a half million cases were committed to the People's courts in 1924 as compared to 1.4 million in 1925. The main cause was the faster growth of economic development in the country, which at that time was adjusting to a peaceful, creative style of living.

In the 1926-1929 period, the Soviet state reached a stage of economic development where conditions for the construction of socialism were created. The general trend of crime reduction continued during this period. By 1930, the number of criminal cases was reduced by 15 percent.

Socialism was victorious in the USSR during the second half of the 1930s. The Soviet people built a powerful material and technical structure, developed a multi-faceted economy, and reached a state of mature social relations.

These important economic and socio-economic factors naturally influenced criminality, which is a social phenomenon. The reduction of crime, a feature of the new type of society, was already visible during the period of strengthening socialism and the gradual transition to communism. By 1967, the number of persons who committed crimes, taking into consideration population growth, decreased more than two times compared to 1946.

A discussion concerning the value of social and biological factors in explaining criminal behavior has taken place in Soviet criminology for a number of years. This discussion has brought the conclusion that social factors play the dominating role in shaping human behavior. At the same time, psycho-physiological mechanisms involved in the social content of an action should be taken into consideration.

Biological factors in turn play the role of conditions favoring or preventing a proper building of the personality. Soviet criminologists believe that consideration of these factors should result in a diversified approach to the people's education, especially adolescents and young adults.

Although social processes are characterized by regularity, some deviations may be observed. Therefore, it is not surprising that the trend for crime reduction in the USSR is developing unevenly, with alterations in different regions of the country. A slight growth of criminality was registered in 1958, 1962, and in the late 1960s. The phenomenon can be explained by both an activization of the struggle against some kinds of widespread crimes and by sociodemographic changes of the quantity, structure, and distribution of the population.

The present recorded crime level is considerably lower than during the post-war period, not to mention the 1920s.

In general, contemporary criminality can be defined as follows:

(1) A rather insignificant number of particularly dangerous state crimes, committed by the agents of Western Powers or certain Soviet citizens enticed by imperialist propaganda;

(2) The bulk of crimes are insignificant;

(3) Professional crime has practically been eliminated;

(4) The number and dangerousness of crimes committed by organized groups is diminishing. There is no organized crime of the gangster type;

(5) All in all, crime is on the decline with occasional growth of certain crimes at certain periods.

STRUCTURE AND FUNCTIONING OF LAW ENFORCEMENT AGENCIES

Soviet courts include the Supreme Court of the USSR, the Supreme Courts of Union Republics, the Supreme Courts of Autonomous Republics, Territories, Regional and city courts, courts of Autonomous Areas, and district or city people's courts. Popular election of judges and people's assessors (lay judges) is the principle on which all courts in the USSR are formed.

Judges of higher courts are elected for five-year terms by the corresponding council of people's deputies.

Judges and people's assessors are responsible and accountable to their constituencies and must report to them and may be recalled by them in the manner prescribed by law.

The Procurator-General of the USSR and the procurators subordinate to him have the supreme power of supervision over the strict and uniform observance of laws by all ministries, state commissions and departments, enterprises, institutions and organizations, executive-administrative bodies of local Soviets of People's Deputies, collective farms, co-operatives, and other public organizations, officials, and citizens.

The Procurator-General of the USSR is appointed by the Supreme Soviet and is responsible and accountable to it, and between sessions, to the Presidium of the Supreme Soviet.

According to the Ordinance on the supervisory powers, the procurator's offices in the USSR have the right to lodge a protest against any acts or decisions of any ministry or department if they contradict the legislation in force.

The Militia operates under the Ministry of the Interior of the USSR and is uniformly structured in all the Union Republics. It registers all crimes and conducts searches and detecting operations in order to find traces of crimes and persons who have committed crimes. The Militia also performs the preliminary inquiry for certain crimes specified by law.

II. SUBSTANTIVE CRIMINAL LAW

GENERAL PRINCIPLES OF RESPONSIBILITY

Under socialism, the criminal law is considered an auxiliary means for the protection of the legal order from criminal abuse. The essential problem seems to be specifying which acts are deemed to be criminal and what punishment should be applied to persons who have committed such acts. In accordance with the Fundamentals of Criminal Legislation, only persons guilty of intentional or careless crimes, provided for in the criminal code as socially dangerous acts, are subject to criminal responsibility. Criminal punishment can be applied only pending court judgment.

Criminal and punishable acts are defined by the law in force at the time the act is committed. A law criminalizing an act or aggravating a punishment is a law declaring as criminal an act which has not been previously deemed so or which increases the maximum and minimum limits of the punishment or introduces additional aggravating circumstances. A law criminalizing an act and aggravating a punishment cannot be applied retroactively. Nationwide criminal laws take legal effect in the entire USSR territory ten days after they are published unless another term is specified.

All persons who have committed crimes in the USSR are subjected to criminal responsibility according to Soviet criminal law. Soviet citizens abroad who have committed acts defined as criminal by Soviet legislation are subjected to criminal responsibility if they are tried in the territory of the USSR. Aliens who have committed crimes outside the USSR are subjected to criminal responsibility according to Soviet criminal law in cases provided for by international convention.

Soviet criminal law defines those socially dangerous acts (either action or omission) considered crimes in the Special Part of the Criminal Codes. These acts include infringing on the Soviet social or state system; socialist economy, socialist property, person, political, labor, property, or other interest of citizens; or any other attempt against the socialist legal order.

The Soviet criminal law is based on the assumption that social danger is a material element of a crime revealing its social character and essence. Social danger is expressed by the substantial damage it causes to socialist social relations. Acts not socially dangerous are not considered crimes.

The introduction of this material element facilitates the implementation of the legality rule. According to this rule, acts falling within the scope of the definitional elements in the Special Part of the Criminal Code are criminal.

The significance of an act is defined by the factual circumstances of the case, considering the nature of the act, the conditions under which it is committed, the absence or insignificance of the damage, as well as some other circumstances.

An act deemed to be insignificant may result in the application of non-criminal social control measures to the guilty person.

Criminal responsibility is the consequence of crimes only.

Acts which are not crimes but which are substantial violations of established legal norms may serve as grounds for application of administrative or social measures such as comrades' courts at the place of work or residence of the offender.

Only persons over the age of 16 when the crime is committed are subject to criminal responsibility.

A person who committed a crime from ages 14 to 16 is subject to criminal responsibility only for homicide; intentional bodily injuries causing serious harm; rape; assault; theft; robbery, malicious hooliganism; intentional destruction or damage to state, public, or personal property resulting in grave consequences; theft of firearms, munitions, or explosives; as well as intentional acts which can bring about a train accident.

If the court establishes that it is possible to rehabilitate without criminal punishments a person under 18 who has committed a crime not presenting greater social danger, the court may apply instead mandatory educational measures. Among them are:

(1) An obligation to apologize to the victim publicly or otherwise as specified by the court;
(2) A pronouncement of a reprimand or a strict reprimand;
(3) A warning;
(4) An obligation of the minor who has reached the age of 15 to compensate financially for the damage, up to twenty roubles, if the minor has an independent income, or to compensate with his work;
(5) Placement of the minor under strict supervision of his parents or guardians;
(6) Placement of the minor under the supervision of a work collective, or social organization, providing the consent, or by private persons at their request. In addition, the court may acknowledge the necessity to appoint a public educator;
(7) Placement in a special medico-educational or educational institution for children and adolescents;
(8) Transfer of a minor to the educational colony for minors.

When a minor is relieved of criminal responsibility he is deemed not to have been convicted.

Only people, not corporations, are subject to criminal responsibility in the USSR.

In accordance with the law in force, a crime can be committed either intentionally or carelessly.

A crime is considered intentional when the perpetrator was conscious of the socially dangerous nature of his act or omission, anticipated its socially dangerous consequences, and willed or consciously allowed such consequences to ensue. The Soviet criminal law recognizes two forms of intention: direct and indirect. A direct intention means that the person anticipated socially dangerous consequences and willed them to ensue; an indirect intention means that the person anticipating socially dangerous consequences of his act or omission has not willed them to ensue but consciously allowed them to ensue.

An establishment of a direct or indirect intention presupposes that the person has realized the dangerous nature of his act or omission. If certain circumstances make it impossible for the person to realize the social danger of his act, then such an act cannot be deemed intentional. The absence of the realization of the illegality of the acts does not, however, exclude criminal responsibility. An offender may be still liable for a non-intentional offense.

A crime is committed by carelessness when the perpetrator anticipated the possibility of socially dangerous consequences ensuing from his commission or omission, but unreasonably relied on their preventions or failed to anticipate the possibility of socially dangerous consequences ensuing, although he could and should have anticipated them.

As one can see from the wording of Soviet criminal law, it distinguishes between two forms of carelessness: recklessness, when the person anticipates the possibility of socially dangerous consequences ensuing from his commission or omission combined with the unreasonable hope of avoiding them, and negligence, a failure to anticipate such a possibility although he could and should have anticipated it.

A careless crime presupposes that the person has relied on the avoidance of the consequences by means of certain circumstances—and this is the essential difference from indirect intention.

Soviet criminal legislation provides criminal responsibility for preliminary activities. They include preparation and attempt. Justification for this type of responsibility is the objectively dangerous nature of the actions comprising preparation or attempt, directed to the commission of a criminal abuse of legally protected interests. Preparation of a crime consists of procurement or adaptation of means or instruments or any other intentional creation of conditions for the commission of a crime. An attempt is an intentional action directed immediately toward the commission of a crime, where the crime has not been brought to completion for reasons not depending on the will of the guilty person.

Punishment for preparation and for attempt is assigned in accordance with the law providing for the given completed crime. In assigning punishment, the court shall take into account the nature and degree of social danger of the actions committed by the guilty person, the extent to which the criminal intention has been carried out, and the reasons the crime has not been brought to completion.

A person who has voluntarily abandoned the completion of a crime shall be subject to criminal responsibility only in the event that the act he has in fact committed constitutes another crime. The motives for abandoning the completion of a crime are irrelevant from a legal viewpoint.

Complicity is the intentional joint participation by two or more persons in the commission of a crime. In such cases, if one person decides voluntarily no longer to participate, that person, to be relieved of criminal responsibility, is obliged to report the crime preparation to the competent agencies. In addition, the failure to report such a crime constitutes a criminal offense.

Perpetrators as well as organizers, instigators, and accessories share equal criminal responsibility for their crimes. An organizer is a person who has arranged or directed the commission of a crime.

An accessory is a person who has promoted the commission of a crime by advice, instructions, provision of means or removal of obstacles, or has promised beforehand to conceal the criminal, the instruments, and means of commission of the crime, traces of the crime, or criminally acquired articles.

In assigning punishment, the court must take into account the degree and nature of participation of each of the accomplices in the commission of the crime.

Insanity, dire necessity, and necessary defense are circumstances which exclude criminal responsibility in Soviet criminal law.

A person who, at the time of the commission of a socially dangerous act, was unable to account for his actions or govern them because of a chronic mental illness, temporary mental derangement, mental deficiency, or other morbid condition, is not subject to criminal responsibility. Compulsory medical measures may be applied to such a person by order of the court.

In accordance with the Decree of the Presidium of the Supreme Soviet of the Russian Soviet Republic of March 1, 1974, persons excessively consuming alcoholic beverages (chronic alcoholics) are subjected to measures of an administrative-medical nature, namely, are sent to special medical-labor institutions.

Only those chronic alcoholics who reject treatment, who violate labor discipline, break social order, and to whom disciplinary or administrative measures had been applied previously are sent to institutions.

The question concerning a person's assignment at a medical facility is examined by a district or city people's court in open session. The court gives a written decision defining the reasons for and the term of compulsory medical treatment and labor re-education.

Persons sent to a medical facility by a court decision are not deemed to have been convicted. The term of the medical treatment is established by the court after considering the opinion of a medical commission. Persons in such facilities work and receive the identical salary as other workers. The amount of money covering their expenses is subtracted from their salaries, including the cost of food, clothing, and medicines. The amount of money left, pending the person's consent, is sent to his family or transferred to his account and can be spent for buying any goods, except, obviously, alcohol.

In accordance with the Republican Penal Codes, if an alcoholic or a drug addict commits a crime, the court can subject him to medical treatment in addition to criminal punishment, if the medical expertise states the necessity of such.

The court does not specify the term of medical treatment for alcoholics or drug addicts. It depends on the gravity of the disease. Treatment is terminated when the court receives a favorable report from the medical institution where the person was treated.

In the case when a convict turns out to be an alcoholic and in need of compulsory medical treatment in the place of confinement, the administration of the establishment must apply to the court to assign such treatment. A medical opinion is necessary in this instance.

As medical experience has shown, the effectiveness of compulsory anti-alcoholic treatment depends on the attitude of the person treated. Such treatment gives the person a chance to lead a normal life. In many cases the treatment is indeed successful.

A formally prohibited action which has been committed in a state of necessary defense, that is, in protecting the interests of the Soviet State, social interests, or the person or rights of the defender of another person against a socially dangerous infringement by causing harm to the infringer, shall not be a crime, provided that the limits of necessary defense have not been exceeded.

A defense which caused harm to the attacker, accomplished by means and methods disproportionate to the nature and danger of the attack and to other circumstances, is considered excessive.

To establish that the limits of necessary defense have been exceeded it is not sufficient to mechanically assess the circumstances surrounding both the attack and the defense. The Supreme Court of the USSR has spoken on this subject: "The degree and nature of the danger threatening the defending person as well as his strength and possibility for the defense should be taken into consideration."

The Judicial Chamber on Criminal Cases of the Supreme Court of the Russian Soviet Republic stated that the necessary defense was excessive in the following instance: "R" and his friends were attacked by drunken "G". "R" struck "G" on the head several times with a wooden club after "G" had already fallen from a stroke. In this case the means of defense clearly exceeded the means and nature of the attack. It may be noted that the law provides for the possibility of insignificant deviations in the relationship between the severity of the defense and the intensity of the attack. In deciding this question it is necessary to consider the state of excitement provoked by the unexpectedness of the attack, when the person defending cannot properly evaluate the nature of the danger and is not able to choose the appropriate means of defense. This may result in "naturally more grievous consequences for which the defendant cannot be responsible."

An action committed in a state of dire necessity is not a crime if such danger could not have been eliminated by other means, and where the harm caused is smaller than the harm prevented.

PENAL MEASURES

In accordance with the Soviet theory of criminal law, punishment is a retribution for the crime committed. It is a retribution since it is: (a) assigned for the committed crime; (b) corresponds to the gravity of the crime committed; (c) is of a coercive character and brings about suffering to the convicted person.

Retribution is the essence of punishment since the law establishing it introduces certain restrictions in the life of a convict, laying unpleasant duties on him.

It is quite obvious that not all restrictions bring about suffering to the convicts, but undoubtedly some restrictions (e.g., deprivation of liberty) cause deep suffering and may have unpleasant consequences.

Punishment as a retribution for the commission of a crime possesses a strong repressive force compared to other measures of social control such as administrative or disciplinary measures.

In Soviet legal writings one can distinguish three aims of punishment: correction and re-education of the convict, prevention of a new crime by the convict, prevention of crime commissions by other people.

The terms correction and re-education have two meanings: first, they refer to the impact on the person who has committed a crime; second, they mean the educational process taking place during the execution of punishment.

Punishment is a special measure of State enforcement, applied in the name of the State by a specially authorized agency—the court. The essence of punishment is the restriction of rights established for each type of offense by the law. Punishment is aimed at making the offender re-evaluate his actions which served as a foundation for his conviction by evoking in him unpleasant feelings.

Correction and re-education of the convict are among the goals of punishment. The law, having established the goal of correction and re-education, requires individualized work with each convict by the officials executing punishment. The emphasis on working with the convicts is directed to their internalization of such ideas and notions that would demonstrate the value of a socially useful way of life and prevent the offender from the commission of fresh crimes.

The fact that punishment must "contribute to the eradication of crime" is emphasized in the Soviet corrective-labor law. Punishment is not the only means of crime prevention. Measures directed to combatting crime may be of an economic, educational, organizational or other social nature. Punishment is an auxiliary measure.

The law establishes the following types of punishment: (1) deprivation of liberty, (2) exile, (3) restricted residence, (4) corrective labor without deprivation of liberty, (5) deprivation of the right to hold specified offices or engage in specified activity, (6) fine, (7) dismissal, (8) restitution, (9) social censure, (10) confiscation of property, (11) deprivation of military and other ranks. Application of the death penalty—by shooting—is allowed as an exceptional measure of punishment for intentional homicide under aggravating circumstances and certain other crimes of special gravity. Abolition of the death penalty is pending.

According to the law, the death penalty may be applied by the court only in a case when its necessity is predetermined by special circumstances aggravating the responsibility and by the exceptional danger of the person who has committed the crime. However, as a rule, sentences of death are not carried out but commuted to a 15-year term of deprivation of liberty.

Conditional corrective labor, conditional deprivation of liberty, social censure, and immediate deprivation of liberty are the principal types of punishment applied by Soviet courts. The trend is to reduce the scope of the application of deprivation of liberty. Only 0.5 per cent of those convicted to deprivation of liberty serve it in prison.

Corrective labor is one of the basic types of punishment mentioned in the Special Part of the Republican Penal Codes. For example, in accordance with the Penal Code of the Russian Soviet Republic, corrective labor can be assigned for 149 types of offenses. It is an often used measure by the courts: approximately every fourth convicted offender in the Soviet Union receives a corrective labor sentence.

The Fundamentals of the Corrective Labor Legislation stipulate that corrective labor without deprivation of liberty is executed by agencies of the Ministry of Interior of the USSR and those of the Union Republics. Among agencies of the Ministry of Interior there are city, district and inter-district sections on corrective labor which are directly engaged in the execution of this type of punishment.

The corrective labor sections are responsible for: (a) keeping records of the persons convicted to corrective work; (b) job placement at places specified by the agencies responsible for punishment execution as well as the control over a correct use of work of the persons convicted to corrective labor at their former places of work; (c) participation in educational activities with such persons; (d) strict observance of the rules dealing with the execution of corrective labor, deductions from their salaries and their timely transfer to the State Treasury; application of measures of encouragement and penalties towards persons serving corrective work, as well as a presentation to the court of the materials for placing responsibility on those persons willfully refusing to work; (e) presentation to the courts of materials on the conditional pre-term release of persons convicted to corrective work or replacing part of the unserved term of punishment by a milder punishment; (f) conducting via militia agencies the search for those persons convicted to corrective work who cannot be located.

The Fundamentals of the Corrective Labor Legislation further stipulate that the correction and re-education of persons serving punishment without deprivation of liberty is accomplished through their participation in socially useful work. Thus, work is recognized as the most important method of rehabilitation.

During the entire period of punishment, educational work is conducted with the convicts. The section in charge of the corrective work performs the educational function from the moment of the convict's registration.

The registration is combined with the convict's summoning to the section, where the current legislation on corrective work is explained to him, as well as his rights and responsibilities.

The officers of the section regularly inspect the enterprises where the convicts work, meet with them, speak to the administration of the enterprises, the convicts' colleagues. If labor discipline violations occur, it is the officer's duty to clarify the causes. If necessary, the inspectors summon convicts to their office, visit the places of their residence, and speak to the family members.

The individual educational work allows consideration of the peculiarities of the convict's personality, his interest and milieu.

In addition to the individual approach, group sessions are held where the legislation in force as well as the convict's behavior and other issues of current interest are discussed. The educational activities are performed also at the place of the convict's work. Social organizations and the administration take part.

The convict is assisted in learning a professional skill if he does not possess one. An active participation in social life helps to develop the self-consciousness of the convict and teaches him to live in accordance with the collective's interests.

There can be no doubt that corrective labor entails a punitive element. In accordance with the Fundamentals, deductions in salary ranging from five to

20 per cent are made. The money deducted is transferred to the State Treasury.

One article of the Fundamentals deals with evading serving corrective work. This may result in a warning or in case of a willful shunning, even in corrective labor with deprivation of liberty. The evasion may be of various kinds, but it is considered malicious if the break lasts more than a fortnight.

Research conducted by Soviet criminologists shows that recidivism among persons who served corrective labor is rather low. Preliminary studies conducted by researchers of the Federal Institute of the Study of Causes and Development of Measures of Crime Prevention have shown that only about nine per cent of the persons convicted by the courts commit fresh crimes within three years.

Deprivation of liberty may be assigned for a three-month to ten-year term and in cases of especially dangerous crimes and for especially dangerous recidivists for a term not exceeding 15 years.

Persons convicted to deprivation of liberty, exile, restricted residence or corrective labor may be subject to a pre-term conditional release or a substitution of the unserved term of punishment by a milder punishment, as in the case of a convict who proves his correction by exemplary behavior and honest attitude towards labor. Pre-term conditional release from punishment and substitution of a lighter punishment of the unserved term is applied by the court at the place the convicted person is serving his punishment on the strength of a joint recommendation by the agency in charge of executive punishment and the supervisory commission under the Executive Committee of the local Soviet of people's deputies.

Conditional pre-term release from punishment or substitution of a lighter punishment for the unserved term may be applied after the convicted person has served at least one half of the assigned term.

RELIEF FROM PUNISHMENT

A person who has committed a crime may be relieved from criminal responsibility if it is deemed that by the time of investigation or court trial the act has, in consequences of a change in the situation, lost its social danger or the person has ceased to be socially dangerous.

One cause eliminating the social danger of an act may be a change of living conditions compared to those under which the crime had been committed.

These changes may be political, economic, social, or organizational. They must be evident by the time of the court trial.

These changes may be of a general character, for example, conditions existing all over the country; or of an individual character, referring to the offender's personality only, for example, an alteration by the time of the trial of personal or family conditions which have influenced the crime commission.

The change of circumstances may result in different consequences: in some cases they may eliminate both social danger of an act and of a person who has committed the act, in other cases only that of the offender. For example, a person may be relieved from criminal responsibility if he changes his job connected with the sources of excess danger, although he may have committed a criminal violation of labor discipline.

Such a change may be caused by objective circumstances not depending on the offender, for example, if his supervisors change his occupation; or by the offender's behavior, for example, if he changes his job on his own initiative.

If an act loses its social danger it follows that the social danger of the offender is eliminated since the latter is predetermined by the former. A person who has committed a crime may be relieved from punishment where it is deemed that, in virtue of his subsequent faultless conduct and honest attitude to work, he may not, by the time of the trial of the case in court, be considered socially dangerous.

The Soviet criminal law stipulates relief from criminal responsibility for committed acts of non-significance with the case being transferred to comrades' courts.

Moreover, if the person, by the circumstances of the case, presents no social danger, if the act committed by him is of no great social danger and has not entailed grave consequences, and if the person repents sincerely, he may be relieved from criminal responsibility and on the basis of a petition filed by a working collective or a social organization be placed under supervision of the collective which has entered the petition for re-education and correction.

A person who pleads not guilty cannot be placed under social supervision. He has the right to demand court examination of his case. The placement of a person under social supervision is an individual act of relief from criminal responsibility and it does not affect the grounds for responsibility of the accomplices of the crime.

III. CRIMINAL PROCEDURE

PRINCIPLES OF CRIMINAL PROCEDURE

In the USSR justice is administered only by the courts. No person can be found guilty of the commission of a crime other than by the judgment of a court. None of the militia, the procurator, or the local Soviet of People's Deputies can do this. There are no separate courts in the USSR for specific groups of the population. Courts are not based on racial or national differences. "Justice is administered in the USSR on the principle of equality of citizens before the law and before the court."

The hearings of civil and criminal cases in all courts is collegial; in courts of first instance cases are heard by one judge and two people's assessors; in the higher courts (courts of appeal and supervision) by three professional people's judges. In some rare cases of administrative violations (e.g., petty hooliganism, petty speculation, etc.) a single people's judge hears the case. Maximum administrative penalty in such cases is 15 days' detention.

People's assessors hear all cases in the first instance. They are elected at general meetings of workers and employees at the place of their work or residence for a two-and-a-half-year term. People's assessors of higher courts are elected at sessions of the corresponding Soviets for a five-year term. In the administration of justice, people's assessors have all the rights of a judge; all decisions are adopted by majority vote.

As the Constitution states, "Judges and people's assessors are independent and subject only to the law." Any pressure or influence on judges aimed at making them pronounce certain decisions are condemned by the law.

Membership in the Communist Party does not restrict the actual independence of judges. On the contrary, the Party Central Committee has strictly forbidden the local party organs to interfere with the administration of justice. If such a prohibition is not observed by a local party leader, the latter is strictly punished, maybe even dismissed from his post, and the event is published in newspapers and magazines.

The Constitution of the USSR provides for public hearings in all courts. Closed hearings are only allowed in cases provided for by the law (e.g., sex offenses, juvenile delinquency, cases connected with state secrets). Even in closed hearings all rules of judicial procedure must be observed.

The USSR is a multinational state. In consequence, judicial proceedings are conducted in the language of the Union or Autonomous Republic, autonomous Region or the majority of the population of the area. Persons participating in court proceedings who do not know the language are insured the right to become fully acquainted with the materials of the case. The services of an interpreter during the proceedings and the right to address the court in their own language are rights provided by the Constitution.

The principle of presumption of innocence is attributable to the whole Soviet criminal procedure. It is expressed as follows: "No person may be prosecuted as an accused other than on the grounds and in accordance with the procedure established by the law" (Article 4, CP Fundamentals).

The court, the procurator, the investigator, and the person conducting the inquiry have the duty to take all measures stipulated by law for a comprehensive, thorough, and objective scrutiny of the circumstances of the case, and to bring out equally the circumstances which aggravate and mitigate guilt.

The court, the procurator, the investigator and the person conducting the inquiry do not have the right to lay the duty of proof on the accused. They are prohibited from seeking to obtain testimony from the accused through the use of force, threats, or any other illegal means.

The law contains a very important principle: "A judgment of conviction must not be founded on assumptions and shall be rendered only where, in the course of judicial examination, the prisoner's guilt in committing the crime has been proved." This leads to the rule expounded by the Supreme Court of the USSR on June 30, 1969: "All doubts concerning the prosecutorial evidence are counted in favor of the accused unless the doubts can be eliminated."

And, finally, presumption of innocence is expressed most clearly in Article 160 of the new Constitution of the USSR: "No one may be adjudged guilty of a crime and subjected to punishment as a criminal except by the sentence of a court and in conformity with law." The presumption of innocence was stipulated by the previous legislation as well, but was formulated less categorically. For the first time it has become a constitutional rule, not just part of criminal legislation. Worth mentioning is the fact that Decree of the Plenum of the Supreme Court of the USSR of June 16, 1978 interprets article 160 of the Constitution in the following way: "Courts must strictly observe the constitutional principle that an accused person is deemed to be not guilty until his guilt is proved according to the legal proceeding and established by the sentence which has come into force."

PARTICIPANTS IN CRIMINAL PROCEEDINGS

The court is the main and principal participant in the trial. During criminal proceedings the other participants may address the court with different petitions, present evidence, etc., but they are not able to make any decisions. This is a unique right of the court. The first duty of the court is to establish the truth.

Soviet theories of criminal procedure as well as practice do not recognize "formal" (judicial) truth as grounds for judgment. The judgment should contain objective (material) truth. This means that the conclusions should correspond to what has really taken place. Doubtful as well as unlawful evidence may never be taken as grounds for a judgment.

Preliminary (pre-trial) investigation of criminal cases is conducted by the investigators from the Procurator's office, the Ministry of Interior or the State Security Committee. Their responsibilities are defined by law. Only some simple cases are examined by other agencies of inquiry, e.g., militia, fire brigade, etc. They function according to the same procedures, with minor exceptions, as the investigator does.

In the criminal procedure the procurator supervises observance of the law. He directs the investigator's activities, examines the lawfulness and gives advice on the conduct of the investigation. During the trial, the procurator supports the state prosecution. Generally, he insists on the conviction of a guilty person, but he must withdraw the accusation if the judicial investigation does not confirm the accusation. The procurator submits a protest to a higher court concerning each unlawful or ungrounded judgment. The procurator has no authoritative or directive power in court. He himself must obey the court's rulings.

The procurator directs and supervises all investigators—including those of the State Security Committee and Ministry of Interior. His powers are very broad; he may vacate unlawful decisions, discharge an investigator, give the investigator binding directives, terminate cases, etc. The procurator's responsibilities are provided for by a federal law—the Ordinance on Procurator's Supervision in the Soviet Union—and are therefore identical in all the Republics.

The State Security Committee has its own investigation body. Investigators of the Committee examine cases of crimes against the State (high treason, espionage, terrorism, etc.) listed precisely in the Code of Criminal Procedure. During an investigation, investigators of the State Security Committee are bound by exactly the same rules as investigators of the Procurator's Office and Ministry of Interior. The Procurator's Office supervises investigations conducted by the Committee. The Committee investigator must obtain the procurator's consent to a search, to detain a suspected person, and to commit a case to trial.

Upon completing an investigation the investigator or the procurator should advise orally or in writing the enterprise, the office or the collective farm that its employee is a crime suspect and that his case is transferred to the court. Such information is made public at a general meeting of the workers or employees of the given enterprise or at a trade union meeting. People discuss the news and make a decision to authorize one of its members to represent them in the court. The appointed person is charged with either supporting the prosecution or defending the colleague on behalf of the collective. The public representative is guided by his conscience and facts exposed at the court's hearings. Depending on the course of events he may change his position even if it differs from the one supported by the collective which appointed him. At present, a social accuser or a social defender participates in about every eighth case in court.

Different forms of public participation in combatting crime (law assessors, social accusers, social defenders, charging work-teams with offender's rehabilitation, etc.) reflect the main trend in the development of the Soviet society's political system—further extension of socialist democracy.

The new Constitution of 1977 calls for "ever broader participation of citizens in managing the affairs of society and the state . . . , heightening of the activity of public organization . . . and constant responsiveness to public opinion" (Article 9). Soviet political theory asserts that the USSR at the present stage of its development is an all-people State, deriving its power from the consciousness of the masses.

ACCUSED PERSON

The accused person because of the presumption of innocence enjoys ample rights which allow him to defend himself. The accused person has the right to know what he is accused of; to present evidence; to enter petitions; to file complaints over the actions and decisions of the investigator, the procurator, the court; to make challenges; to acquaint himself, upon completion of the preliminary investigation, with all the material of the case; and to have a defense counsel. The accused person may be detained only by a court decision or on the warrant of a procurator. This, again, is a constitutional principle.

As a general rule, pre-trial detention is allowed only for a two-month term. This term may be extended only by a procurator at a higher level. The longest term possible, nine months, may be sanctioned only by the General Procurator of the Soviet Union. In practice, the average term is two to three months.

In exceptional cases the person suspected of a crime may be detained without the warrant of a procurator if he has been caught committing a crime, if stolen objects have been found on him, etc. Detention in custody may not continue for more than three days after which the person must be released or the procurator's warrant for detention issued.

Advocates (professional defense attorneys), representatives of trade unions, and other social organizations may act as defense counsels. The defense counsel is invited to participate by the accused or his relatives. On the accused person's request, the investigator, the procurator, and the court must assign a defense counsel for him. This request of the accused should be granted regardless of the ground which prevented the accused from selecting an advocate. The defense counsel is appointed free of charge but the court in its judgment may oblige the defendant to pay the defense counsel.

The defense counsel participates in the criminal case from the moment when the preliminary investigation is completed and the accused person is handed a record of the proceedings. However, if the accused person is a minor, or deaf or blind, etc., the defense counsel may participate from the moment the indictment has been presented. In any other case, the procurator may grant defense counsel the right to participate from the moment the indictment has been presented.

The defense counsel has the right to meet the accused privately without any limits on the number and length of meetings; to acquaint himself with the materials of the case and to make extracts of any necessary information; with the permission of the investigator to attend a part of the investigation; and to file complaints against the actions and decision of the investigator, the procurator, and the court.

The advocate has no right to abandon the defense of the accused once he has accepted it. But the accused may reject the defense counsel at his own initiative at any stage of the investigation or court trial.

Besides the above mentioned, the participants of criminal proceedings may be: a victim, that is, a person who suffered moral, physical, or property damage caused by the crime; a civil plaintiff, the person or organization whose property is damaged by the crime; and a civil respondent, the person who bears responsibility for the property damage caused by the crime (often it is the accused himself, it may also be his parents, legal representatives, etc.). The right of these participants are equal: they may present evidence, enter petitions and make challenges, acquaint themselves with the material of the case, and file complaints over the cases and decisions of the investigator, the procurator, and the court.

Finally, social accusers and social defenders may participate in the trial. These persons represent interests of labor collectives or public organizations and express public opinion concerning the personality of the accused, the crime which has been committed and the possible penalty. In practice, social accusers and social defenders take an active part in criminal trials. Their role is constantly growing. At present, about 12 per cent of the cases are tried with their participation.

STAGES OF CRIMINAL PROCEEDINGS

Initiation of Case: Case initiation is the primary stage of criminal proceedings. At this stage, the agency conducting inquiry, the investigator, the procurator, or the judge having received the crime report, prepares a special procedural act called "the decree on the initiation of a criminal case." It is only after this action that acts directed to the detection of evidence (searches, examinations, etc.) are allowed.

Preliminary Investigation: This is the second stage of the proceedings. During preliminary investigation accusation, defense and decision-making are functions of a single person—the investigator. As a result, the proceedings are not as adversary as they are at trial where these functions are separated into accusation, defense, and judgment.

The investigator must first establish the circumstances of the crime. Having this aim in mind, the investigator conducts searches, interrogations, examinations, and other investigatory actions. When the necessary evidence is obtained he presents a decree in which he names the accused and gives details of the charge. Then he makes decisions concerning preventive measures such as pre-trial detention and he continues to collect evidence. An investigation must be terminated if the period of limitation has expired, if it has been established that the accused person did not commit the offense charged, in cases of amnesty, etc. But if the evidence collected confirms the guilt of the accused, the investigator prepares an indictment and with the procurator's consent submits the case to the trial court.

Committal for Trial: In this next stage, some criminal proceedings are terminated and persons accused without sufficient grounds have an additional guarantee not to be tried. The question of guilt is not yet being decided. The court does not verify the evidence here but just examines whether any evidence exists in the case, whether the indictment is based on facts, and whether formal legal requirements are being observed. In consequence, the decision to commit a person for trial does not mean he is guilty.

Committal for trial is accomplished by a single judge. But in some instances, for example when the judge does not agree with the conclusions or in cases of minors, the question is decided collegially—by the judge and two people's assessors. Procurator's opinion must be attached. As a result, the case may be terminated, sent back for an additional investigation, or committed for trial.

The filtering function of this stage is mostly expressed by the fact that a great percentage of cases are returned by the court to the procurator for an additional investigation. This happens when the court finds out that procedural rules have not been observed; e.g., the accused has not been fully acquainted with the case, the evidence gathered is not satisfactory (e.g., if the accused's alibi has not been verified or the age of a minor has not been established accurately). Besides that, at this stage issues such as the participation of a defense counsel, expert, etc., are decided.

The court trial is the central stage of the criminal proceedings. Evidence is examined orally, directly, and without interruption. The adversary-inquisitorial model is fully reflected here: the parties (accuser, accused, defense counsel, victim, civil plaintiff, and civil defendant) enjoy equal rights in presenting evidence, participating in the scrutiny of the evidence, and in entering petitions.

A court hearing has several stages: a preparatory stage where the appearance in court of all summoned is checked, possible challenges raised, etc.; a judicial investigation where the court and the parties interrogate the accused, the witnesses, assess the evidence and read the documents; court debates where the parties express their opinion on the results of the assessment of evidence and the judgment; and the final statement of the accused.

The court hearing is completed by pronouncing judgment. The court may base its judgment only on the evidence which has been examined during the court trial. The judgment is formed in the consultation chamber where the judge and the two people's assessors examining the case are present. All questions are settled by a simple majority vote. A judge or people's assessor in the minority may write a dissenting opinion.

Any participant in the trial has the right to appeal the judgment to a higher court within a seven-day period. The convicted person is guaranteed that his punishment shall not be aggravated by his appeal. The appeal court is not bound by the specifics of the appeal and may review the entire case.

The procurator, the defense counsel and the victim may participate in the appeal session. Witnesses are not interrogated, only case files are examined.

As a result of the examination of the case by way of appeal, the court may leave the judgment unchanged, vacate the judgment and refer the case for a fresh investigation, vacate the judgment and terminate the case, or change the judgment to a milder or harsher one.

In the final stage of criminal proceedings, the final legal judgment is executed. Serving punishment is beyond the limits of criminal procedure. But at this stage, questions are decided concerning a suspension of the execution of punishment, relief from punishment because of illness, conditional pre-release from punishment, etc.

Besides the stages described we may also mention judicial supervision and re-opening of cases because of newly discovered circumstances. These stages are aimed at an examination of the judgments which have taken legal effect and in such a way are exceptions. We shall not dwell upon them.

Summary Criminal Proceedings are not widespread. Some cases of petty hooliganism or petty thefts are tried according to a simplified procedure, but court hearings are usually performed according to regular criminal procedure.

As far as crimes of minors are concerned, criminal responsibility begins at 18, in some cases 16, and for especially grave crimes at 14. The proceedings in these cases do not differ in principle from those of adults. However, there are additional guarantees: the conditions of life and education of the minor must be carefully established, as well as the participation of adult instigators; custody and detention is allowed in exceptional cases, more often the minor is placed with his parents, trustees or guardians; the interrogation of a minor is conducted in the presence of an educator; the participation of the defense counsel is mandatory; committal for trial is always made collegially; and parents, or persons replacing them, are invited to court hearings and have the right to present evidence, to scrutinize it, and to enter petitions and make challenges. Minors more often than adults are sentenced to different measures of the educational nature, such as making apologies to the victim and paying damages, instead of criminal punishment.

DIFFERENCES AMONG REPUBLICAN CHOICES

There are some differences among the codes of the various Republics of the USSR. For example, bail as a measure of securing an accused's appearance in the future proceedings is provided for only in the Code of Criminal

Procedure of the Russian Soviet Republic. Codes of other Republics do not contain such a measure.

The right of a victim to participate in court trials differs from Republic to Republic. For instance, in Estonia this right is not restricted. In Lithuania and Uzbekistan a victim has the right to speak in court, if the procurator does not take part in the trial. In Moldavia a victim has such right only in a certain category of cases. In the Russian Soviet Republic, Georgia, and Armenia and some other Republics a victim has no right to participate in court debates.

IV. EXECUTION OF PENAL MEASURES (CORRECTIONS)

PRINCIPLES OF EXECUTION OF PUNISHMENT

The basic means for the reform of convicted persons shall be: the regime of serving sentence, socially useful work, educational work, or general and vocational instruction.

The means for correction and reform must be applied with due consideration to the nature and degree of danger to society of the committed act, the personality of the convicted person, and his behavior and attitude to work.

The execution of punishments in the Soviet Union is based on the following principles: strict observance of socialist legality, ample participation of the public in the correction of convicted persons, compulsory enlistment for socially useful work, individualization of the execution of punishment and differentiated application of means and methods of correction and reform, and building the spirit of collectivism and initiative in convicted persons.

The execution of punishment under law provides for the functioning of agencies charged with the execution of punishment, and thus creates the conditions necessary for achieving goals of corrective labor institutions— the education of convicted persons in the spirit of respect for the law, and the guarantee of the protection of the rights of convicted persons.

Further, persons serving punishment are obliged to steadily observe law requirements dealing with the order and conditions of the execution of punishments.

The procurator's supervision of the execution of punishment guarantees strict observance of legality. Corrective Labor Law Fundamentals assigns supervision of the execution of sentences to the Procurator-General of the USSR and the procurators subordinate to him in conformity with the Ordinance on the Supervisory Powers of the Procurator's Office in the USSR. In exercising supreme supervision of the observance of the law in the name of the state, the procurator is obliged to take measures in good time to prevent and eliminate any breaches of the law and to bring the guilty to account.

The administration of corrective labor institutions and agencies which execute punishment are obliged to carry out the decisions and proposals of the procurator.

During execution of punishment the law stipulates wide responsibilities for the procurator, including the right to suspend execution of orders and rulings by the administration of the places of confinement, if they are contradictory to the law; to present to the administration mandatory proposals concerning the conditions of the convicts' keeping; and to release from custody persons who are kept in places of confinement illegally.

The same responsibilities are valid for all places of confinement and all categories of convicts.

TYPES OF CORRECTIVE-LABOR INSTITUTIONS

Corrective-labor institutions occupy an important place in the system of agencies executing criminal punishment assigned by the court, since such institutions are for criminals who are to be isolated from society due to their high social danger and the gravity of their crimes. Deprivation of liberty is more often imposed on a person who had been convicted previously and whose re-education may prove more expedient under conditions of corrective institutions.

The convict population in such institutions is heterogeneous. Corrective institutions of different types have been established to provide differential treatment for each category of convicts and to eliminate the negative influence of one category of convicts on another (considering age, sex, degree of social danger of the crime committed and criminal career).

Three basic types of corrective labor institutions are established in all the Union Republics: corrective-labor colonies, prisons, and educational-labor colonies. In turn, corrective-labor and educational-labor colonies are subdivided into several types, ranging from the most to least restrictive.

Male adults serve deprivation of liberty in corrective-labor colonies with a general regime, reinforced regime, strict or special regime, or in settlement colonies.

Men serving punishment in corrective-labor colonies are assigned as follows: those sentenced for the first time for crimes which are not grave are sent to colonies with a reinforced regime; those who are either convicted of especially dangerous crimes against the state or who had earlier served punishment in the form of deprivation of liberty are sent to colonies with a strict regime; those who are deemed especially dangerous recidivists go to the colonies with special regimes.

Women serve punishment in corrective-labor colonies of two types: general and reinforced regimes. Women are assigned to colonies of reinforced regimes who are deemed especially dangerous recidivists or whose original sentence of capital punishment is replaced by a deprivation of liberty by way of amnesty or pardon. In practice, women are not sentenced to the death penalty.

Colonies-settlements are a special type of corrective-labor institution for persons convicted of crimes of carelessness. In addition, persons convicted of other types of crimes who have served part of their sentence in colonies of general, reinforced or strict regimes can be transferred to such colonies to encourage their rehabilitation if they have decidedly chosen the way of correction.

In the corrective-labor settlement colonies, the convicted persons are kept under surveillance without guard. They have the right of free movement within the bounds of the colony in the hours from the waking signal to the retirement signal; with the permission of the colony's administration they may, for work or study, travel without surveillance outside the colony but within the bounds of the respective Region, Territory, Autonomous or Union Republic which has no regional division. They may wear civilian clothes, carry money and valuables, and use money without restriction. They also may, with the sanction of the colony's administration and if housing conditions permit, live in the colony with their families, buy a dwelling house in accordance with the law in force, and set up a personal household in the colony's territory.

Convicted men and women are kept together in one settlement colony irrespective of the regime in the colonies where they were previously kept.

Corrective-labor colonies are the main type of corrective-labor institutions for adults sentenced to a deprivation of liberty. Deprivation of liberty is very rarely served in prison in the USSR. Deprivation of liberty in the form of committal to prison for a full or partial term of punishment may be assigned to especially dangerous recidivists, to 18-year-olds who have committed very serious crimes, or to those who have been sentenced to deprivation of liberty for more than five years. In the great majority of cases courts assign prison sentences only for a partial term. After serving this time, the convict is transferred to a corrective-labor colony to serve the balance.

A convict may be transferred from a colony to a prison for a malicious violation of the regime in the corrective-labor colony. In exceptional cases, according to procedures established by the corrective-labor codes of the Union Republics, those sentenced to a deprivation of liberty for the first time for crimes which are not deemed grave, and who are assigned to serve their punishment in the corrective-labor colonies of a general regime, may, pending their consent, be left at a prison to do household work.

Prisons have two regimes: general and strict. Persons sentenced for the first time to imprisonment or transferred from a strict regime are kept under a general regime. A strict regime is applied to persons who have previously served a term of imprisonment; persons sentenced to imprisonment for crimes committed in places of confinement; persons transferred from colonies to prison; and persons transferred to a strict regime as a penalty in accordance with statutory procedure. A strict regime may be imposed two to six months.

Minors serve their punishment in educational-labor colonies. Male minors are kept in educational-labor colonies of two types: general and reinforced regimes. Male minors sentenced for the first time to a deprivation of liberty for crimes which are not grave, or sentenced for the first time for grave crimes for a term up to three years, are assigned to colonies with a general regime. Accordingly, those who had earlier served punishment in the form of a deprivation of liberty for grave crimes for a term of more than three years are kept in colonies with a reinforced regime. Minor females are kept only in educational-labor colonies of a general regime. Convicted persons who reach the age of 18 are appropriately transferred, depending on their crime.

For the purposes of consolidating the results of correction and reform and completing general or vocational studies, convicts who reach the age of 18 may complete their sentences in the educational-labor colony, but not after the age of 20. The decision about remaining is made on the basis of a reasoned application to the colony's chief, which must be agreed upon by the juvenile commission, and sanctioned by the procurator, according to the provisions of the corrective-labor codes of the Union Republic.

The type of corrective-labor institution and the corresponding regime for the convict to serve is defined by the court. When assigning punishment in the form of a deprivation of liberty, the court of first instance in all cases defines the type of corrective-labor institution. The court's decision as to the type of corrective-labor institution and its regime is binding upon the administration of places of confinement.

The Supreme Court of the USSR has drawn the attention of courts to the fact that a legally established order in assigning the type of colony is directed to the improvement and reform of the convicted person as well as to the prevention of fresh crimes. This order should be strictly observed.

In defining the type of corrective-labor institution, the courts take into account the nature of social danger of the crime committed and any previous convictions that make the person an especially dangerous recidivist. At the same time, criminal legislation of the Union Republics provides for the possibility for a court (pending the nature and social danger of the crime committed, the offender's personality and other circumstances) to sentence offenders to a deprivation of liberty at colonies of any type except a special regime which is designed for especially dangerous recidivists. Convicted male minors may be placed in educational-labor colonies of a general regime instead of a strict regime.

Commenting on these provisions, the USSR Supreme Court, in a decision of 1961, emphasized the necessity for courts to observe general rules established by the Corrective-Labor Law Fundamentals in assigning punishment. When defining the type of corrective-labor, the courts must take into account the nature and degree of social danger of the crime committed, the offender's personality, and mitigating and aggravating circumstances of the case. When circumstances mitigating responsibility are present, the court may take them into account and assign the convict to the corresponding type of corrective labor-colony with a milder regime. When there are circumstances aggravating responsibility, the court may in most cases assign the person to a colony of a stricter regime. In all such cases the court is obliged to explain the motives of the decision adopted in the sentence.

As a rule, a person sentenced to a deprivation of liberty must serve all the term of punishment in the same correctional-labor colony or prison or educational-labor colony. Keeping convicts during their term of deprivation of liberty in the same corrective-labor institution creates more favorable opportunities for the study of their personalities and makes it possible to establish a program and systematically accomplish educational treatment.

Article 17 of the Corrective-Labor Law Fundamentals reads: "The transfer of a person from one colony to another with the same kind of regime or from one prison to another shall be allowed in cases of sickness or of a radical change in the amount or nature of the work performed by the convicted person and also in the case of other exceptional circumstances preventing the further keeping of the convicted person in a given colony or prison."

The legislation provides for the possibility of transferring a convicted person from one colony to another with a less strict regime or from a prison to a corrective-labor colony as a measure of encouragement. Persons who have firmly chosen the road to correction may be singled out for the transfer for the remaining part of their punishment.

Nonetheless, transfers of convicts from one type of institution to another are possible in various situations.

The decision to transfer a convict from one type of regime to another is made by the court where the convict is serving his punishment upon petition by the corrective-labor institution administration.

The Corrective-Labor Law Fundamentals discuss the main principles of the assignment of persons sentenced to a deprivation of liberty to corrective-labor institutions and define the requirements for their placement. According to the regulations, persons sentenced for the first time to a deprivation of liberty shall serve their sentence, as a rule, within the bounds of the Union Republic in whose territory they resided prior to detention or conviction. In exceptional cases, to insure more successful correction and reform of the convicted offenders, they may be sent to serve sentences in the corresponding corrective-labor institutions of another Union Republic.

Persons who have previously served a sentence of deprivation of liberty, persons whose death sentence has been commuted to a deprivation of liberty by way of pardon or amnesty, persons who have been convicted of particularly dangerous crimes against the state, and convicted aliens and stateless persons are to serve their sentences in corrective-labor institutions set aside for these categories of offenders, regardless of the Union Republic in which they resided prior to detention or conviction.

In the absence of an appropriate corrective-labor institution in the Union Republic where they resided prior to detention or conviction, women sentenced to a deprivation of liberty, persons in need of special medical treatment, and minors may be sent to serve their sentences in a corrective-labor institution of another Republic.

PUNISHMENTS WITHOUT DEPRIVATION OF LIBERTY

They are executed under the auspices of the court's special inspection-officers whose task is to supervise the persons sentenced to corrective-labor and some other categories of offenders. The officers' activities are fully coordinated with those members of the public participating in the convicts' re-education.

8

POLISH PEOPLE'S REPUBLIC

Stanislaw J. Frankowski

I. GENERAL INFORMATION

Poland is over 1,000 years old. Once one of the great powers in Europe (sixteenth-seventeenth centuries), late (nineteenth century) divided by her three neighbors (Prussia, Austria, Russia), it is now a middle-size country located in the very heart of Europe. It has a population of 35 million and covers a territory of 120,359 square miles (about the size of New Mexico).

Poland is a socialist country; there is no private ownership of the major means of production. The single important exception is the land; over 80 percent is owned and cultivated by individual farmers. This is a phenomenon unique to Poland compared with other socialist countries.

Historically, Poland was almost ceaselessly a battleground, especially during World War II, when Poland lost one-sixth of her population and her economy was destroyed. In the days of final victory in 1945 Poland was literally in ruins. Its capital, Warsaw, a flourishing city of 2.5 million before the war, was almost completely destroyed; there was no family that had not lost at least one member. No wonder that even today the memories of war are still vivid and the war's effects are still felt psychologically and economically. From this point of view it is important to realize that for the first time in history all of Poland's neighbors are now her allies. It is bordered by three other socialist countries: the Soviet Union in the East, the German Democratic Republic in the West, Czechoslovakia in the South. The Baltic Sea is a natural frontier in the North.

The political order is based on the Constitution of 1952. The Constitution defines the rights and duties of Polish citizens, emphasizing such social rights as the right to work, free health care, and free education. In fact, these rights have been fully implemented in practice: there is no unemployment—on the contrary, labor is in short supply; free health care is available to everyone, including farmers; and ten-year free elementary school is mandatory. The highest governing body is an elected Parliament; all citizens over 18 are eligible to vote.

In accordance with the Constitution, the Polish United Worker's Party is a leading political force in Poland. Out of 460 members of Parliament, 261 belong to the Party, 113 to the United Peasant Association, 37 to the Democratic Association, and 49 have no political association. In the last group, there are a few representatives of the Polish Catholic movement. The second phenomenon unique to Poland is that it is a socialist country with a largely Catholic population. Many foreign visitors say Poland is a country of paradoxes, and this phenomenon is certainly one of them. On Sundays, churches are as full as a New York subway during rush hour; during Christmas season everything is paralyzed for a week. Moreover, the Polish Church plays an important social and political role in contemporary Poland. This has been clearly acknowledged by Party leader Edward Gierek when he met in 1977 with the head of the Church—Cardinal Stefan Wyszynski. In 1979 Gierek, in his official capacity as First Party Secretary, greeted Pope John Paul II.

Poland is an industrialized country. Her economic growth has been rapid since the war. In the last few years, however, the Polish economy has experienced some difficulties, especially regarding agriculture. Nevertheless, in the period from 1971 to 1976 the GNP increased on average about 9 percent per year. Per capita income is a little under $3,000, and one must take into account the many free social benefits available to citizens.

GENERAL DESCRIPTION OF THE LEGAL SYSTEM

Polish law belongs to the socialist family of laws, but historically it is the Romano-Germanic family with emphasis placed on the codified law—the law built in a systematic manner and phrased in general, abstract language. Formally, judicial decisions are not the source of law. For all practical purposes, however, Supreme Court decisions, especially the so-called practice directives, must be viewed as universally binding, legal rules. Particularly until 1970, when the old, prewar legislation was still in force, the role of Supreme Court decisions was immense.

In 1969 the new codes were passed: the Penal Code, the Code of Penal Procedure, the Code on the Execution of Penal Penalties. They all entered into force on January 1, 1970. In 1971 a Code on Violations, acts of minor importance, formally not criminal offenses, was passed. In this way the Polish criminal law almost in its entirety has become codified.

AMOUNT, STRUCTURE, AND DYNAMICS OF CRIMINALITY

Leaving aside all the reservations dealing with the value of crime statistics in measuring criminality, we may state that the crime rate in contemporary Poland is much lower than in Poland before the war. This decline has been indeed dramatic, especially in some categories of crimes. For example, while in 1937 1,306 persons were convicted of homicide, in 1966 the number fell to 306. The decrease in criminality is usually attributed to the new sociopolitical conditions which promote behavior patterns typical of a socialist society—behavior based on mutual respect and cooperation as opposed to individualism and competitiveness typical of capitalism.

The structure of recorded adult criminality in Poland may be described briefly in the following manner: Offenses against property amount to approximately 40 percent of recorded crimes, traffic offenses to about 20 percent, offenses against the person to about 15 percent, offenses against family to about 10 percent, the remaining categories of offenses to about 15 percent. Political criminality is, for all practical purposes, nonexistent. From time to time there are occasional convictions for espionage.

Road traffic offenses are on the increase and it is probable that in the years to come they will become a major problem. The relative share of other categories of crimes has remained surprisingly steady in the last 20 years.

Juvenile delinquency does not create as serious a problem as in some Western societies. It is, however, a source of concern that over 50,000 people under 17 are every year in with the criminal justice system.

SCOPE OF CRIMINAL LAW

In general, the Polish criminal law may be described as modern in the sense that it does not attempt to regulate public morals. Adultery, sodomy, prostitution, homosexuality, and self-use of drugs are not criminal offenses. In addition, social parasitism is not considered a criminal offense, unlike in most socialist countries.

Since the state is directly involved in running the economy, criminal law interferes in this sphere to a greater extent than in capitalist countries. For example, one can be criminally liable for nonfraudulent mismanagement while running a state firm if serious losses result from negligence. In a capitalist country the manager would simply be out of business.

In the last decade the process of decriminalization has taken place, including the differentiation of crimes into offenses and violations. The latter are, as a rule, minor breaches of legal order, usually of a regulatory character, that are removed from the ambit of criminal law in the strict sense by being classified as violations. They are tried by semiadministrative tribunals. In some cases, when the sentence is deprivation of liberty for up to three months the verdict is subject to judicial review. The conviction does not blur one's criminal record. From the mid-1960s the process of reclassifying minor misdemeanors into violations has been ongoing. First, minor theft, even of social property, was removed from the reach of criminal law. In the 1970s driving under the influence of alcohol became a violation. Those are just two examples illustrating the continuing process of decriminalization via reclassification of minor offenses.

STRUCTURE AND FUNCTIONING OF LAW ENFORCEMENT AGENCIES

The police are centralized, as in most countries. They are attached to the Ministry of Internal Affairs. The functions of the police (called People's Militia) are manifold: to prevent the occurrence of social conflicts, not necessarily criminal; to solve some social conflicts on the spot; and to detect and investigate crime. Regarding the latter function, it must be stressed that police do not act on their own but always under the supervision and guidance of the procurator.

The procurator's office is hierarchically organized on a countrywide basis with the procurator general at the top. The procurator general is responsible directly to the Council of State which is a collective body performing various functions, most important passing decrees when Parliament is not in session. The principal function of procurators is to ensure the strict observance of law by all state organs as well as by citizens. It may be said that the procurator is the key element in the Polish legal system, as in other socialist countries. In the field of criminal justice the procurator is the one who either conducts preliminary investigations or supervises investigations carried on by other agencies. It is up to the procurator to indict suspects and act as a public accuser at trial.

Courts are of three levels: local, district, and the Supreme Court. Most criminal cases are heard by local courts. District courts are primarily appellate in their function; they are also first instance courts in cases of serious offenses. The Supreme Court has appellate functions only. Its role is also to ensure some degree of uniformity of judicial practice. To attain this objective, the Supreme Court is empowered to issue practice directives which are binding on all the courts.

Finally, a few words about attorneys. In order to become a practicing attorney one must be admitted to the bar. The bar is a self-governing body composed of many collectives of attorneys. There are now 402 collectives of lawyers in Poland, comprising 3,468 active members specializing in court proceedings. The collective is organized on a cooperative scheme. Profits are evenly divided among its members, but only up to a certain limit; the remainder goes to those who contributed most. Expenses are shared equally. An attorney may take any case; however, in practice, especially in large cities, most attorneys specialize either in civil or criminal matters. The social prestige of attorneys is quite high and they usually make more money than either judges or procurators.

Judges, procurators, as well as attorneys must be legally educated at the university level. An apprenticeship of two years for judges and procurators and at least five for attorneys is required. As a matter of interest it may be noted that many Polish judges and procurators, especially at the lower levels, are women. Special efforts are now being made to attract more male candidates to the local courts and procurator offices in order to restore the sex balance. Currently, women constitute 20 percent of attorneys in practice but this will change rapidly, since almost half of those currently undergoing apprenticeship are female.

II. SUBSTANTIVE CRIMINAL LAW

GENERAL PRINCIPLES OF RESPONSIBILITY

There are several principles adopted by the Polish criminal law which might be of special interest to a foreign reader, but only a few can be discussed here.

Let us start with some rules related to the problem of legality. One of the fundamental principles is the rule, expressed clearly in the Penal Code, that there can be no crime and therefore no punishment without law. This means that no one can be subjected to criminal liability without having committed an act prohibited by the law in force, and no punishment other than that provided by the law may be applied. It must be stressed that, in consequence, the analogy rule, according to which criminal responsibility may also be based on the commission of the act which is only similar but not identical to the one prescribed explicitly by the law in force, is alien to the Polish criminal justice system. Incidentally, the analogy rule was known in most socialist countries, especially in the 1950s, but has never been accepted in Poland. So, for example, the Supreme Court quashed in 1977 the conviction of an offender charged with an escape from a penal institution when it turned out that the offender was, in fact, a youth kept in a special correctional center. According to the ruling, the escape from a facility of that kind is not covered by the statute which refers only to penal institutions. This example demonstrates also that although the rule of strict construction of criminal laws has not been adopted in Poland, when in doubt, the courts tend to accept in practice the interpretation.

The code further requires that an offense be not only formally prohibited by law but also socially dangerous. This statement is characteristic of socialist criminal law. This law is not satisfied with the legal prohibition: If the social danger of a formally prohibited act is not existent or insignificant, the act shall not constitute an offense. In such situations, the case may be transferred to a social court, to a disciplinary commission, or to another similar organ. The criterion of social danger reduces the scope of criminal responsibility. To avoid any misunderstanding, it must be emphasized that the social danger of an act cannot be itself make the act criminal. It is absolutely necessary that the act be formally prohibited under the threat of penalty by law. On the other hand, the concept of social danger makes, without any doubt, the law more flexible, but always in favor of the accused! Some cases may be dismissed as noncriminal if their social danger is deemed to be insignificant. This power in turn gives a great deal of discretion to law enforcement agencies, procurators, and judges charged with evaluating the degree of social danger of the act committed.

Concerning retroactivity of criminal laws, as has been clearly spelled out by the code, criminal responsibility may be incurred only when an act is prohibited by the law in force at the time of the commission of the act. This means that criminal laws in Poland are not retroactive. The principle of nonretroactivity was violated at least twice in Poland's not-too-distant past, during World War II and immediately after the War. The decree passed then provided for harsh treatment for "the traitors of the Polish Nation." This was applied to those Polish nationals who, during the war, voluntarily changed their nationality by becoming German subjects. Another decree dealt with those responsible for the September 1939 defeat against Hitlerite Germany. The two decrees were soon repealed; the second decree was never used.

The rule of nonretroactivity is not applicable, however, to judicial decisions. As a result, more extensive judicial interpretation is adopted immediately in the case under review despite the fact that the act, at the time of its commission, was considered noncriminal in light of previous judicial decisions related to the same statute. The most striking example is the Supreme Court decision in the mid-1950s pertaining to willful nonsupport of a family member. In accordance with the law in force at that time (the relevant article of the 1932 Penal Code), the offense was not committed unless the nonsupport resulted in the poverty of a person entitled to support. Nevertheless, the Supreme Court decided that it was enough if the person were bound "to live under very difficult conditions"—clearly something less than the poverty required by the law. The law remained unchanged, but the scope of criminality was de facto extended. The new interpretation of the law (quickly abandoned) was applied instantly to the offender whose case was reviewed by the Supreme Court. It must be noted that this evidently unjust solution is fairly typical of the Romano-Germanic family of law, based on the fictitious (from a practical point of view) idea that judicial decisions do not constitute the source of law. The function of the court is only to declare what the law is, not to create it. In consequence, the rule of nonretroactivity can be applied only to laws, not to judicial decisions, since those are not supposed to change the existing legal order.

Finally, a few words on the concept of "void for vagueness." In short, the concept, in the American sense, has no place in the Polish legal system. First, there is no constitutional rule requiring that criminal laws be specific. Nevertheless, all Polish scholars emphasize that it is absolutely necessary to have laws constructed in a precise and clear manner. This, in fact, is a necessary prerequisite for socialist legality. It is submitted that, with few exceptions, criminal laws in Poland meet the demand for precision and clarity, at least to an extent typical of laws belonging to the Romano-Germanic family. Second, the supremacy of Parliament is understood in such a way that all properly passed acts are unconditionally valid and may not be subject to any external control, including judicial. To avoid the possible conflict between constitutional provisions and acts of Parliament, a special Parliamentary Commission was created some years ago to check whether bills submitted meet constitutional requirements, and whether they are in accord with the existing legal order. The rule that criminal law must be clear and precise is part of this order. There seems to be a growing awareness of the importance of the issue. It is indicative that among the constitutional amendments of 1976 there was one that made the Council of State responsible for making sure the laws are in accordance with the Constitution.

AGE OF CRIMINAL RESPONSIBILITY

A person over 17 at the time of the commission of an offense incurs criminal responsibility on a general basis. A person under 17 is a juvenile and is treated differently. A juvenile over 16 may be treated as an adult in exceptional cases, if he commits one of several very serious offenses listed by the code and if it seems highly probable that correctional or educational measures designed for juveniles would be ineffective. In these cases, however, the death penalty cannot be the sentence. For less serious offenses the court may treat an offender who is 17 or 18 years old as a juvenile and apply correctional or educational measures in place of penal measures.

The last category of offenders differentiated on the basis of age is a youth: a person under 21 at the time the court verdict is passed. While imposing a penalty on a youth, the court aims first to rehabilitate him by, for example, educating him or teaching him a trade. Some scholars, commenting on this rule, reached what seems to be a very controversial conclusion: A youth should be sent to a penal institution for a period longer than that warranted by the gravity of the offense, if the longer stay in the institution enables the youth to complete his education at a given level. So, a youth should be sent to a penal institution for nine instead of six months if the court deems it advisable for the sake of rehabilitation. It is clear also in light of some other provisions of the code that a youth should be treated not always in a more lenient manner. For example, while conditionally suspending the execution of penalty the shortest trial period is regularly two years, but in the case of a youth it has been raised to three. It is clear from those examples that the increased stress on rehabilitation means sometimes increased social control.

RESPONSIBILITY OF CORPORATIONS

Criminal responsibility of corporations is unknown in Poland, as in all other socialist countries. It is claimed that the personal responsibility of corporation officers is far more effective. Further, the soundness of corporate criminal responsibility is highly questionable in our conditions: All large corporations are social (state) property. It is doubtful whether it would be advisable for the state to criminally punish its own enterprises. Some scholars claim, however, that especially in such areas as the protection of the environment, where it is almost impossible in practice to identify the individual offender and where in most cases only those on the lowest echelons are brought to responsibility, corporate criminal responsibility would be far more effective and just.

MENTAL ELEMENT *(MENS REA)*

Another basic rule of Polish criminal law is that no crime can be committed without a guilty mind *(mens rea)*. In particular, strict liability—that is, liability irrespective of offender's fault—is absolutely not accepted as a matter of principle. The code makes the following distinction regarding the forms of *mens rea:* intention (direct or oblique), recklessness, and, finally, negligence. The dividing line has been drawn by the code between intention and recklessness: All offenses based on intention are considered intentional; all other offenses, nonintentional. This distinction is of a vital importance, since nonintentional offenses are punishable only in cases provided explicitly by law. In fact, there are very few nonintentional offenses known to the code; basically, only intentional commission of an act constitutes the offense. It is imperative to have this in mind while analyzing the scope of criminalization.

Ignorance of the law does not exclude responsibility; the penalty, however, may be mitigated. Only exceptionally, when the ignorance is excusable, will the responsibility be excluded. So, for example, if a foreign tourist is misinformed by a Polish public official and, as a result, commits an illegal commercial transaction involving currency exchange, he will be absolved if his ignorance is considered unavoidable.

PREPARATION, ATTEMPT, COMPLICITY, CONSPIRACY

Mere preparation is not punishable, unless the law provides otherwise. Instances of this kind are very rare. For example, preparation to participate in espionage, treason, and similar serious offenses is punishable. Curiously enough, mere preparation to commit a homicide is not punishable. Attempt is, as a rule, punishable within the limits provided for the accomplished offense. Theoretically, one could be sentenced to death for attempted murder. In practice, attempts are obviously treated more leniently.

When dealing with complicity, the code distinguishes among the perpetrator, coperpetrator, aider, and instigator. The perpetrator is not only the person who has committed an offense by himself, but also the person who has directed the commission of a prohibited act by another. This original form of perpetration was introduced by the new code to deal with organized crime, mainly of an economic nature. In consequence, the "brain" of the group organized to appropriate social property is to be regarded as the perpetrator even if he personally has not participated in the acts of appropriation.

Aiding and instigating are considered separate and independent forms of the commission of an offense. Theoretically, the instigator and aider are criminally responsible even if the person instigated or to whom the aid was given has made no attempt to commit an offense. In practice, such cases are never prosecuted because an act whose social danger is insignificant shall not constitute an offense; this legitimizes the nonaction of law enforcement agencies.

The concept of conspiracy in the American sense is not known. Entering into agreement with another person for the purpose of committing an offense constitutes a separate form of preparation, punishable as preparation in general, in rare cases when the law explicitly provides. In addition, participation in an association having as its purpose the commission of an offense constitutes a separate offense.

DEFENSES

The code lists the following circumstances that exclude penal responsibility: necessary defense, higher necessity, insanity, and insignificant social danger.

The limits of defenses have been delineated rather broadly. For example, while describing higher necessity, the code states that it is permissible (from the point of view of criminal law) to sacrifice the good of even a slightly greater value in comparison with the good protected, if the danger is imminent and cannot be averted otherwise. It means that one can destroy a neighbor's house valued at $50,000 in order to protect his own house valued at $45,000. Even if the limits of higher necessity are exceeded, the court may apply extraordinary mitigation of the penalty or waive its imposition. The same applies to necessary defense.

The definition of insanity is composed of two parts. In the first, the code specifies that an offender, to be adjudged insane, at the time of commission of a prohibited act must have been incapable of recognizing its significance or controlling his conduct. In the second part, the code specifies the grounds of the above-mentioned psychological dysfunctions: mental deficiency, mental illness, or any other disturbance of the mental function. Insane offenders are not subject to criminal liability because they are not capable of committing an offense. In consequence, they cannot be punished. However, special preventive measures discussed later may be applied. In practice, the defense of insanity is raised only when the offense charged is a capital one. In all other cases it is better, from a defendant's point of view, to be punished than to be acquitted on reason of insanity and put in a closed institution such as a psychiatric hospital. Finally, insanity does not exclude criminal responsibility if the perpetrator has put himself into the state of insanity, for example, by excessive drinking of alcohol. Due to widespread consumption of alcohol in Poland, the legislature decided to violate the rule "no crime without guilty mind" in order to protect society from aggressive offenders acting in the state of acute insobriety. To afford them the defense of insanity would be contrary to public interest.

Other defenses such as consent, custom, and justified risk have been elaborated by scholars and judicial decisions. Special attention should be given to justified risk. This concept may be applied in many spheres of social life—for example, sports activities. Under a socialist system, in which most enterprises are social property, the concept of justified risk is important in economic life. Therefore, the code introduced the concept of "economic risk" while describing the offense of mismanagement. This offense is not committed if the alleged offender acted within the limits of admissible risk—that is, the risk justified in light of the current state of science. This clause is aimed at exonerating the managers of the state-owned enterprises who undertake risky decisions resulting in economic losses if they intended to bring an advantage to the socialized economy or to conduct technical or economic experiments.

PENAL MEASURES

Polish criminal law is, in essence, based on the idea of just punishment or "desert." Punishment is related primarily to the gravity of an offense. One could say that this is nothing but retribution in its modern shape, but free of any feeling of vengeance or hate toward the offender. Probably this description would be fair.

The proportionality of the sanction to the degree of social danger of an offense found expression first in the way in which the penal laws were built. A typical article of the Special Part of the code consists of two sections: In the first is a detailed description of a prohibited act; in the second, the minimum as well as the maximum limits of a penalty are fixed by the legislature. This minimum and maximum reflect, above all, the gravity of the given kind of an offense. The role of a judge is to fix—within the limits.

The legislature, while fixing the minimum as well as maximum limit of the penalty, takes into account the degree of social danger of the given offense in the abstract (homicide as the type of an offense) while the judge has to assess the degree of social danger of the offense of this type in specific cases (the homicide committed) and then fix the penalty accordingly.

It must be stressed, however, that the gravity of the offense is not the only factor to be taken into account by the judge in the process of sentencing. Attention should also be paid to the idea of special and general prevention. Incidentally, it is symptomatic that the code does not utilize the term "general prevention," not to mention "general deterrence," but speaks instead of the "social impact of punishment." The former term has certain connotations (intimidation of large masses of the population by excessively harsh penalties) which the legislature wanted to avoid.

The code, specifying the guidelines for judicial sentencing, attempts to reconcile the above-mentioned, sometimes conflicting, aims of punishment: to satisfy the social feelings of justice, the idea of "desert," special prevention, rehabilitation of the offender, and, finally, general prevention, forming desirable attitudes in the society at large. It may be added that it is debatable whether the above-mentioned aims of punishment have been placed by the legislature in any specific order in the sense that one aim clearly predominates. The Supreme Court seems to favor the social feeling of justice as the main guideline. However, it should be recalled that while sentencing offenders under 21, the court must give priority to special prevention.

Penal policy accepted by the code is usually described by the term "polarization of criminal responsibility." According to this concept, first-time offenders committing relatively minor offenses shall be given considerable leniency, sometimes even outside of the system of criminal justice, while recidivists and those committing especially grave crimes shall be dealt with harshly. As can easily be seen, no answer is given for how to deal with offenses of average seriousness. The policy of polarization, pursued for about the last 10 years, brought about some specific consequences, discussed in the next subsection.

KINDS OF PENAL MEASURES AND THEIR DISTRIBUTION IN PRACTICE

Polish criminal law is characterized by a great variety of penal measures at the disposal of the judge. They may be divided into penalties and preventive measures. The death penalty is described by the code as "of an extraordinary character." It must not be applied to persons who were under 18 at the time of commission of an offense, nor to a pregnant woman. In no case is the imposition of the death penalty mandatory. The judge is always empowered to impose a penalty of deprivation of liberty for 25 years, even if this penalty is not explicitly mentioned by the law under which the offender is prosecuted.

The death penalty is provided by the code (excluding the military part) for the following offenses: treason, espionage, seditious conspiracy, terrorist acts, sabotage, murder, armed robbery, and organizing or directing a major economic swindle. The last offense deserves some comment. It might seem as if the death penalty could be imposed for the offense of an economic nature. However, this is not the case according to the Polish theory of criminal law. The offense in question is directed, as has been pointed out by many scholars, against the basic economic interests of the state. The prohibited act must cause serious disturbance in the functioning of the national economy. It is the kind of economic assault against the very foundations of the system. It does not seem correct to view this offense within the framework of economic crimes the essence of which consists usually in the usurpation of social property.

The list of offenses threatened by the death penalty in Poland may seem rather extensive, but in practice it is imposed almost exclusively for especially heinous cases of murder. Annually, an average of 15 death sentences for murder are announced, yet most are commuted to 25 years of deprivation of liberty. In recent years there was one conviction using the death penalty for espionage. The sentence of death for other crimes has not been used, at least not in the 1970s.

The problem of the death penalty is not debated. In particular, there is no strong abolitionist movement. However, on most occasions it has been emphasized again and again that the death penalty as such is irreconcilable with the principles of socialism. Karl Marx's words that a society that wants to be called civilized cannot tolerate the death penalty are often quoted in scholarly writings. Nevertheless, the prevailing attitude seems to be that nowadays there are no reasons for the complete abolition of the penalty. Sometimes it is pointed out that this penalty is considered by society as the only just penalty, especially in the case of murder. In fact, a poll conducted several years ago revealed there exists strong public support for the death penalty, particularly in the case of murder and especially among those less educated and those having had a difficult childhood.

Deprivation of liberty, formerly called imprisonment, may be adjudged for a period of three months to 15 years or, exceptionally, for 25 years. If the penalty imposed does not exceed two years (or three years, in the case of a nonintentional offense), the execution of penalty may be conditionally suspended. This is often called "suspended sentence." The offender remains under supervision during the test period and several restrictions may be imposed on him. The suspended sentence is a favorite noncustodial measure of Polish judges.

Immediate imprisonment is also widely used by Polish courts, despite often-expressed opinions based on many empirical studies that it neither deters nor rehabilitates. Perhaps even more important, the average length of sentence has increased considerably in recent years. This is, one can assume, the intended consequence of the policy of polarization of criminal responsibility discussed earlier. Another result of this policy, however, is the significant decrease in the number of those sentenced to deprivation of liberty. In other words, fewer people are now sent to prison than before, but those sent remain there longer.

Limitation of liberty is a new kind of penal measure introduced by the code to limit the use of the widely criticized deprivation of liberty. Its essence is mandatory unremunerated work for social purposes performed at liberty under supervision. In addition, several restrictions are imposed, such as a prohibition on freely changing place of residence and duty to report regularly to administrative authorities. Finally, the court may impose an obligation to make restitution for damages caused or to publicly apologize to the injured person. As can be seen, in Poland the emphasis has been shifted from compulsory work as the key element of the penalty to the conditions under which the work is to be performed and to the restrictions to which the convicted person is subjected.

The newly introduced measure was, especially immediately after the code went into force, considered in practice as a substitute for the fine, not—as intended—for the deprivation of liberty. Second, it was used very rarely. Recently, the situation has changed. The percentages of limitation of freedom sentences is now quite impressive and probably this noncustodial measure will be used with increased frequency. Those sentenced are in practice required to perform simple, manual works, such as cleaning the streets, gardening, and road-building.

A fine may be levied by itself or it may be adjudged in conjunction with deprivation of liberty. In the second situation, the purpose of the fine is clearly to intensify criminal repression, to hurt an offender financially, especially when the offense was directed against social property.

For many years, fines were viewed in Poland with great suspicion as supposedly incompatible with some basic ideological premises of socialism. It was claimed that fines were a penal measure typical of capitalist systems in which almost everything, even the criminal justice system, is profit-oriented. It was also maintained that fines are, by their very nature, clearly discriminatory because they cannot seriously affect the rich while they are unbearable for the poor. For the indigent, if the fine is applied excessively, it may lead in practice to imprisonment due to nonpayment. Nowadays, the approach to fines is definitely less critical. On the contrary, it is emphasized that, particularly in a socialist country in which economic differences are not so acute, reasonably assessed fines are deprived of their discriminatory character. Moreover, it is claimed that in the future the role of fines will be increased in socialist countries as the economic conditions of all strata of population gradually improve.

Consequently, the new code gave greater power to the judge to apply fines. However, despite clear legislative intent, the percentage of fine sentences decreased. Only recently can the reverse trend be noticed. More offenders are fined now than, for example, three years ago. It must be noted that the fines adjudged are also considerably higher. Inflation is only one cause of this phenomenon.

Conditional quashing of criminal proceedings is another new measure introduced by the code. It occupies an intermediate position between the unconditional withdrawal of charges and all other penal measures. It may be applied toward offenders without prior conviction if the social danger of the act is not substantial, if the circumstances of its commission are not in doubt, and if the applicable penalty would otherwise be a fine, limitation of liberty, or deprivation of liberty not exceeding three years. The Code of Criminal Procedure empowers not only the court but also the procurator to conditionally quash the proceedings. This solution evoked some controversy, since many scholars and practitioners were opposed to conferring on the procurator the power (establishing that the person has, in fact, committed a criminal act) that is considered to be the prerogative of the judiciary. The conditional quashing has been used often in practice, mostly by procurators. In 1976, in the case of every sixth defendant deemed guilty criminal proceedings were conditionally quashed.

At this point, having outlined the system of basic penalties in Poland and having given some information on the frequency of their use in practice, we can now describe in a more comprehensive way the distribution of penal measures.

The death penalty is statistically without significance. Noncustodial penal measures—fine, limitation of liberty, suspended sentence, and conditional quashing of criminal proceedings—account for approximately 75 percent of penal measures applied in 1976. Quite recently, a strong tendency exists to apply such measures more often. On the contrary, immediate imprisonment seems to be on the decline. Nevertheless, in 1976, still 30 percent of those convicted by the courts were sent to closed penal institutions, compared to 37 percent in 1972. At the same time, the average length of sentence rose significantly to the unprecedented level of 25 months in 1976. Out of 100 persons sentenced to deprivation of liberty in 1976, only 10 received sentences under one year, but 20 over three years. The number of sentences for 25 years of imprisonment rose from 40 in 1972 to 77 in 1976.

In general, it seems to be a fair characterization of the criminal justice system in contemporary Poland to say that penal measures are being used now much less often than, for example, 10 years ago, but are more severe when used. Most scholars consider that the severity of the system is excessive.

SPECIAL TREATMENT OF JUVENILES, RECIDIVISTS, INSANE, DRUG, AND ALCOHOL OFFENDERS

With juveniles (those under 17 but over 13), measures of educational and correctional character replace penalties. The most severe measures are placement in educational or correctional centers. These are semiclosed institutions designed for rehabilitation. In practice, correctional centers to some extent may resemble adult penal institutions especially nowadays when, in regard to the latter, the stress also has been put on rehabilitation. The length of stay in the center is indeterminate, and a juvenile may be kept in an educational center until he is 18 or in a correctional center until he is 21. The decision to place a juvenile in a correctional center may be conditionally suspended. This is, in fact, a common practice of the Polish juvenile courts. In 1975, in 4,614 instances the decision was suspended and only in 1,336 instances was the immediate placement ordered.

The average length of stay in an educational center is about three years and a little over two years in correctional centers. The failure rate of those released conditionally from correctional centers is about 10 percent.

Recidivists, in particular the multiple ones, are treated in a harsh manner. The imposition of deprivation of liberty is, practically speaking, mandatory. In addition, the code introduces two other special measures. The first, protective supervision, runs for a period of three to five years from the time of release from a penal institution. The recidivist under supervision is subjected to many restrictions, including a prohibition on freely changing his place of residence. The second measure is assignment to a social readaptation center. It is designed for those multiple recidivists who have served deprivation of liberty, but are deemed not fully adapted to regular life in society. The minimum length of stay is two years; the maximum, five years. The center is a semiopen institution. Socially useful work is a basic measure of resocializing treatment. In 1975, 463 recidivists were sent to the center.

Offenders declared insane are committed to a psychiatric hospital or to another appropriate medical institution if their remaining at liberty presents a serious danger for the legal order. It must be emphasized that the commission of an act prohibited under the threat of penalty by the law in force is a necessary prerequisite for the use of this preventive measure. The length of stay is not fixed in advance and depends on treatment result. The same rules apply to those whose responsibility at the time of the commission of an offense was partially diminished. In practice this measure is used infrequently. In 1975, 253 persons were sent to psychiatric hospitals.

With drug and alcohol abusers, the code allows placement in detoxification treatment centers prior to serving the penalty adjudged. The minimum length of stay is six months, the maximum two years. The court decides on the release, taking into account results of the treatment. There are a few other code provisions dealing with drug and alcohol offenders. For example, when conditionally suspending the execution of deprivation of liberty, the court may impose a duty to refrain from abusing alcohol and/or to submit to medical treatment. In 1976 this obligation was imposed on about 30 percent of those whose penalty was conditionally suspended. The same duty may be imposed on the multiple recidivist remaining under protective supervision.

PAROLE

Every person serving a deprivation of liberty term may be conditionally released early if several specific requirements are met. First, there must exist a positive prognosis that the perpetrator, after his release, will respect the legal order—in particular, that he will not commit a new offense. The decision regarding conditional release is based above all on the evaluation of the offender's behavior in the penal institution. Conditional release may take place after at least two-thirds of the penalty has been served. When a youth is involved, at least one-half of the sentence must be served; when a multiple recidivist, at least three-fourths. The portion of the penalty remaining to be served constitutes a test period.

DIVERSION FROM THE CRIMINAL JUSTICE SYSTEM

Priority has been given in Poland to the principle of legality, which requires that every person who has committed an offense should incur criminal responsibility. The concern seems to be how to make the system of criminal justice flexible enough so that minor breaches of the law are not dealt with excessively harshly. Conditional quashing of criminal proceedings is the best example of this concern. In general, the new code gives many opportunities to deal in a humane manner with offenses of less severe importance. It must also be recalled that many acts previously considered misdemeanors are now classified as semiadministrative violation. Probably this is the most effective diversionary method that has been adopted in Poland.

III. CRIMINAL PROCEDURE

Criminal trials in Poland are not as spectacular as in some other countries. In most cases there are no surprises: all the evidence is known in advance to the court and to the parties. It has been gathered during the pretrial investigation conducted either directly by the procurator or by the People's Militia

under the procurator's guidance and supervision. The emphasis put on pretrial investigation is one of the principal features of Polish criminal procedure. The second characteristic feature is active participation of the court
during the trial. In practice, a trial is aimed at verifying the accuracy of
evidence collected during the investigation. The leading role in this process
is played by the judge. He is supposed to be familiar with all the relevant
findings of the investigation as they appear in the files submitted with the
indictment, a document in which the charges and the evidence in the case are
specified in detail. It is up to the judge to hear the accused, to interrogate the
witnesses and experts, and to undertake all actions he deems necessary to
reach a just verdict. For the duty of the Polish judge is not to decide who is
the winner in a duel played in front of him between the defense attorney and
the accusing party, but to establish the guilt or innocence of the accused by
all legally accepted means. With some exaggeration it might be said that the
defense attorney, the accusing party, and other parties play only supporting
roles. For example, their lack of initiative would not relieve the court from
the duty of clarifying a given matter if this seems indispensable from the
point of view of justice. If the defense attorney fails to summon an important
witness who might help establish the accused's alibi, the witness should be
summoned by the judge.

ADVERSARY OR INQUISITORIAL?

It may already have become clear that Polish criminal procedure is a
mixture of the so-called inquisitorial and adversary system, with "inquisi-
tional" elements prevailing especially during the pretrial investigation. According to the majority of Polish legal scholars, the advantages of an adversary system are indisputable, but only when there exists a true equality of
parties involved. If, for example, only a small fraction of defendants can
afford a good defense attorney of their choice, the adversary system in its
pure form may lead to inequality based on economic differences, not to
mention the potental for unjust verdicts. It is assumed that, especially under
socialism, where economic and social differences are not so acute, the
adversary system may be successfully implemented. In fact, in the last 20
years the tendency to introduce more adversary elements to our model of
criminal justice is very clear.

We will now briefly discuss three fundamental principles of Polish criminal procedure.

The first is called the "principle of objective truth." According to this
principle, all decisions in criminal proceedings should be based only on
well-established facts, not on legal fictions. It is therefore the duty of all
official bodies, including the procurator, to do everything in their power to
establish relevant facts, regardless of whether those facts speak in favor of

the accused. This duty is in a way restricted by another basic principle underlying Polish criminal procedure: all facts may be established only in a manner not prohibited by law.

The second principle is "objectivity of official organs." This means that all official organs must be impartial while performing their duties. The rule, closely related to the principle of objective truth, is binding not only upon the court but upon the procurator as well as on all officials dealing with a given criminal case. In consequence, the Code of Criminal Procedure provides that if for whatever reason impartiality cannot be assured, the official must be excluded from the case. It should also be mentioned that, according to the code, all officials are required to inform the parties concerned about their rights in those situations where the law so provides. In all other situations, the official is required to provide the information if this information may be useful to the party concerned.

Finally, the principle of "presumption of innocence" is without doubt one of the most fundamental rules on which our criminal procedure is based. Only the exact meaning of the principle is currently debated in Poland. Two interpretations may be distinguished: the objective and the subjective. According to the first, due to the principle discussed, a certain objective, legal situation is created: From the point of view of the legal order, the accused must be deemed innocent. According to the second interpretation, which seems to prevail among Polish scholars, all official agencies are required to consider and treat the accused as innocent until he is declared guilty by the court. The code also seems to favor the subjective interpretation while stating that the accused is deemed to be innocent until his guilt has not been proved in the manner required by the code.

The principle discussed is, in itself, of great value, but it must be accompanied by at least two other rules in order to create a fully satisfactory legal situation for the accused. The first rule deals with the burden of proof. For ages it has been a golden principle of Polish criminal procedure that the burden of proof is on the accusing party, in the sense that if this party does not succeed in proving the guilt of the accused, the accused must be declared innocent and unconditionally acquitted. On the other hand, the accused is not obliged to prove his innocence. In other words, the failure to prove guilt is detrimental to the "interests" of the accusing side. The second rule strictly connected with the presumption of innocence is often referred to as *"in dubio pro reo, in dubio pro mitius."* As expressed briefly by the code, "doubts that cannot be eliminated must not be interpreted in disfavor of the accused." Again, there exist different opinions among Polish scholars on the scope of this rule. Most claim the rule must be applied to questions of facts as well as of law. In each case, the version more favorable to the accused must be adopted.

RIGHTS OF A DEFENDANT

Three phases may be distinguished: preparatory proceedings, the court proceedings, and appellate proceedings. In each phase a defendant enjoys somewhat different rights.

Preparatory proceedings are conducted either directly by a procurator or by another authorized state organ, which in most cases is the militia, under the procurator's supervision and guidance. When the suspect has been identified, the first step is to inform him immediately of the charge against him. From this moment on, the suspect may hire a defense attorney. In some instances a defense attorney must be appointed ex officio. The suspect is then to be interrogated, but has the privilege of refusing to answer any question asked. He may demand that the reasons justifying the charge be put in writing and delivered to him. Later, the suspect, or his defense attorney, may submit motions to have certain actions performed during preparatory proceedings. He may also request to participate in the actions undertaken by an investigating agency. In some cases the suspect's presence is mandatory—for example, if certain actions cannot be repeated, such as a highly complicated reconstruction of events which allegedly had taken place. Upon the completion of preparatory proceedings, the suspect has an unrestricted right to acquaint himself with all collected evidence which has been selected by the investigating agency to be used in his case. Also, a defense attorney must be given access to the files. Then each of them may file a motion that certain actions be performed to supplement the evidence. If it is decided to perform the actions indicated by the suspect or his defense attorney, the latter's request to be present during these actions cannot be denied. On average, preparatory proceedings do not take more than six weeks. Of course, some investigations take much longer, especially when there are several suspects and many witnesses and experts involved, as is often the case in large-scale fraudulent usurpations of social property.

It must be emphasized that preparatory proceedings are the crucial part of criminal proceedings in Poland, since at this stage the most vital decision is rendered: to prosecute or to quash the proceedings (unconditionally or conditionally). It has been a well-established practice for many years that doubtful cases are not sent to court. In consequence, the decision to prosecute is practically tantamount to conviction. The conviction rate in Poland is in consequence very high—about 95 percent.

The next step is the preparation of the indictment. A written form is required. The public prosecutor (who is in most cases the procurator) must immediately notify the suspect (who from this moment on is called the accused) about this action.

Now starts the next phase—the court proceedings. The court, having examined whether the indictment conforms to the formal requirements, sends a copy of it to the accused. Later, the date of the main trial is set and the accused must be notified about it at least seven days in advance. Since there is no problem of court congestion, the case is usually scheduled to be heard within two or three weeks.

The trial takes place in a courtroom, some architectural elements of which are worthy of our attention. As almost everywhere in continental Europe, at the very end of the room there is a rostrum, approximately two feet high, on which stands a large, rectangular table. Judges sit in front of the table. On their right, by the same table, sits a public prosecutor and on the left, a court clerk recording the proceedings. The accused sits on a bench at ground level on the extreme right. Just in front of him is a bench for his attorney so that they can communicate freely. On the opposite side there are two benches: one for a private prosecutor or for a civil plaintiff and one for their attorneys. A witness box is in front of the main table. It is intriguing that the public prosecutor sits on the same level as the judges, while the defense attorney is on lower ground with his client. The explanation is usually given that both the public prosecutor and the judge represent the state, so there should be no distinction made in regard to location.

The trial begins with a brief judicial interrogation of the accused as to his name, address, occupation, family situation, criminal record, and so on. Then the prosecuting party reads the indictment. Afterward, the judge addresses the accused by asking him whether he understood the charge, whether he pleads guilty or not guilty, and whether he intends to offer any explanations. Also at this stage the accused has the unrestricted right to remain silent or not to answer specific questions if he deems it advisable. As recalled in 1977 by the Supreme Court, this way of defense must *not* be interpreted in disfavor of the accused. In practice, the accused usually pleads not guilty and decides to present his version of the events, considering it to his advantage to do so at the beginning of the trial. The accused's explanations usually are not interrupted by the judge. After he has finished, the judge will ask questions. Already at this point the main purpose of the judicial activity is to establish the truth. Therefore, some of his questions will be absolving, some accusatory; some throwing a favorable light on the accused, some clearly demonstrating his blame. When the judge completes his interrogation, the floor is given to a public prosecutor, then to a defense attorney, assuming that, as in a typical case, there are no other parties involved. It must be emphasized that the accused does not testify under oath, but merely voluntarily offers explanations that will be evaluated as any other evidence.

Later, witnesses and experts are called and other evidence is presented. As before, the leading role is played by the judge. He is the one who starts asking questions and asks most of them, while other parties sit mute, taking notes. Obviously, the public prosecutor, as well as the accused and his attorney, also have a right to question people summoned by the court and they exercise this right in almost every instance. The judge may waive or modify any question, since he is in charge of conducting the trial in the manner required by law.

The trial ends with concluding speeches. The prosecutor speaks first, followed by other parties such as the civil plaintiff. The final word belongs to the defense attorney and to the accused. If the prosecutor decides to reply, the defense attorney and the accused must be given the floor once again. This is a rule without exception—the defending side is always allowed to speak last. In a typical case, the court hearing takes no more than one and a half hours. Concluding speeches are usually condensed, free of rhetoric. Sometimes a defense attorney speaks longer than might seem necessary, mostly to show his client that he is doing his best.

After the speeches, the court recesses to prepare the verdict. The debate is secret and only the judges and the court clerk may be present. No records are made. First, the question of guilt or innocence must be decided. As in all other circumstances, a majority vote is binding. The professional judge casts his vote last. If the outcome is against the accused, as is usually the case, the debate centers on the kind and amount of punishment. When this issue is resolved, the verdict is immediately announced in public. The reasons justifying the verdict must be orally presented. This presentation may be compared to a postscriptive summing-up of the case during which a chronological account and review of the events, the legal aspects of the case, and the reasons justifying the penalty imposed are discussed at length. As has been emphasized many times in Polish legal writings, this oral presentation is of great significance: It helps the accused understand why he was convicted and it shows the public that the court verdict had been passed after a thorough scrutiny of the case.

At the very end, the presiding judge asks the accused whether he understood the meaning of the verdict passed; if he answers in the affirmative, the judge informs him of the legal requirements regarding his right to appeal and gives him some details on this subject. In sum, a typical criminal case in Poland involving one accused defended by one attorney, a procurator, and two or three witnesses would take about two hours of courtroom time.

Appellate proceedings may be instituted by the defendant as well as the prosecutor. Both have equal rights in this respect: both may appeal against the conviction or acquittal, both may appeal against the sentence claiming the penalty is manifestly disproportionate. Their appeal may be based on either legal or factual grounds. Most appeals instituted by the procurator are in disfavor of the defendant, but sometimes it does happen that the procurator acts in favor of the convicted person because legally, as has been mentioned previously, he is obliged to seek justice. If the appeal had been instituted only by the convicted defendant, the appellate courts may not worsen his situation.

Unless the case is sent for a retrial, the verdict passed by the appellate court becomes final. At this time there is very little room for maneuver. In exceptional cases only, the so-called extraordinary appeal may be launched to the Supreme Court either by the procurator general or by the minister of justice or, finally, by the chief justice of the Supreme Court. Also, in some narrowly defined situations, there exists a possibility of reopening the case. This may happen, for example, when the conviction was based on perjury. In practice, these two legal remedies are used extremely rarely.

In 1977, about 15 percent of the verdicts passed by local courts were subject to appeal. In about two-thirds of the cases, the original verdicts were upheld by the district courts. Similarly, about 60 percent of the verdicts meted out by the district courts and subject to appeal were by the Supreme Court.

PRETRIAL DETENTION

Pretrial detention is a fairly common occurrence in Poland. Among those deprived of liberty, people awaiting trial amount to about 15 percent. The decision to detain the suspect may be made either by the procurator or by the judge. In the former instance, the decision is subject to judicial review if the suspect appeals; in the latter, it is up to a higher court to check the propriety of the measure applied.

The initial period of pretrial detention must not exceed three months. In practice, the suspect remains in custody no longer than that, since investigations in Poland are performed swiftly. Only in exceptional cases the period of pretrial detention may be extended to six months and, later, for a term necessary to complete the investigation. In the latter instance, the decision is to be taken by the district court. The suspect's appeal will be reviewed by the Supreme Court.

The code specifies several reasons justifying the application of pretrial detention, such as (a) danger that the suspect may hide or tamper with evidence; (b) the suspect is charged with a felony or is a multiple recidivist; or (c) the suspect is charged with an offense of considerable social danger. Most decisions rely on the last clause, which has been the subject of immense criticism in scholarly writings for being vague.

As a rule, those under pretrial detention are later convicted by the courts. Almost always they are sentenced to immediate imprisonment. Incidentally, the time spent in custody must be fully credited to the penalty adjudged. As some studies have demonstrated, the chances of being convicted are much higher for those awaiting trial in custody; also, the sentences meted out are usually harsher. Finally, it must be mentioned that instead of pretrial deten-tion, bail or police supervision may be applied. It is also possible for a third party to guarantee the suspect's further participation in the case. In practice, these measures are used infrequently.

SPECIAL MODES OF CRIMINAL PROCEEDINGS

Regarding petty offenses of a hooligan character (a legal term defined in the Penal Code) speedy proceedings may be adopted. The idea behind this mode of criminal proceedings is very simple: offenders committing offenses manifestly violating the public feeling of safety should be brought to justice quickly to demonstrate that the law will be effectively enforced against them. The proceedings are therefore initiated by the militia's information; no formal indictment is necessary. The offender must be brought to court within 48 hours and his case must be heard immediately. The sentence is subject to appeal within seven days instead of the regular 14 days. The appellate court must review the case within one month.

Also, so-called summary proceedings are known in Poland. While deal-ing with minor offenses, some procedural rules are not applied. The most substantial deviation from standard proceedings is that the case may be mentioned that plea-bargaining, in its American form, is unknown. The court conviction may take place only after a court trial. Any attempt to influence the judge's decision constitutes a criminal offense in Poland.

LAY PARTICIPATION IN CRIMINAL PROCEEDINGS

The jury system, as known in the United States, does not exist in Poland. There are, however, other forms by which lay participation in criminal proceedings have been achieved perhaps in a greater extent than in many other countries. First, it must be emphasized that about 90 percent of crimi-nal cases heard by the local courts are tried by a panel comprised of one professional judge and two people's assessors, elected by the local govern-ment agencies for a period of four years. Each member of the panel has equal rights. It may therefore happen that the professional judge will be in a minority and the verdict will be the result of the joint efforts of the two assessors. If we take into account that only a slight percentage of the district court's sentences are successfully appealed, the role played by the people's assessors must be viewed as considerable.

Another form of lay participation in criminal proceedings in Poland is a social representative. He is not a party in the trial but may be admitted by the court on a special basis. He may submit motions to the court, or he may be given the floor, but he is not supposed to act in favor of or against the accused. His only role is to represent the public interest allegedly harmed by the offense. There are several civic organizations are empowered to appoint a social representative who would act on their behalf. For example, the League of Polish Women is entitled to appoint a social representative to take part in the case involving mistreatment of a wife by her husband. Of course, it is up to the court to decide whether to admit a social representative appointed by a civic organization. In practice, there are very few cases in which social representatives take part.

Finally, on several occasions the Penal Code requires the participation of the public if certain measures are to be applied. For example, while conditionally quashing the proceedings the court may require that surety be given by a social organization to which the perpetrator belongs, or by a collective where he works. Similar conditions may be attached when the decision to conditionally suspend the execution of the penalty of deprivation of liberty is at stake.

IV. EXECUTION OF PENAL MEASURES
(CORRECTIONS)

AIMS AND BASIC PRINCIPLES

The Code on the Execution of Penalties states clearly that the only aim of the execution of deprivation of liberty is to rehabilitate the offender, to accustom him to socially useful work and thereby prevent his relapse into crime. It is highly significant that no reference to the idea of general deterrence has been made in this context. The code further specifies that penalties "shall be executed in a humanitarian manner and with respect for the human dignity."

USE AND IMPLEMENTATION OF DEATH PENALTY

When the court sentence imposing the death penalty becomes legally valid, the files must be sent to the Council of State (the collective organ exercising functions of the Head of State) for review. The sentence is not implemented until the Council of State announces its decision whether the sentence should be carried out or commuted. In practice, in approximately two-thirds of the cases the death sentence is commuted (usually to 25 years of deprivation of liberty, sometimes to 15, but almost never to shorter terms). If the Council of State decides not to commute the death sentence, the court verdict is implemented immediately. The execution is imposed by hanging. Only the next of kin, the defense attorney, and prison officials may be present. The mass media always report that the sentence has been carried out. Only details such as the name of the person and the nature of the offense are given.

EXECUTION OF DEPRIVATION OF LIBERTY

In the years 1944-1955, the administration of penal institutions was under
the authority of the Ministry of Internal Affairs (then called the Ministry of
Public Security). At the same time, it was the responsibility of the Procura-
tura to supervise implementation of the penalties in accordance with the law.
Because the ministry was formally and factually independent from the Pro-
curatura, a procurator charged with the supervision of penal institutions was
in practice concerned mostly with purely legal aspects of imprisonment (the
length of stay, legal validity of a warrant, and so on) and did not interfere in
the internal life of penal institutions. In 1956, the administration of penal
institutions was transferred to the Ministry of Justice (a special department
charged with the administration of penal institutions was then created). This
move was considered a major step toward the elimination of serious abuses
of law which were fairly prevalent in the early 1950s. The supervision
performed by the procurator, however, was retained. The above model was
accepted by the code. It declares, first of all, that all penal institutions are
subordinate to the minister of justice (the special department in charge of
penal institutions is now called the Main Bureau of Penal Institutions).
Second, the code introduced two new institutions: the penitentiary court and
the penitentiary judge. The code specifies that supervision exercised by a
penitentiary judge shall consist primarily of ensuring the propriety of the
execution of the penalty and particularly the methods and measures of
penitentiary treatment employed. The supervision exercised by the procurator primarily includes ensuring the legality of the execution of the penalty
and observance of the rights and duties of inmates. It must be noted that the
penitentiary judge and the prosecutor have an unlimited right to enter the
premises of any institution. They also have the right to examine documents
and demand explanations from administrators, to converse in private with
inmates, and to investigate inmates' grievances and petitions.

The code declares that all inmates shall be classified, directed to the
appropriate penal institution, and assigned an appropriate regimen (depending on the regimen, inmates have different duties and privileges). The purpose of classification is to prevent mutual demoralization and to create
favorable conditions for the application of individualized treatment measures. The classification group to which an inmate belongs is determined by
a penitentiary commission, the collective organ existing within each penal
institution. The type of penal institution and the conditions of incarceration
are prescribed either by the court imposing the sentence or by the penitentiary court. The latter is also empowered to order modifications in the
process of the execution of penalty; only exceptionally may the decision be
made by the penitentiary commission. It must be noted that this practice is a
consequence of the principle of progression accepted by the Polish correc-

tional system. Depending on progress in the rehabilitative process, the inmate may be transfered from one type of penal institution to another, and the regimen under which he serves the penalty may also be changed (for the better, which is the predominant rule, but also for the worse).

The classification group, the type of penal institution, and the conditions of incarceration are supposed to be determined on the basis of such factors as age, previous criminal record, length of sentence, susceptibility to resocialization, and character of the offense. In practice, it is the gravity of the offense which decisively influences the decision. It is especially true in the first stage of the execution of penalty. Before we describe penal institutions, it must be made clear that they are conceptually different from prisons in a traditional sense (a huge building behind thick walls where convicts are kept in absolute isolation either doing literally nothing or performing hard, sometimes senseless work). Instead, penal institutions in Poland are supposed to be at the same time educational and rehabilitative centers as well as economically productive units, actively reshaping convicts' attitudes in socially desirable directions.

The Polish correctional system is highly complex and diversified. There are six types of institutions. In addition, inmates placed in whatever types of penal institution may be subjected to one of four different regimes: mitigated, basic, intense, and severe. Briefly, the six types of penal institutions may be described as follows. Labor-centers are semiopen institutions in which two types of regimes (basic, mitigated) may be applied. They are for convicts who begin serving a penalty not exceeding five years. In practice, the majority of convicts are placed in labor-centers. Ordinary penal institutions are for those serving long-term sentences and for those convicted of offenses of a hooligan character. Transitional penal institutions are open-type institutions for those who have served at least two years in another type of institution and who are in the last stage of serving the penalty. Youth institutions are for those who are under 21 and who were under 21 at the commencement of their term and have a relatively short time to serve. The emphasis in these institutions is on vocational training and sports activities. Special penal institutions are reserved for multiple recidivists. In those institutions the mitigated regimen is not applied.

Penal institutions for those requiring special medical-educational measures house alcoholics, drug abusers, and all convicts with mental disturbances. Those who require these special measures constitute at least 10 percent of all inmates.

In this context mention must be made of a new form of treatment for alcoholics. These prisoners are to be treated either in special dispensaries or wards. It is interesting to note that the dispensaries are organized and run by the health service of the penal institution with the help of the local health authority providing the necessary medical staff, equipment, and medicines. The ward for addicts is also a unit run by the local health service where intensive medical treatment is applied to imprisoned alcoholics. In 1977, there were 11 such wards with a total of 700 beds. Their number is to be increased to 15 with 1,000 beds. A total of 23 dispensaries were in existence in 1977. In December 1976, over 9,000 alcoholics requiring medical treatment were registered in penal institutions with 3,500 actually undergoing treatment.

The effectiveness of the treatment is difficult to be ascertained. In most cases the prisoner is released before the treatment has been completed. A survey carried out in the early 1970s revealed that at least 45 percent of those treated abstained from alcohol for at least six months. The percentage decreased to 25 percent after one year. The last test estimates are more optimistic: 60 percent abstaining after six months, and 40 percent after one year. Conclusive data are still lacking.

The sentenced person is obligated to perform assigned work or to pursue training, to observe the order and discipline of the institution, to maintain proper relations with other inmates, and to have a conscientious attitude toward work. It is clear, however, from the foregoing summary of pertinent code regulations that emphasis has been placed on socially useful, productive work as the inmates' basic duty. In practice, it is strictly enforced. The employment of the sentenced person is also considered to be one of his basic rights. Remuneration for the work performed and working hours correspond with generally accepted standards. However, substantial deductions to cover maintenance costs of inmates and for other purposes are made; as a result the convict receives not less than 19 percent from the amount due for labor.

The kinds and scale of rewards are specified in the Prison Rules. The code mentions only that rewards are granted by the director of the penal institutions to those who distinguish themselves by their exemplary attitude and particularly by diligence in work or training. The code also declares that the highest reward is a pass to leave the penal institution for a period up to five days.

The code is more detailed when describing the most severe disciplinary penalties, such as reduction in the remuneration for work performed, deprivation or limitation of visits, a hard bed in a solitary cell for up to 14 days, and placement in an isolated section from one to six months. Penalties are imposed by the director of the institution, who may request an opinion from the penitentiary commission. Placement in an isolated section requires the prior consent of the penitentiary judge. It is important to observe that the judge is obligated to annul or modify any decision concerning the disciplinary punishment if that decision is contrary to law or to the principles of penitentiary policy.

EXECUTION OF NONCUSTODIAL MEASURES

The way the limitation of liberty is carried out in practice depends mainly on the type of work imposed. In general, it is the duty of the local government to decide on the type of work performance. In rural areas, sentenced persons are usually required to work manually on such communal projects as building roads or constructing drainage. In the city, they are usually directed to garden or to clean public parks or streets. In all cases, the court exercises overall supervision to ensure that the penalty is imposed properly both from the legal and educational point of view.

9

GERMAN DEMOCRATIC REPUBLIC

Erich Buchholz and Horst Luther

I. GENERAL INFORMATION

The German Democratic Republic (GDR) was established on October 7, 1949 as a socialist German state on the territory of the former Soviet occupation zone. To implement the Potsdam Agreement signed on August 2, 1945 by the US, Great Britain, the Soviet Union, and, later, France, a new, consistently and truly democratic, peace-loving society was established. With new political and ownership relations and the leadership of the Socialist Unity Party of Germany (SED) this antifascist, democratic, antimperialist society has gradually developed into a socialist society.

Free from exploitation, oppression, and economic dependence, every citizen of the GDR has equal political, economic, social, and cultural rights and manifold opportunities to develop his abilities in the socialist community for the welfare of society and for his own benefit. The right to work is guaranteed. The Constitution stipulates—and this is a reality in our country—that every citizen has the right and free choice of employment in accordance with social requirements and personal qualifications. Men and women, adults and young people get equal pay for equal work; an equal right to education for all citizens is ensured by compulsory, general ten-year secondary schooling or vocational training, both of which are free of charge, as well as by opportunities of further education. Every citizen has the right to the protection of his health and working capacity. Material security and medical care are granted free of charge in cases of illness and accident, as is social care in the case of invalidity and old age. Marriage, family, and motherhood are under the special protection and promotion of the socialist state.

The GDR is located in central Europe. Neighboring countries include the Federal Republic of Germany, the Polish People's Republic, and the Czechoslovak Socialist Republic. Its territory covers 41,923 square miles and contains approximately 17 million inhabitants (density about 400 people per square mile). Its capital is Berlin, the only city with over one million people.

The Constitution of 1968, as amended in 1974, established the foundations of the socialist social and state system, the status of the citizens and communities in socialist society, the structure and system of state management, and the principles of the administration of justice. As to combating crime, the Constitution says that it is the joint concern of the socialist society, the state, and all its citizens to combat and prevent crime and other violations of law. To an increasing extent this is becoming part of extensive social planning.

The following are the most important legal acts in combating crime:

(a) The 1968 Penal Code as amended in 1974 and 1977.

(b) The 1968 Code of Criminal Procedure as amended in 1974 and 1977.

(c) The 1974 Law on the Constitution of Courts (Court Constitution Act).

(d) The 1968 Law on the Social Courts.

(e) The 1977 Law on the Procurator's Office.

(f) The 1977 Law on the Execution of Penalties involving Imprisonment (Penal Execution Act).

(g) The 1977 Law on the Reintegration of Citizens released from Prison into Social Life (Reintegration Act).

The development of crime in the GDR is distinctly different from that in prewar Germany; that is, it has shown a downward trend. After liberation from Hitlerite fascism the comparatively high crime rate caused by the war and the economic, intellectual, and cultural chaos left behind by fascism were considerably decreased in a relatively short time. This is credited to overcoming the aftermath of the war and beginning the new democratic development. The further stabilization of the new society added to the downward trend of crime. The trend, irrespective of temporary variations, continues to determine the dynamics of crime development in the GDR.

Similarly, the structure, quality, and character of crime have changed considerably. In the GDR there are no such phenomena as professional criminals, criminal underworld, gangs or rackets, counterfeitings, or crimes involving drugs or narcotics. Armed robberies and similar serious crimes are virtually unknown. Violent crimes occur rarely.

Crime, the rate of which is low, mostly consists of minor thefts and frauds. Motoring offenses, including fatal accidents, account for a relatively high number of punishable acts. Of some importance are also some sex offenses (among them a few serious cases), a few cases of bodily injury, crimes against public order and general security, and a few planned and organized serious crimes against state-owned national property. Voluntary manslaughter and murder occur very seldom.

This overall picture of crime has been rather constant for years. In contrast, the crime rate of the Federal Republic of Germany (FRG) has been constantly increasing since 1953, and the crime rate in the FRG per 100,000 inhabitants is about seven times higher than in the GDR. We attribute these diametrically opposed trends in crime and resulting significant quantitative and qualitative differences in the two German states to their contrary social developments. The entirely different development of crime in the neighboring FRG and the underlying social causes exert, no doubt, an influence on the development of crime in the GDR.

The success in combating punishable acts is a result of the construction of a socialist society in which the socio-economic basis of crime has been abolished, social security for all citizens has reached a high level, and human rights are fully guaranteed. Consequently, crime in the GDR has become a phenomenon which is absolutely foreign to the basic socioeconomic and politicosocial structure of society. Under present social conditions, the prevention of crime grows in importance. The favorable social prerequisites are also manifest in the citizens' willingness to participate actively, and in many ways, in preventing punishable acts. This participation is encouraged and recognized by society.

ORGANS OF ENFORCEMENT

The organs of law enforcement are court, procurator, investigating agencies, lawyers, and the agencies responsible for the execution of sentences.

The GDR has state and social courts. State courts are the district and county courts whose responsibility corresponds to the territorial and administrative division of the country. A Supreme Court controls the jurisdiction of all other courts. Two kinds of social courts exist: one is the dispute commissions found in enterprises and institutions and the other is neighborhood dispute commissions in residential areas and cooperatives.

Whereas the state courts employ professional judges, the 52,910 lay judges and the members of the social courts work exclusively on a voluntary basis. The German Democratic Republic has 25,358 dispute commissions with 225,623 citizens, and 5,124 neighborhood dispute commissions with 53,448 citizens. Social courts review and solve annually over 20,000 cases involving criminal offenses. Minor breaches of law (violations) are not included in this number.

All professional judges, lay judges, and members of social courts are elected by popular representative bodies or directly by the citizens. They are independent in their jurisdiction and bound only by law. In case of violation of their legal obligations they may be recalled by the popular representative bodies. For the period of their court duty, the lay judges are released from work, paid their normal wage, and reimbursed for expenses.

Jurisdiction in criminal cases is incumbent upon independent state and social courts only. Punishments may be inflicted only by the state courts. The law requires that no one will be deprived of his legally guaranteed judge. Special courts are inadmissible. As a rule, courts hear and decide on criminal cases as collective bodies consisting of one professional judge and two lay judges in courts of first instance or three judges in courts of second instance. Most criminal procedures are decided by district or social courts. County courts as courts of first instance hear and decide major offenses exclusively.

The procurator's office is of key importance for uniform socialist state power. Its task is to see that socialist legality is strictly observed in all spheres of state and social life. It guides the combat against punishable acts and ensures that persons having committed crimes are called to account in court. The procurator general is elected by the People's Chamber for the duration of its electoral term. The People's Chamber may recall him at any time. All procurators of the counties and districts are subordinate to him; he appoints and recalls them.

The investigating organs of the Ministry of the Interior, the Ministry of State Security, and the Customs Administration are responsible for investigation in criminal procedures under the control of the procurator. The procurator is entitled to give binding instructions for the investigation and to cancel illegal regulations and measures. Appeal against decisions and actions taken by the investigating organs are decided by the procurator.

In criminal procedures lawyers have the task of defending accused and indicted persons. Most lawyers belong to lawyers' collectives set up in all counties. In addition, there are lawyers with private practices who have the same rights and duties as counsels for the defense. The lawyers' collectives work on the basis of self-administration of their members under the guidance of the executive boards and of a Central Auditing Commission. They are not state institutions.

II. SUBSTANTIVE CRIMINAL LAW

The laws (especially the Penal Code) passed by the supreme popular representative body outline in a comprehensive way prerequisites and limits, content and scope of personal criminal responsibility in the GDR.

The principle "No punishment and no crime without law" *(Nulla poena, nullum crimen sine lege)* applies without reservation. Retroactivity and analogous application of penal laws to the disadvantage of the person concerned are inadmissible. Equality before the law is guaranteed as a fundamental principle of socialist justice. No one may be prosecuted or discriminated against for reasons of nationality, race, religious beliefs, philosophy, or class or social stratum.

The only ground for criminal liability is a punishable act—that is, a culpably committed act which is either incompatible with social conduct or endangers society as described in the penal law. A distinction is made between crimes endangering society *(verbrechn),* about five percent of all criminal acts; and offenses incompatible with social conduct *(vergehen).* All criminal acts due to negligence, even the most serious ones, are offenses.

The adoption of the 1968 Penal Code meant a considerable restriction of spheres subject to the penal law (so-called decriminalization). This was especially apparent among economic offenses, sex offenses, and acts of negligence as well as formerly criminal acts now considered violations or infringements of civil or labor law. Since 1968 the following offenses, among others, have ceased to be subject to the penal law: simple illicit sexual relations (homosexuality); the obtainment, by false pretenses, of extramarital intercourse; adultery; squandering family possessions; denial of help for a pregnant woman; resistance to forestry officials and forest guards, hunting officials and gamekeepers, and fishery officials and guards; simple cases of disturbing domestic peace and security; instigation of acts of violence or instigation to class struggle; misuse of sermons for nonreligious purposes; and unauthorized issue of negotiable instruments. The whole immense complex of the 1948 legislation on penalties for economic offenses and numerous other so-called supplementary penal laws, as well as provisions on bankruptcy (or the Bankruptcy Code) and on punishable acts committed for personal gain, and usury were eliminated from the penal law. Various offenses due to negligence were also eliminated from the supplementary penal laws. Criminal liability due to negligence was generally limited through the new provisions contained in the General Part of the Penal Code. Moreover, those valid penal provisions which are, as far as their number is concerned, easy to survey and which are not covered by the Penal Code are published fully in a list which has to be updated periodically.

The main purpose of legislation in the GDR is to ensure that criminal liability is limited to acts endangering society or incompatible with social conduct which must be prosecuted with no other but penal measures. On the other hand, it may be necessary in individual cases to criminalize certain acts, especially on the basis of international conventions (such as hijacking) or in connection with scientific and technological progress (for example, environmental protection). Sometimes it is necessary to sharpen criminal liability. Prosecution is also restricted by the creation of offenses that are prosecuted only at the request of the injured party.

The penal law of the GDR knows only individual personal liability of persons of responsible age (over 14 years) and sound mind—that is, not institutions, organizations, or enterprises. In the case of juveniles (14 to 18 years of age), individual responsibility for the criminal acts committed by them must be clearly established.

The commitment of persons of unsound mind (insane persons) to an appropriate medical institution may be ordered by virtue of a decision of the civil court, if this is imperative for the public interest.

In the case of certain recidivists, legislation provides for more severe punishments and for the application of special measures connected with reintegration into society after release from the penal institution. Beyond this, there are no special provisions for distinct categories of offenders.

Criminal liability presupposes that there is a causal connection between the incriminated act and the harm brought to society or individual citizens (or even only exposing them to danger) and that the offender has caused the effects of his action (or omission) through his own fault—with intent or through negligence. There is no objective liability.

Guilt consists, according to the Penal Code, of the fact that the offender has committed, by acting in an irresponsible manner, a punishable act in terms of law. In the case of guilt through negligence, an offender will be called to account only if he expected the harmful consequences of his action, or deliberately acted contrary to his duty, or if he was unaware of the breach of duty which in itself constituted neglect of duty. In this way, the scope of negligent offenses has been restricted. The establishment of a juvenile's guilt and especially of his degree of guilt has to allow for the special characteristics conditioned by his development.

If the offender is unaware of the circumstances constituting the definitional elements of the offense, criminal liability does not apply unless the offender's lack of awareness of these circumstances is based on negligence as provided for by law.

To exclude excessive demands made on the individual in certain situations, the penal law of the German Democratic Republic includes—in addition to the generally accepted defenses, justifications, and legal reasons for exemption, such as self-defense, state of distress, and undue influences—a number a provisions pertaining to the exclusion of guilt. Of special importance are the provisions on the conflict of duties and on justifiable risk, which, though restricted by law to a few economic issues, is theoretically of a more general application.

Attempt is punishable in the cases provided for by law. Even mere preparation is punishable in cases of certain especially serious criminal acts.

As forms of participation, the law distinguishes between perpetrators (in the case of intentional offenses), accomplices, abettors, and aiders. Some special cases of punishable acts against property, public order, and bodily security are considered to be more dangerous if committed by a conspiracy.

There are some justifiable exceptions to the principle that every offender has to be called to account for his act. In order to do justice to the specific circumstances of the individual case, the law provides for the possibility of inflicting no punishment if the offender shows a distinct positive change in his attitude and if the punishable act has, as a result of the development of socialist social relations, caused no harmful effects. For example, neither a penalty nor any other measure following criminal liability is applied to an offender against property who, shortly after the offense, has redressed or begins to redress of his own accord and for honest motives the damage caused by him, provided that his conduct after the offense gives reason to believe that he will respect the legal order in the future. This implies that an application of penal measures in the case of this offender will no longer be necessary from the view of the reeducational tasks inherent in the penal law. Penalties and other measures following criminal liability are also dispensed with if—in the case of an economic offense, for instance—the social, and particularly the economic, conditions have changed so fundamentally since the commission of the offense that this very offense no longer endangers society. This implies that, from a social viewpoint, a punishment would be anything but appropriate. Should the reasons stated in the Penal Code not fully apply, an extraordinary commutation of the sentence may be granted.

PENAL MEASURES

Punishments and other measures following criminal liability do not serve the purpose of retaliation or revenge. Their objective is to protect society, to prevent punishable acts, and to reeducate any offender to observe the law. The penal laws of the GDR cover a wide range of different punishments and other measures following criminal liability. This enables the courts to do justice to a high degree to any individual offender and to deliver fair decisions.

For a long time not just punishments have been inflicted as legal consequences of punishable acts. Remarkable in this respect are the reeducational measures ordered by the social courts, which apply to nearly one-third of all punishable acts. These reeducational measures include compensation for damages, apology to the injured party, reprimand, or imposition of a fine.

In the case of juveniles, the matter may be transferred to the youth services agencies or to collective groups or institutions capable of reeducating young people (for example, schools) so that only about two-fifths of all penal matters involving juveniles come before a court. The court may impose special duties on a juvenile (such as work during leisure-time) that do not constitute a criminal punishment.

Noncustodial measures—probation, fines, and public reprimands—which for many years have been imposed in about one-third of all cases are increasingly important. Of these three, sentences of probation account for most of the punishments, and this approach clearly demonstrates the connection of state and social influence on the offender, which is typical of socialist criminal law. The offender is given the opportunity to prove himself and redress injuries. The probationary period is fixed by the court for one to three years; if the conditions of probation are broken, imprisonment from three months to two years is possible.

In the vast majority of cases the process of probation is successful so that no prison sentence has to be ordered. When revocation of probation occurs, most often it is due to the fact that the person placed on probation commits another punishable act during the probation period, as with about 15 percent of all persons placed on probation.

If material damage has been caused, the offender is under obligation to redress this damage during the period of probation. Additional obligations may be imposed with a view to supporting probation and giving it a lasting effect (for example, obligations such as not to change one's job, to engage in certain leisure-time activities, to avoid certain places, and to use one's earnings in a certain way for one's family and for other commitments).

A special form of assuming responsibility for the reeducation and proper conduct of the offender by society is a guarantee for the offender undertaken by his work team or some other collective group to promote his reeduction. To ensure social reeducation is, in fact, the legal duty of the managers of enterprises and institutions, of heads of departments, as well as of the executive bodies of social organizations.

As far as juveniles are concerned, punishment not involving imprisonment may be applied to a larger extent. Most important, probation is intended to secure the completion of school or vocational training.

Prison sentences are inflicted in only about one-third of all punishable acts. Usually they are inflicted in serious cases and in the case of particularly obstinate recidivists, even if their punishable acts were not very serious.

The minimum prison sentence is six months (in exceptional cases, three months) and the maximum is two years in minor cases. In major cases (felonies), the maximum is 15 years. With regard to especially serious crimes, adult offenders may be sentenced to life imprisonment. This applies in particular murder cases. Even in these cases life imprisonment is inflicted very rarely.

In case of proper conduct, the court may put a convict on parole. As with probation, there is a parole period and it is possible to impose special duties.

Lesser offenses (such as hooliganism) are subject to imprisonment up to six weeks for disciplinary purposes.

Beyond the basic punishments, additional punishments such as fines, confiscation of objects, withdrawal of licenses, or restriction of residence, may be imposed.

The court may order special curative treatment for people such as alcoholics, sex offenders, and the like.

The legislation in force provides for the death penalty. It may be applied only for the most serious crimes against peace and humanity, war crimes, particularly serious crimes against the state, and in aggravated cases of murder. Its practical application is limited to an infinitely small number of cases, and in most cases it is commuted to life imprisonment. It must not be used with juveniles, pregnant women, and insane persons.

As to foreigners, the court may order their expulsion.

III. CRIMINAL PROCEDURE

The sole legal basis of criminal proceedings is the Code of Criminal Procedure. It regulates the procedures to be applied in investigating and establishing criminal liability and includes provisions for the execution of sentences.

Criminal proceedings consist of three main phases: preliminary proceedings, court trial, and appeal.

Preliminary proceedings include an examination on the part of the investigating agency or the procurator as to whether there is an indication of a punishable act.

Appeal proceedings and retrials are special court proceedings for examining the legality and justification of final judicial decisions. Appeal proceedings are heard and decided by the executive board of the county court or by the Supreme Court.

Investigations are made by the state investigating agencies. The state procurator supervises the preliminary proceedings; he is responsible for the strict observance of the law during all investigations, for the respect of citizen's dignity, for seeing that no citizen is wrongly accused and that no citizen's rights are illegally restricted.

When the investigation is completed, the criminal case is transferred to the state or social court. Decisions of social courts always are made by a collective body of at least four members. As a rule, decisions of state courts are made by a body of three members consisting of one professional judge and two lay judges. Lay judges possess equal rights with professional judges during all proceedings.

After the procurator has brought in an indictment to the state court and the trial has opened, the court hears the criminal case in a public trial in the presence of the procurator and the defendant. Generally, trials are open to the public. In certain cases exclusion of the general public is provided for by the legislation.

The defendant must always be at the trial. His presence is compulsory in every case. The law permits the trial to continue without the defendant only if he had already been heard on all points of the charge and if the court does not consider his presence to be necessary.

All decisions of social courts as well as district and county courts of first instance may be appealed. The decisions of the state courts may be appealed by legal remedies (such as defendant's appeal or procurator's protest).

Appeals are decided upon by the next higher court. Decisions of state courts are appealed in 10 to 15 percent of all cases. Approximately 50 percent of the appeals result in a reversal or commutation of the initial verdict. If only the defendant appeals the decision, no court dealing with his case at some later date is entitled to increase the punishment.

Decisions of social courts may be appealed to the district courts. In practice, this happens rarely (in less than five percent of all cases).

The objective of a criminal procedure is to secure the fair application of criminal law and thus to guarantee that anyone guilty of a punishable act will be called to account according to the degree of his guilt, and that innocent persons will not be punished. Double jeopardy is expressly forbidden by law.

An accused person may be punished only if his guilt has been proven beyond doubt. The burden of proof rests only on law enforcement agencies. Under no circumstances may it be transferred to the indicted or accused person. As long as guilt has not been duly proved by positive evidence, the defendant is considered not guilty. The presumption of innocence is provided for in the Constitution and is one of the most important legal guarantees for the defendant.

The right of defense applies throughout the criminal procedure. From the beginning of the preliminary proceedings the accused person may call upon a counsel for the defense or he may defend himself. The investigating agencies, which also have to examine mitigating circumstances, are obliged during the investigation to give the accused person the opportunity to eliminate with exonerating evidence (such as producing witnesses and bringing forward motions). In criminal cases only lawyers may act as counsels for the defense. The counsel for the defense always has the right to speak to, and correspond with, the accused person while the latter is in pretrial detention. During the preliminary proceedings the procurator may impose certain conditions for these contacts in order to safeguard the investigation process.

Counsel for the defense must attend the trial before the county courts, the proceedings before the Supreme Court, and such proceedings before the district court which, because of the complicated state of facts or legal situation or because of the defendant's character, necessitate his presence. If in such cases the defendant fails to designate his counsel, one will be appointed by the court.

The trial is governed by the principle of adversary procedure. Both the accuser and the representative for the defense have the same procedural rights to participate in taking evidence in open court. The defendant is entitled to the final statement before the court session is closed for consideration of the findings.

A typical feature of socialist law is the broad participation of citizens in criminal proceedings. Mainly, these are the representatives of the public, especially of social organizations and of the collectives in which the indicted or accused person lives or works. Three main groups take part in criminal proceedings: (a) the representatives of collective bodies (work teams); (b) social accusers; and (c) social defenders. Representatives of work teams participate in approximately 60 percent of all criminal proceedings. They contribute to clearing up the criminal case by, above all, comprehensively assessing the indicted person's character. Their participation in the proceedings creates important prerequisites for a successful reintegration of the offender into social life, especially during the probation period and is a characteristic of socialist relations between the individual and society. This demonstrates the help of society for the offender as well as the individual's responsibility for conduct in keeping with the norms of socialist society.

These collective bodies (work teams)—and, in exceptional cases, even individual citizens—may vouch for defendants or convicted persons. They are entitled to suggest that the court impose a sentence without imprisonment and to pledge themselves to safeguard the reeducation of the convicted person. Also, they may propose to the court a sentence of probation. As is clear, participation of the citizens is one of the fundamental principles of criminal procedure in the GDR.

Another important principle is the requirement for speedy trial. The obligation for a speedy conclusion of criminal proceedings finds its expression in the periods of time allowed by law. The maximum time is three months for preliminary proceedings (only the county procurator or the procurator general may extend this period), and four weeks each for court proceedings of first and second instances (in the case of juveniles, three weeks). One of the main duties of the procurator consists of making sure the investigation is carried out in due time. He determines concrete terms for the investigations, which in simple cases amounts to only a few days.

The preconditions for temporary apprehension and pretrial detention are laid down in detail by law. An arrest warrant may be issued only by a judge. The law contains detailed provisions as to judicial interrogation of the arrested person right after his capture, right of complaint, as well as obligations such as the periodic review of the detention, notification of the arrested person's family, and ordering of social welfare measures (for minors or persons in need of care, or for the protection of the arrested person's property and dwelling).

Pretrial detention serves no other purpose but to clear up the punishable act and to conduct the criminal procedure. A maximum time period for pretrial detention is not fixed by law, but the terms for the investigations and the court proceedings prevent an excessive period of pretrial detention. In deciding the length of imprisonment, time already served while awaiting trial has to be fully credited.

According to the Code of Criminal Procedure, pretrial detention may be ordered or prolonged only if this is indispensable for criminal proceedings. The nature and seriousness of the accusation, the personality of the indicted or accused person, and his health, age, and family background have to be taken into account. Pretrial detention may be ordered if the indicted person is under strong suspicion of having committed a crime (felony) or some other serious punishable act for which more than two years of imprisonment are to be expected, if the indicted person attempts to flee or to obstruct the investigation, if the speedy conclusion of the criminal proceedings has to be secured under all circumstances, or if there is a danger that the indicted person who is repeatedly penalized will commit further punishable acts. Due to the structure of crimes and the fact that punishments without imprisonment are preferably applied, pretrial detention is ordered infrequently. Bail is applied only to accused and indicted persons who are not citizens of the GDR. The reason for this restriction is that, in regard to GDR citizens, there are sufficient other possibilities so that pretrial detention can be avoided.

The Code of Criminal Procedure contains detailed provisions on the prerequisites and implementation of a search and seizure. Usually, the relevant warrant is issued by the procurator; in urgent cases, by the investigating agency. The very act of search and seizure is attended by the procurator or two disinterested parties who must not belong to the investigating agency. At any rate, all searches and seizures require judicial confirmation within 48 hours.

The application of the speedy procedure presupposes that (a) the punishable act must not be a very serious one and the facts of the case must be uncomplicated; (b) the indicted person does not deny the punishable act; and (c) the purpose of the punishment requires an especially speedy criminal procedure. In such cases the procurator may bring forward a motion for a speedy proceeding with the district court. In practice, speedy proceedings are rare. This form of proceeding is most often applied in cases of hooliganism. The maximum admissible penalty is one year imprisonment when this type of proceeding is used.

The order of punishment by the court is the only kind of procedure in which a citizen's criminal liability is decided on in writing, without trial. Such a procedure presupposes a comparatively minor offense and the indicted person's admission of guilt. Fines, imprisonment up to six weeks, withdrawal of licenses (such as driving licenses), confiscation of objects, and expulsion are punishments that may be applied. In practice, orders of punishment are rarely used. Most often they are applied in traffic offenses. If the defendant appeals the order of punishment, a regular court procedure including trial will be held. This kind of procedure is not admissible with juvenile offenders.

A separate chapter of the Code of Criminal Procedure regulates the specific circumstances that have to be taken into account in criminal proceedings against juvenile offenders (everyone over the age of 14 and under 18 is a juvenile). As with adults, in each case the juvenile's responsibility for the criminal act is to be examined because the juvenile is criminally liable only if his responsibility is verified. In case of doubt, psychologists are called as experts. The circumstances that induced the juvenile to commit the punishable act have to be examined very carefully. In establishing a juvenile's criminal responsibility the court has to take into account special characteristics of his development. Measures have to be taken to influence positively and reeducate the juvenile and to support effectively his personality development and his growing responsibility. For this very reason the juvenile's parents, youth service agencies, teachers, representatives of social organizations, and others are called upon to take part in the criminal proceedings.

All judicial proceedings must be attended by a counsel for the defense, who in most cases is a legal adviser without legal training but with the rights and duties of a regular defense attorney.

What matters most is the reeducation of the juvenile offender. Therefore, minor juvenile offenses need not be prosecuted if the youth services agencies or other state or social bodies in the field of education take appropriate measures of reeducation. Punishments not involving imprisonment may be applied even if they are not provided for in the specific section of the law that was violated. The professional judges, lay judges, procurators, and members of the investigating agencies involved in juvenile cases must have special expert knowledge and be able to exert a positive influence on juveniles. In larger offices (especially in larger towns) there are investigating agency case workers, procurators, and judges appointed especially to deal with juvenile cases.

IV. EXECUTION OF PENAL MEASURES
(CORRECTIONS)

The application of measures following criminal liability is intended to serve the purposes of protection, prevention, and reeducation of the offender. In practice, the focus is on the systematic reeducation of the offender, with emphasis placed on the joint efforts of state bodies and social forces to make him adopt proper conduct, redress injuries, and lead him to a law-abiding attitude. Such an approach implies that the offender is not just the object of punishment or of the execution of sentences; it is rather his own activity and attitude, his own efforts for proper conduct, redress and reeducation (that is, his actual role in the process) that matters.

Under the socialist social order in the GDR, this uniform process of the execution of measures of criminal law and also of the social reintegration of the offender takes place mainly in work teams and in the process of work. Here the offender's responsible attitude toward his work team as his closest and most natural collective representative of society and toward fulfilling fundamental social duties is strengthened. This also forms the basis for developing his ability and readiness to fulfill in the future his responsibility toward society, to meet his civic duties, and never to break criminal laws.

The success of adequate conduct and restitution following criminal liability depends first on the offender's willingness and efforts. At the same time, socialist society assumes its tasks and obligations in the form of definite duties incumbent on state and enterprise managers, on the executive bodies of social organizations (especially the trade unions), as well as on work and other teams or individual citizens, probation officers, sponsors, and the like. Although their main task in their daily close contacts with the offender is to assist him, they also make demands and supervise him with a view to encouraging proper conduct, restitution, and strengthening his readiness and positive attitude. This mutual responsibility is an essential element of socialist democracy and also contributes to developing collective relations and collective consciousness. Most important, this mutual responsibility encourages the offender's sense of responsibility for conforming to socialist legality and to the people around him.

In the case of juveniles, both probation and compensation for damages are linked with their education and vocational training. Parents and educational institutions, youth organizations and youth teams, instructors and teachers (in the case of socially maladjusted juveniles, also youth services agencies) in this respect have to fulfill an especially responsible and demanding task to which quite a number of citizens, collective groups, and youth teams have devoted themselves with great enthusiasm, effort, and success.

The application of measures following criminal liability lies in the competence of various state agencies. For example, courts are responsible for punishment not involving imprisonment; agencies of the Ministry of Interior are responsible for the execution of punishment involving imprisonment, as well as for expulsion and the death sentence; and relevant state agencies, especially those of the Ministry of Interior and the District Councils, are responsible for additional punishments.

Judgments as well as decisions important for the execution of sentences may be implemented only if they are final; the death sentence, only if a petition for mercy has been decided upon. The execution of the death penalty (by shooting) falls into the purview of the Ministry of Interior.

Probation is the most frequent sentence not involving imprisonment. In probation, the attention of the competent court (the court in whose jurisdiction the convict is a resident) focuses on supervision of conduct and the compensation of injuries on the part of the convict. Particularly, the fulfillment of duties connected with the conviction is to be controlled. In doing so, the court often cooperates with the lay judges acting at the court or working in the convict's enterprise; it seeks information from the relevant state or enterprise managers or the work team and requires the convict to report on any progress he has made with regard to adequate conduct, especially on the fulfillment of his duties. According to the circumstances of the case and the convict's personality, the court sets differing periods of time for supervision and reporting.

In cases of exemplary conduct, the court may, after at least one year, drop the remainder of the probation period. Should the convict fail to discharge properly his duties, the court may summon him, caution him, and point out to him that in case of recurrence the execution of the adjudged sentence will be ordered.

The adjudged prison sentence must be executed if, during the probation period, the convict intentionally commits a new punishable act which is subject to a penalty involving imprisonment (so-called revocation of probation). The suspended prison sentence may be executed if a new punishable act, which is not subject to a penalty involving imprisonment, was committed or the duties imposed were not fulfilled.

In practice, the courts in the GDR apply revocation only with a conviction subject to a prison sentence. Only every eighth convict on probation commits a new punishable act of this category.

The court is responsible for recovering fines, if necessary with the help of a bailiff. For their payment the courts may lay down time limits and instalment amounts. It is possible to change a fine to a prison sentence if the convict evades payment. This exists only in theory.

The agencies for the enforcement or execution of sentences, in particular penal institutions (including prison hospitals) and reform schools—attached and subordinate to the Ministry of Interior—are responsible for the application and execution of punishments involving imprisonment. In the Ministry of Interior itself, responsibility lies with the head of the Department for the Execution of Sentences, who, in application of the laws and other statutory provisions, issues the appropriate orders and instructions and, if necessary, revokes decisions on the execution of sentences made by the heads of penal institutions.

The execution of sentences in the GDR is carried out on the basis of the 1977 Law on the Execution of Sentences. Its principles and contents are governed by the humane nature of the socialist state. Strict observance of legality, respect for human dignity and personality, and application of equality and justice are indispensable principles of the execution of sentences in the GDR. This implies the protection of the legally determined rights of persons imprisoned (the protection of their life, health, and working capacity included) and also insistence on the discharge of their duties. The procurator's office controls adherence to the law in connection with the execution of sentences.

Prisoners must be made aware of their responsibilities as members of society. They are taught to observe legislation and to arrange their lives responsibly. Punishments in the GDR have nothing in common with any sort of retaliation, vengeance, or atonement, and the same applies to the execution of sentences which are not oriented to atonement, retaliation, vengeance, humiliation, or debasement of the prisoners. Priority is given to the convicts' preparation for life in society after their release from the penal institution. One of the main objectives of this preparation is to train the convicts to fulfill their civic duties and to enable them to do so.

Consequently, reeducation during the execution of sentences includes socially useful work (predominantly in modern manufacturing enterprises), education on civil rights and duties, reinforcement of order and discipline (safe custody included), general education and vocational training measures, and cultural and sports activities.

Typical of the execution of sentences in the GDR is enlisting social forces (for example, work teams and representatives of social organizations) and other state bodies and experts as well as the prisoners' own active participation in this process of reeducation. This is known as collective self-education. The concept is realized with growing success also under the condition of the executions of sentences.

Prisoners who are put to work are subject to the same economic, social, legal, and production-technological conditions as any normal worker. Work in nationally owned enterprises (whether in or out of the penal institution) is free from any form of exploitation. Work is organized on the basis of the annual economic plans and benefits both society and the individual. This implies remuneration according to the principle of work output. Remuneration for work paid to prisoners as a rule amounts to 18 percent of payment for the same work output of normal workers. The determination of this percentage allows for deductions for the cost and expense incurred by the penal institution for a prisoner's accommodation and maintenance. If the prisoner accomplishes more than his production quota, he gets a higher percentage. In addition, he is entitled to premiums and other extra pay (for example, allowances for work which is injurious to health are paid in full). A considerable part of a prisoner's remuneration for work is given to him on release as a reserve fund. The other part may be used for purchasing consumer goods and publications in prison.

In addition, the work makes it possible for the prisoner to meet his maintenance obligations and other liabilities. Persons entitled to maintenance receive it through the penal institution out of public funds, irrespective of the prisoner's performance. In fact, anyone who is liable under the Family Code to pay maintenance is bound, in principle, to meet his maintenance obligation out of his own means, in particular out of his earned income. This applies to all citizens, prisoners included. The very fact that prisoners are put to socially useful, productive work during the execution of sentences is a guarantee for the penal institutions that these prisoners will be able to meet their legal obligation to provide maintenance. Besides, with a view to avoiding, as far as possible, any financial effects of the punishment on those entitled to maintenance, permanent maintenance is provided on time, regularly, and without cut in public funds, independent of the remuneration paid to the prisoner who is under the obligation to provide the maintenance. An important condition is that the amount of maintenance is fixed, dependent on the earned income of normal workers for the work concerned (it is subject to general principles).

The extensive equality of working conditions both of prisoners and other working people is also reflected in the application of labor safety and health protection measures, of the scheduled hours of work, in the payment of premiums for outstanding performance, and in the competitive participation of prisoners in the production sphere, in production conferences, and in the movement to introduce innovations to the production process.

Prison sentences for adults may be executed under the conditions of an ordinary or eased execution. Should the prisoner's conduct be irreproachable in every respect, a transfer to an easier type of execution may be ordered.

Prison sentences for juveniles are executed in reform schools. This type of execution serves juveniles by providing adequate education, training, and cultural activities. All this permits them to avail themselves in a purposeful manner of those many opportunities offered by a socialist society for their personality development, an opportunity to behave themselves responsibly, and active participation in social life. All these efforts are based on the close cooperation with the young prisoner's relatives, enterprises envisaged for their future training and work, and youth organizations and youth services agencies. Education at school and vocational training are provided on the basis of generally accepted training regimes. Certificates and any other documents for completed training must not mention that such training was acquired in a penal institution.

Personal contacts, visits, correspondence, and parcels are regarded as important means to stimulate personality development. Positive overall conduct may be appreciated by extension of personal privileges (for example, permission to receive visitors out of the penal institution), by greater freedom of movement, or by free use of leisure time. Another form of appreciating such overall conduct is permission to wear private civilian clothes and to have leave from the institution.

The highest form of stimulating proper conduct and compensating damages is parole, which may be granted by an order of the court after relevant applications have been received and an assessment made of the prisoner. With a view to encouraging the convict's proper conduct after release from the penal institution, parole may be linked with certain obligations (similar to those imposed on persons put on probation). A new violation of the legal order involves the question of the execution of the remainder of the sentence.

Legislation in the GDR pays special attention to the *reintegration* of previously convicted persons after release from the penal institution because this reintegration period is critical for many offenders. This phase in the development of a released person, which no longer forms part of the execution of a penalty, is regulated by a special law, the 1977 Law on Reintegration. This is intended to facilitate the reintegration of the previously convicted person and particularly to prevent him, as far as possible, from incurring a new penalty. This duty is also regarded as a concern of society as a whole; it is realized day by day during the social process of work and of mutual relationships. The local authorities are bound to provide, if necessary, a job and accommodation; they control the progress of reintegration. The managers of enterprises and institutions are responsible for seeing that persons released from penal institutions are incorporated into the work process and the work team in an adequate manner, and that they are given necessary assistance (for example, in further professional training). Special attention is directed to a successful reintegration of juveniles, which is done in close cooperation with parents and guardians, educators, and other qualified people. The youth services agencies bear a special responsibility in this respect.

As far as particularly endangered citizens are concerned, special measures of reintegration may be initiated by court decision. Special measures concerning the social reintegration of persons released from penal institutions apply if an offender who has already had a previous conviction has become liable to penalty for the second time and if this new punishable act is attributable mainly to lack of discipline during reintegration. In such a case, the court may stipulate, when pronouncing a sentence of imprisonment for this new offense, that it will check, prior to release from the penal institution and with due consideration of the offender's conduct and development during his prison term, if special measures of reintegration are necessary. Such special measures can be ordered by the court—prior to release from the penal institution—for a period ranging from 12 months to three years and include conditions and obligations similar to those applied during probation (such as reeducation by a collective group, obligation not to change one's place of work, or limitations of residence). The important point is that these are legal forms of social influence and control which also comprise appropriate activities of enterprise managers, just as in the case of probation.

Under the Penal Code, the court may decide on the admissibility of public control measures on the part of the police. This may occur in three situations: if the offender serving a prison term has already had a previous conviction for a crime (felony); if in view of his personality only such public control measures ensure an orderly reintegration; or, if in cases of hooliganism, the very personality of the offender requires such public control measures even if he serves a term of no more than six weeks or has been placed on probation. This provision emphasized control by the state—in particular by the police—in the form of special obligations to register, limitations on residence, and searches of premises.

Anyone who violates these provisions or evades measures of reeducation is liable to punishment. Depending on requirements, doctors, psychologists, teachers, and other experts are called upon to promote the process of reintegration of given categories of citizens, particularly endangered ones.

The enlistment of such experts is based on the Law on the Reintegration of Citizens Released from Prison. The experts have both consultative functions in individual cases, and general functions vis-à-vis local authorities, particularly the special departments of interior affairs. These specialists are in charge of psychically weak or ill persons (alcoholics, psychopaths, feeble-minded persons, and others), which often requires all their energy. They advise the local authorities (such as the health officer) as to what medical, social, work-related, or administrative measures should be initiated. Many local authorities have gained good insight due to periodically held collective deliberations devoted to current problems, and discussions of shared experiences.

In addition, citizens are increasingly enlisted on a voluntary basis for cooperation with the departments of interior affairs. These citizens' personality patterns guarantee the necessary conditions for giving support to those persons who are to be reintegrated into social life after release from penal institutions. Together with the work teams of the released persons, they care for individual persons or cooperate in the joint efforts of enterprises, social forces, and communal institutions in residential areas.

The comprehensive and differentiated regulation both of the execution of sentences and reintegration of previously convicted persons by legislation in the GDR indicates that the demands of the standard minimum rules established by the United Nations are not only complied with in this country but are even surpassed in many important respects.

BIBLIOGRAPHY

This bibliography is composed of the major books and articles in English describing the criminal justice systems of the foreign countries included in this book. The bibliography was gathered through a search conducted by the National Criminal Justice Reference Service and supplemented by the authors and editors.

ENGLAND

BALDWIN, J. and M. McCONVILLE (1979) "Plea bargaining and the Court of Appeals." British Journal of Law and Society, 6:200-218.

BALDWIN, J., et al. (1978) "The metropolitan police blacklist of lawyers." Justice of the Peace, 142:731-733.

BANTON, M. (1964) The Policeman in the Community. London: Tavistock.

BOTTOMLEY, A. (1973) Decisions in the Penal Process. London: Robertson.

BOX, S. (1971) Deviance, Reality and Society. London: Holt, Rinehart & Winston.

BURT, C. (1944) The Young Delinquent (4th ed.). London: University of London Press.

BURWOOD, J. B. (1979) "Compensation and restitution." Magistrate, 35:122-123.

CARTER, J. A. and G. F. COLE (1979) "The use of fines in England: could the idea work here?" Judicature, 63:155-161.

CLARKE, A. T. (1979) "Volunteer work with the probation service." Justice of the Peace, 143:37-38, 51-52, 54.

DENT, H. R. et al. (1979) "An experimental study of the effectiveness of different techniques of questioning child witnesses." British Journal of Social and Clinical Psychology, 18: 41-51.

DOWNES, D. (1978) "Promise and performance in British criminology." British Journal of Sociology, 29:483-499.

EDWARDS, G. (1979) "British policies on opiate addiction: ten years working of the revised response, and options for the future." British Journal of Psychiatry, 134:1-13.

HAMRICK, W. S. (1979) "Towards a phenomenology of legal rules." Journal of British Society for Phenomenology, 10:9-22.

JONES, R. (1978) "Intermediate treatment and adolescents' perceptions of social workers." British Journal of Social Work, 8:425-438.

KOFFMAN, L. M. (1978) "A critique of penal philosophy and recent penal policy." Cambrian Law Review, 9:27-39.

McCLINTOCK, F. H. and N. H. AVISON (1968) Crime in England and Wales. London: Heinemann.

MIRFIELD, P. (1980) "Alteration of sentences and order in the Crown Court." Leeds Criminal Law Review, January:17-28.

MORRIS, T. (1957) The Criminal Area. London: Routledge & Kegan Paul.

MURPHY, N. (1979) "Community service—Whither South Yorkshire probation and aftercare service." Justice of the Peace, 143:391.

OSCAPELLA, E. (1980) "A study of informers in England." Criminal Law Review, March: 136-146.

RADZINOWICZ, L. (1966) Ideology and Crime. London: Heinemann.

REINER, R. (1978) "The police in the class structure." British Journal of Law and Society, 5:166-184.

RETTIG, S. (1964) "Ethical risk sensitivity in prisoners." British Journal of Criminology, 42:582-590.

SAMUELS, A. (1980) "Prison for the motoring offender." Justice of the Peace, 144:95-96.

SOFTLEY, P. (1980) "Sentencing practice in magistrates' courts." Criminal Law Review, March:161-169.

WALKER, N. D. (1965) Crime and Punishment in Britain. Edinburgh: Edinburgh University Press.

WEST, D. J. (1963) The Habitual Prisoner. London: Macmillan.

WILKINS, G. (1979) "Fine enforcement in Birmingham." Justice of the Peace, 143:386-388.

WOOTTON, B. (1959) Social Science and Social Pathology. London: George Allen & Unwin.

CANADA

AKMAN, D. D. (1966) "Homicides and assaults in Canadian penitentiaries." Canadian Journal of Criminology and Corrections, 8:284-299.

———— and A. NORMANDEAU (1967) "The measurement of crime and delinquency in Canada." Criminal Law Quarterly, 9:323-347.

AVIO, K. L. (1973) "An economic analysis of criminal correction: the Canadian case." Canadian Journal of Economics, 6:164-178.

———— and C. C. SCOTT (1976) Property Crime in Canada: An Econometric Study. Toronto: University of Toronto Press.

BELL-ROWBOTHAM, B. and C. L. BOYDELL (1972) "Crime in Canada: a distributional analysis." pp. in C. Boydell et al. (eds.), Deviant Behaviour and Societal Reaction. Toronto: Holt, Rinehart & Winston.

BIENVENUE, R. and A. H. LATIF (1974) "Arrests, dispositions and recidivism: a comparison of Indians and whites." Canadian Journal of Criminology and Corrections, 16:105-116.

CARLSON, K. A. (1973) "Some characteristics of recidivists in an Ontario institution for adult male first incarcerates." Canadian Journal of Criminology and Corrections, 15:397-411.

CHANDLER, D. B. (1976) Capital Punishment in Canada: A Sociological Study of Repressive Law. Toronto: McClelland & Stewart.

EDWARDS, J. L. (1966) "Sentencing, corrections and the prevention of crime." Canadian Journal of Criminology and Corrections, 8:186-201.

———— (1970) "Criminal law and its enforcement in a permissive society." Criminal Law Quarterly, 12:417-436.

FOX, R. G. and M. J. SPENCER (1971) "The young offender's bill: destigmatizing juvenile delinquency." Criminal Law Quarterly, 14:172-219.

FRECHETTE, M. (1975) "Delinquance, socialization et nevrosisme." Acta Criminologica, 8:53ff.

FRIEDLAND, M. L. (1965) Detention Before Trial: A Study of Criminal Cases Tried in the Toronto Magistrates' Courts. Toronto: University of Toronto Press.

GIFFEN, P. J. (1965) "Rates of crime and delinquency." pp. 59-90 in W. T. McGrath (ed.), Crime and Its Treatment in Canada. Toronto: Macmillan. (revised version, 1976)

GREENAWAY, W. K. and S. L. BRICKEY (1978) Law and Social Control in Canada. Scarborough: Prentice-Hall.

GREENLAND, C. (1972) "Dangerous sexual offenders in Canada." Canadian Journal of Criminology and Corrections, 14:44-54.

GROSMAN, B. A. (1969) The Prosecutor: An Inquiry into the Exercise of Discretion. Toronto: University of Toronto Press.

———— (1975) Police Command: Decisions and Discretion. Toronto: Macmillan.

HOGARTH, J. (1967) "Towards the improvement of sentencing in Canada." Canadian Journal of Criminology and Corrections, 9:122-136.

JAFFARY, S. K. (1963) Sentencing of Adults in Canada. Toronto: University of Toronto Press.

KELLY, N. and W. KELLY (1973) The Royal Canadian Mounted Police: A Century of History, 1873. Edmonton, Alberta: Hurtig Publishers.

McDONALD, L. (1969) "Crime and punishment in Canada: a statistical test of the 'conventional wisdom.'" Canadian Review of Sociology and Anthropology, 6:212-233.

McGRATH, W. T. [ed.] (1976) Crime and Its Treatment in Canada. Toronto: Macmillan.

McLEOD, W. E. (1967) Society Behind Bars. Toronto: Social Science Publishers.

———— (1968) Deviant Behavior in Canada. Toronto: Social Science Publishers.

———— (1970) The Underside of Toronto. Toronto: McClelland & Stewart.

———— (1971) Social Deviance in Canada. Vancouver: Copp Clark.

MANN, W. E. and L. G. HANLEY (1968) "The mafia in Canada." In W. E. MacLeod (ed.), Deviant Behavior in Canada. Toronto: Social Science Publishers.

MARTIN, J. C. (1955) The Criminal Code of Canada. Toronto: Cartwright.

MORRISON, W. A. (1973) "Criminal homicide and the death penalty in Canada. Time for reassessment and new directions: toward a typology of homicide." Canadian Journal of Criminology and Corrections, 15:367-396.

NORMANDEAU, A. (1966) "The measurement of delinquency in Montreal." Journal of Criminology and Corrections, 8:592-616.

SCHMEISER, R. L. (1969) Civil Liberties in Canada. New York: Oxford University Press.

SCOTT, F. R. (1959) Civil Liberties and Canadian Federalism. Toronto: University of Toronto Press.

SILVERMAN, R. and J. J. TEEVAN, Jr. [eds.] (1975) Crime in Canadian Society. Toronto: Butterworth and Co.

WALKER, I. (1974) Men Released from Prison. Toronto: University of Toronto Press.

WILKINS, J. L. (1975) Legal Aid in the Criminal Courts. Toronto: University of Toronto Press.

FEDERAL REPUBLIC OF GERMANY

ADLAM, G. (1956) "Juvenile courts in the Federal Republic of Germany." Criminal Law Review.

BAUMANN, J. (1970) "The alternative draft prepared by the criminal-law teachers to the Code of Criminal Law and Execution of Punishment." Law and State, 1:52.

GASPER, G. and H. ZEISEL (1972) "Lay judges in German criminal courts." Journal of Legal Studies, 1:135.

GLEMENS, W. (1960a) "Police detention and arrest privileges: Germany." Journal of Criminal Law, Criminology, and Police Science, 51:421.

——— (1960b) "Privilege against self-incrimination: Germany." Journal of Criminal Law, Criminology, and Police Science, 51:172.

——— (1961a) "The exclusionary rule: Germany." Journal of Criminal Law, Criminology, and Police Science, 52:277.

——— (1961b) "Police interrogation privileges and limitations: Germany." Journal of Criminal Law, Criminology, and Police Science, 52:59.

ESER, A. (1973) "The politics of criminal law reform: Germany." American Journal of Comparative Law, 21:245.

FELSTINER, W. (1979) "Plea contracts in West Germany." Law and Society Review, 13:309.

GOLDSTEIN, A. and M. MARCUS (1977) "The myth of judicial supervision in three 'inquisitorial' systems: France, Italy, and Germany." Yale Law Journal, 87:240.

——— (1978) "Comment on continental criminal procedure." Yale Law Journal, 87:1570.

GRÜNHUT, M. (1961) "The reform of criminal law in Germany." British Journal of Criminology, 2:171.

HERRMANN, J. (1974) "The rule of compulsory prosecution and the scope of prosecutorial discretion in Germany." University of Chicago Law Review, 41:468.

——— (1978a) "Development and reform of criminal procedure in the Federal Republic of Germany." Comparative and International Law Journal of Southern Africa, 11:183.

——— (1978b) "Various models of criminal proceedings." South African Journal of Criminal Law, 2:3.

——— (in press) "The German criminal justice system: the trial phase—appellate and review proceedings." Revue Internationale de Droit Pénal, 51.

JESCHECK, H.-H. (1970a) "The discretionary powers of the prosecuting attorney in West Germany." American Journal of Comparative Law, 18:508.

——— (1970b) "Principles of German criminal procedure in comparison with American law." Virginia Law Review, 56:239.

——— (1974) "Modern criminal policy in the Federal Republic of Germany and the German Democratic Republic." p. 509 in R. Hood (ed.), Crime, Criminology and Public Policy: Essays in Honour of Sir Leon Radzinowicz. New York: Free Press.

——— (1975) "The new German criminal law in the international context." Law and State, 12:85.

KLAUSER, K. and R. RIEGER (1971) "Legal assistance in the Federal Republic of Germany." Buffalo Law Review, 20:583.

LANGBEIN, J. H. (1974) "Controlling prosecutorial discretion in Germany." University of Chicago Law Review, 41:439.

——— (1980) "Land without plea bargaining: how the Germans do it." Michigan Law Review, 78:204.

——— and L. WEINREB (1978) "Continental criminal procedure: 'myth' and reality." Yale Law Journal, 87:1549.

LEFERENZ, H. (1972) "The personality of the criminal with regard to the assessment of punishment and measures of security and reform." Law and State, 8:57.

MEYER, H. H. (1955) "German criminal procedure: the position of the defendant in court." American Bar Association Journal, 41:592, 666.

MUELLER, G. O. W. (1961) "German Draft Criminal Code 1960—an evaluation in terms of American criminal law." University of Illinois Law Forum, 25.

PIEK, M. (1960) "Witness privilege against self-incrimination in the civil law." Villanova Law Review, 5:375.

———— (1962) "The accused's privilege against self-incrimination in the civil law." American Journal of Comparative Law, 11:585.

RADBRUCH, G. (1936) "Jurisprudence in the criminal law." Journal of Comparative Legislation and International Law, 18:218.

ROBINSON, C. D. (1965) "Arrest, prosecution and police power in the Federal Republic of Germany." Duquesne University Law Review, 4:225.

ROXIN, C. (1970) "The purpose of punishment and the reform of penal law." Law and State, 2:66.

SCHRAM, G. (1969) "The obligation to prosecute in West Germany." American Journal of Comparative Law, 17:627.

SCHRÖDER, H. (1965) "German criminal law and its reform." Duquesne Law Review, 4:97.

SCHWENK, E. H. (1941) "Criminal codification and general principles of criminal law in Germany and the United States: a comparative study." Tulane Law Review, 15:541.

SIEVERTS, R. (1957) "The administration of juvenile penal law in the Federal Republic of Germany." British Journal of Delinquency, 7:206.

SWEDEN

ANTILLA, I. (1971) "Conservative and radical criminal policy in the Nordic countries." pp. 9-21 in N. Christie (ed.), Scandinavian Studies on Criminology, Vol. 3. London: Tavistock.

———— (1975) "Probation and parole: social control or social service." International Journal of Criminology and Penology, 3:79-84.

ASPELIN, E. (1975) "Some developments in Swedish criminal policy." In Some Developments in Nordic Criminal Policy and Criminology. Stockholm: Scandinavian Research Council for Criminology.

BULTINA, L. (1971) Deviant Behavior in Sweden. New York: Exposition Press.

FRIDAY, P. (1976) "Sentencing in Sweden: an overview." Federal Probation, 40:48-55.

GEIS, G. and R. GEIS (1979) "Rape in Stockholm: is permissiveness relevant?" Criminology, 17:311-322.

HOLMGREN, P. and O. LINDQUIST (1975) "Lethal intoxications with centrally stimulating amines in Sweden 1966-1973." Journal of Legal Medicine, 75:265-273.

KUHLHORN, E. (1975) Non-Institutional Treatment. Stockholm: National Council for Research and Development Section.

MARNELL, S. (1972) "Comparative correctional systems: United States and Sweden." Criminal Law Bulletin, 8:748-760.

MORRIS, N. (1966) "Lessons from the adult correctional system of Sweden." Federal Probation, 30:65.

ROSLUND, B. and C. A. LARSON (1979) "Crimes of violence and alcohol abuse in Sweden." International Journal of Addiction, 14:1103-1115.

SCHMIDT, F. and S. SHOMHOLM (1964) Legal Values in Modern Sweden. Totowa, NJ: Bedminster Press.

SUNDEEN, R. A. (1976) "Swedish juvenile justice and welfare." Journal of Criminal Justice, 4:109-121.

SVERI, K. (1975) Some Developments in Nordic Criminal Policy and Criminology. Stockholm: Scandinavian Research Council for Criminology.

JAPAN

ABE, H. (1961) "Criminal justice in Japan: its historical background and modern problems." American Bar Association Journal, 47:555-559.

―――― assisted by B. J. GEORGE (1963) "The accused and society: therapeutic and preventive aspects of criminal justice in Japan." Pp. 324-363 in A.T. von Meheren (ed.), Law in Japan. Cambridge, MA: Harvard University Press.

ARMSTRONG, S. (1974) "A perspective on Japanese criminal law and procedure law." Asia, 5:179-204.

BAYLEY, D. H. (1976) "Learning about crime: the Japanese experience." Public Interest, 44:55-68.

BAYLEY, D. H. (1976) "Forces of Order-Police Behavior in Japan and the United States. Berkeley: University of California Press.

BENJAMIN, R. W. (1975) "Images of conflict resolution and social control: American and Japanese attitudes toward the adversary system." Journal of Conflict Resolution, 19:123-137.

CLIFFORD, W. (1976) Crime Control in Japan. Lexington, MA: D.C. Heath.

DANDO, S. (1960) "Basic problems in criminal theory and Japanese criminal law." Indiana Law Journal, 35:423-433.

―――― (1965) Japanese Criminal Procedure (translated by B. J. George, Jr.). South Hackensack, NJ: Rothman.

―――― (1970) "System of discretional prosecution in Japan." American Journal of Comparative Law, 18:518-531.

―――― and K. TAMITA. (1960) "Conditional release of and accused in Japan." Pennsylvania Law Review, 108:323-335.

FUJIKI, H. (1968) "Property and criminal law" (translated by B. J. George, Jr.). Law in Japan, 2:120-139.

GEORGE, B. J., Jr. (1965) "The impact of the past upon the rights of the accused in Japan." American Journal of Comparative Law, 14:672-685.

HANAJIRI, H. (1967) "The courts and lawyers in Japan." New York Law Journal, 162:1-4.

HAYAKAWA, T. (1973) "Age and the judiciary in Japan." Kobe University Law Review, 9:1-10.

HIRANO, R. (1973) "The draft of the revised penal code: a general critique." Law in Japan, 6:49-64.

INGRAHAM, B. L. and K. TOKORO (1969) "Political crime in the United States and Japan: a comparative study." Issues in Criminology, 4:145-170.

KOICHI, M. (1976) "Victimological studies of sexual crimes in Japan." Victimology, 1:107-129.

KOSH, G. M. (1970) The Japanese Advisor: Crimes and Punishments. Rutland, VT: Tuttle.

NAGASHIMA, A. (1969) "Family court in Japan." Juvenile Court Judges Journal, 19:130-133.

SUZUKI, C. (1970) "Problems of disqualification of judges in Japan." American Journal of Comparative Law, 18:727-743.

SUZUKI, S. (1968) "Discovery in Japanese criminal procedure." Kobe University Law Review, 6:13-25.

UEMATSU, T. (1964) "Trends in the revision of the penal code of Japan." Hitotsubashi Journal of Law and Politics, 3:1-15.

UEMATSU, T. (1964) "Control of sex crimes by penal code of Japan." Hitotsubashi Journal of Arts and Sciences, 4:15-21.

WILSON, H. C. and A. J. C. WILSON (1964) "Juvenile delinquency in Japan." British Journal of Criminology, 4:278-282.

YANAGIMOTO, M. (1970) "Some features of the Japanese prison system." British Journal of Criminology, 10:207-224.

―――― (1973) "The juvenile delinquent in Japan." British Journal of Criminology, 13:170-177.

UNION OF SOVIET SOCIALIST REPUBLICS

BEERMAN, R. (1960a) "Criminology and juvenile delinquency reconsidered." Soviet Studies, 11:451-452.

―――― (1960b) "The law against parasites, tramps, and beggars." Soviet Studies, 11:453-455.

―――― (1961) "The parasite law." Soviet Studies, 13:191-205.

―――― (1967) "The Soviet law on commissions for cases of juveniles." British Journal of Criminology, 2:386-471.

BERMAN, H. J. (1959) "Comparison of Soviet and American law." Indiana Law Journal, 34:557-570.

―――― (1972) "The education role of the Soviet court." International and Comparative Law Quarterly, 21:81-84.

―――― (1963a) Justice in Russia: An Interpretation of Soviet Law. New York: Vintage Books.

―――― (1963b) "Soviet comrades courts." Washington Law Review, 38:842-910.

―――― (1958) "Soviet law and government." Modern Law Review, 21:19-26.

―――― and L. B. QUISLEY (1968) "Comment on the presumption of innocence under Soviet law." UCLA Law Review, 15:1230-1239.

BERMAN, H. J. and J.W. SPRINDLER (1966) Soviet Criminal Law and Procedure: The RSFSR Codes. Cambridge, MA: Harvard University Press.

BHATIA, H. S. (1966) "The Soviet procuracy." International Journal of Legal Research, 1:1185-1193.

BINKLEY, J. T. (1960) "The rule of law: the new Soviet criminal procedure." American Bar Association Journal, 46:637ff.

CONNOR, W. D. (1970) "Juvenile delinquency in the U.S.S.R.: some quantitative and qualitative indicators." American Social Review, 35:283-297.

―――― (1973) "Criminal homicide U.S.S.R., U.S.A.: reflections on Soviet data in a comparative framework." Journal of Criminal Law, 64:111-117.

FELDBRUGGE, F. J. (1963) "Soviet criminal law—the last six years." Journal of Criminal Law, 54:247-266.

FLETCHER, G. P. (1968) "The presumption of innocence in the Soviet Union." UCLA Law Review, 15:1203-1225.

GAL'CHENKO, F., P. MATYZHEVISKII, and S. IATSENKO (1973) "The charge of hooliganism." Soviet Law and Government, 2:94-101.

GALKIN, I. (1966) "The court and public passions." Soviet Law and Government. 2:6-7.

GALPERIN, R. I. M. (1967) "Responsibility of recidivists under the penal legislation of the U.S.S.R. and Union Republics." McGill Law Journal, 13:679-682.

GERTSENZON, A. A. (1961) "The community's role in the prevention and study of crime." The Soviet Review, 1:14-27.

GINSBURG, G. (1970) "The Soviet Union and international co-operation in legal matters: criminal law—the current phase." International and Comparative Law Quarterly, 19:626-670.

GREENBLATT, I. M. (1972) "Women, justice, and crime and punishment in the Soviet Union." Women Law Journal, 58:54-57.

GRZYBOWSKI, K. (1960a) "Main trend in the Soviet reform of criminal law." American University Law Review, 9:73-110.

_____ (1960b) "Power's trial and the 1958 reform of Soviet criminal law." American Journal of Comparative Law, 9:425-440.

_____ (1966) "Soviet criminal law." Problems of Communism, 2:53-62.

GSOVSKI, V. (1960) "Reform of criminal law in the Soviet Union." Social Problems, 7:315-328.

GUTSENKO, K. (1957) "Comrades' courts are a collective educator." Current Digest, 42:21.

HAMMER, D. P. (1963) "Law enforcement, social control and the withering of the state: recent Soviet experience." Soviet Studies, 14:379-397.

HAZARD, J. N. (1953) Law and Social Change in the U.S.S.R. London: Stevens.

HEARN, L. V. (1962) Russian Assignment: A Policeman Looks at Crime in the U.S.S.R. London.

JOHNSON, E. L. (1969) An Introduction to the Soviet Legal System. London: Methuen.

JUVILER, P. (1967) "Mass education and justice in Soviet courts: the visiting sessions." Soviet Studies, 18:494-510.

KALASHINK, I. M. (1969) "Medical measures applied to mentally ill persons who have committed socially dangerous acts." Soviet Law and Government, 2-4:102-118.

KARPETS, I. I. (1966) "The nature and causes of crime in the U.S.S.R." Soviet Law and Government, 1:522-559.

KRESTYANINOV, V. I. (1961) "The treatment of crime in new legislation." Soviet Review, 1:28-33.

KUZNETSOVA, N. (1972) "A comparative criminological study of crime in Moscow." Soviet Law and Government, 11:177-186.

LaFAVE, W. R. (1966) Law in the Soviet Society. Urbana: University of Illinois Press.

LAPENNA, I. (1968) Soviet Penal Policy. London: Bodley Head.

MADDOCK, C. S. and K. GRZYBOWSKI (1969) "Law and communist reality in the Soviet Union." American Bar Association Journal, 55:937-942.

MALONE, A. C., Jr. (1961) "The Soviet bar." Cornell Law Quarterly, 46:258-287.

MELNIKOVA, E. (1968) "Delinquency prevention in the Soviet Union." International Journal of Offender Therapy, 12:41-45.

MILLER, R. W. (1954) "Comparison of the basic philosophies underlying Anglo-American criminal law and Russian criminal law." University of Kansas City Law Review, 23:62-93.

MUKEJEE, H. (1949) "Some aspects of Soviet law and justice." Indiana Law Review, 3:148-162.

NAPOLITANO, T. (1965) "Outline of modern Soviet criminal law." Journal of International Communists Jurists, 6:54-81.

NIKI FOROV, B. S. (1960) "Fundamental principles of the Soviet criminal law." Modern Law Review, 23:31-42.

NIFIFORIV, V. (1961) "Whether the Soviet criminal code?" Anglo-Soviet Journal, Autumn: 19-27.

OSBOON, R. J. (1968) "Crime and the environment: the Soviet debate." Slavic Review, 27:395-410.

OSTROUMOV, S. and N. KUZNETSOVA (1968) "The subject of Soviet criminology." Soviet Law and Government, 3:36-44.

PERLOV, I. (1968) "The science of Soviet criminal procedure and improvement of legislation." Soviet Law and Government, 4:11-16.

PETROV, G. (1973) "Rural lawyers." Soviet Law and Government, 11:371-381.

PRUSAKOV, N. (1964) "Court practice in cases of speculation." Soviet Law and Government, 1:51-56.

ROSHCHIN, V. and M. P. CASHIN (1961) "The study and treatment of crime: characteristics of criminals." The Soviet Review, 1:3-14.

ROVECK, J. S. (1959) "The sociological aspect of Soviet legality." Ukranian Quarterly, 15:363-366

_____ (1974) "Capital punishment in the U.S.S.R." Ukranian Quarterly, 30:166-172.

SCHLESINGER, R. (1964) Soviet Legal Theory. London: Routledge & Kegan Paul.

SHUMAN, S. I. (1959) "Soviet legality as revealed by Soviet jurisprudence." Wayne Law Review, 5:209-225.

SOLOMON, P. H., Jr. (1969) Soviet Criminology. Cambridge, MA: Cambridge University Press.

TARAS, J. (1963) "Social courts in the U.S.S.R." Soviet Studies, 13:398-407.

UTEVSKII, B. S. (1963) "Certain questions in the further development of the theory of criminal law." Soviet Law and Government, 2:22-29.

VICTOROV, B. A. (1969) "Public participation and crime prevention in the Union of Soviet Socialist Republics." International Review of Criminal Policy, 27:38-39.

_____ (1974) "The preliminary investigation agencies of the U.S.S.R. Ministry of International Affairs in the struggle against crime." Soviet Law and Government, 1:63-75.

POLISH PEOPLE'S REPUBLIC

BIERZANEK, R. (1974) "Planning of human resources for crime prevention in Poland." International Review of Criminal Policy, 31:42-47.

CIESLAK, M. (1972) "The problem of depenalization in contemporary Polish criminal law." Revue Internationale de Police Criminalle, 25:193-200.

KOSTASZUK, S., T. MARCINKAWSKI, and A. PRZYBYLSKI (1974) "Frequency of various seralogical characteristics in the Polish population." Forensic Science, 3:31-37.

MAREK, Z., J. WIDACKI, and T. HANAUSEK (1974) "Alcohol as a victimogenic of robberies." Forensic Science, 4:119-123.

NASILOWSKI, W. (1972) "Medicolegal certification of insobriety." Forensic Science, 1:197-205.

PELKA-SLUGOCKI, M. D. and C. SLAGOCKI (1976) "Advance pay to ex-prisoners in Poland." International Journal of Offender Therapy and Comparative Criminology, 20:73-76.

_____ (1977) "Alcoholism and female crime in Poland." International Journal of Offender Therapy and Comparative Criminology, 21:174-183.

WALCZAK, S. (1976) "The evaluation of probation measures in Poland: conditional suspension of criminal proceedings." International Journal of Offender Therapy and Comparative Criminology, 20:33-40.

GERMAN DEMOCRATIC REPUBLIC

BUCHHOLZ, E. (1979) "The role of penal law in combating crime in the German Democratic Republic." International Review of Criminal Policy (United Nations), No. 35.

HOLBROOK, S. (1968) Germany: East and West. New York: Hawthorne Books.

INGELTON, R. D. Police of the World. London: Ian Allan.

KIRCHHEIMER, O. (1959) "The administration of justice and the concept of legality in East Germany." Yale Law Journal.

LUDZ, P. C. (1959) The German Democratic Republic from the Sixties to the Seventies. Cambridge, MA: Harvard University Center for International Affairs.

ABOUT THE AUTHORS

ERICH BUCHHOLZ holds the Chair for Penal Law and Penology and is Dean of the Faculty of Law, Humboldt University, Berlin. Among his many publications is *Socialist Criminology* with R. Hartmann, J. Lekschas, and G. Stiller (D.C. Heath, 1974, English translation). Professor Buchholz is a member of the Presidency of the Council for Scientific Investigation of Legal Science at the Academy of Science of the GDR and the International Association of Penal Law.

GEORGE F. COLE is Professor of Political Science at the University of Connecticut. His published works include *Politics and the Administration of Justice* (Sage, 1973) and *The American System of Criminal Justice* (Duxbury, 1979). He recently completed research on criminal prosecution in England under the auspices of the Fulbright-Hays Program.

STANISLAW J. FRANKOWSKI is Professor of Law and a member of the Institute of Penal Law, University of Warsaw. He has lectured at various universities throughout Eastern and Western Europe as well as in the United States and Mexico. As an authority on comparative criminal law, Professor Frankowski has contributed to many law journals.

JOHN C. FREEMAN, J.P., now lectures on criminal law, criminology and penology at University of London King's College. He is Vice President of the Scientific Committee of the International Sociological, Penal and Penitentiary Research and Studies Centre, Messina, Treasurer of the British Society of Criminology, and a member of the Parole Board of England and Wales.

MARC C. GERTZ holds a Ph.D. in political science from the University of Connecticut and is currently Associate Professor of Criminology at Florida

State University. His published articles have appeared in *Justice Systems Journal* and *Journal of Criminal Justice*.

BRIAN A. GROSMAN, formerly Professor of Law at the University of Saskatchewan and McGill University, is now a senior partner in the law firm of Greenglass and Grosman, Toronto. His published works include *The Prosecutor* (University of Toronto Press, 1969).

JOACHIM HERRMANN has been Professor of Law at the University of Augsburg since 1972. He holds degrees from Freiburg and Tulane Universities and has been a visiting professor at the University of Virginia, University of Chicago, and University of Tokyo. His main publications in English include "The Rule of Compulsory Prosecution and the Scope of Prosecutorial Discretion in Germany," *University of Chicago Law Review*, (1974) and "Reform of the German Penal Code-Sanctions—The German Law and Theory," *American Journal of Comparative Law* (1976).

HORST LUTHER holds the Chair for Criminal Procedure at Humboldt University, Berlin, where he is also a member of the Scientific Council of the Departments of Law and of Criminalistics. His research interests focus on problems of juvenile delinquency and on the principles of criminal procedure, subjects about which he has published frequently.

KENICHI NAKAYAMA is Professor of Law at Kyoto University where he is a specialist in criminology and socialist law. His published books include *Soviet Criminal Law* (1958), *Causality in Criminal Law* (1970), and *Law and Society in Poland* (1978).

ALVAR NELSON is Professor of Penal Law at the University of Uppsala. He has practiced law in Sweden and served in the judiciary and on various governmental commissions. The author of many books and articles, his works in English include *Responses to Crime* (1972), *The Swedish Penal Code* (1972), and "Youth Conflicts in the Welfare State" (1981).

VALERY M. SAVITSKY is a graduate of the Moscow Law Institute and is currently Chief, Section on Theoretical Problems of Justice Administration, Institute of State and Law, Academy of Sciences of the U.S.S.R. He is a member of the Scientific Advisory Council of the Supreme Court of the U.S.S.R., and Vice General Secretary of the International Association of Penal Law. He is the author of many papers, and has a special interest in criminal procedure, human rights, and procuracy.

VALERY P. SHUPILOV is at present Chief of the Section on Problems of Crime in Foreign Countries, All Union Institute for the Study of Causes and Development of Measures for Crime Prevention. The author of many papers on criminology, international criminal law, and the execution of punishment, he was elected Vice General Secretary of the International Society for Social Defense in 1975.